STANDARDS
FOR OUR SCHOOLS

How to Set Them,
Measure Them,
and Reach Them

Marc S. Tucker
Judy B. Codding

JOSSEY-BASS
A Wiley Company
www.josseybass.com

Published by

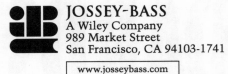

JOSSEY-BASS
A Wiley Company
989 Market Street
San Francisco, CA 94103-1741

www.josseybass.com

Jossey-Bass books and products are available through most bookstores. To contact Jossey-Bass directly, call (888) 378-2537, fax to (800) 605-2665, or visit our website at www.josseybass.com.

Substantial discounts on bulk quantities of Jossey-Bass books are available to corporations, professional associations, and other organizations. For details and discount information, contact the special sales department at Jossey-Bass.

We at Jossey-Bass strive to use the most environmentally sensitive paper stocks available to us. Our publications are printed on acid-free recycled stock whenever possible, and our paper always meets or exceeds minimum GPO and EPA requirements.

Jossey-Bass also publishes its books in a variety of electronic formats. Some content that appears in print may not be available in electronic books.

Library of Congress Cataloging-in-Publication Data

Tucker, Marc S.
    Standards for our schools : how to set them, measure them, and
reach them / Marc S. Tucker, Judy B. Codding. — 1st ed.
      p. cm.
    Includes index.
    ISBN 0-7879-3894-7 (cloth : acid-free paper)
    ISBN 0-7879-6428-X (paper)
    1. Education—Standards—United States.   2. Educational
accountability—United States.   3. Academic achievement—United
States.   I. Codding, Judy B., date.   II. Title.
    379.1'58'0973—dc21   97-45242

HB Printing   10 9 8 7 6 5
PB Printing   10 9 8 7 6 5 4 3 2 1

FIRST EDITION

Contents

Preface to the Paperback Edition   v

Acknowledgments   xiii

The Authors   xvii

Prologue: The View from the Plains   1

Introduction: Failure Is Not an Option   17

Interlude: What Do You Mean, Tiffany Won't
    Get Credit for Algebra I?   25

1. Setting High Standards for Everyone   31

Interlude: But How Will We Actually Get These
    Kids to Algebra II?   65

2. Teaching to the Standards   73

Interlude: Upset Victory: Student Achievement 1,
    Everything Else 0   101

3. Leading and Managing for Success   107

Interlude: The School Nobody Wanted   133

4. Rethinking the Elementary and Middle Schools   139

Interlude: The Graphic Arts Academy   169
    5. Beyond the Comprehensive High School   175

Interlude: Accountability, Chicago-Style   209
    6. Rebuilding "Central" for Accountability   217

Epilogue: What We Owe Jeff   245

Resources
    A. The National Center on Education
        and the Economy   251
    B. New Standards Performance Standards   255
    C. New Standards Reference Examinations   291
    D. Resources for Standards-Based Education   301
    E. Glossary   313
    F. Annotated Bibliography   323
Notes   331
Afterword to the Paperback Edition: The America's
    Choice School Design   335
Index   351

Preface to the Paperback Edition

HARWICH, MASS.—In this Cape Cod town where children of service workers and the leisure class attend school together, a substitute now teaches eighth-grade social studies. The regular teacher, James Bougas, has been suspended for three weeks after refusing to give a state exam.

Mr. Bougas is part of a growing antitest backlash that challenges state officials to match reality to their rhetoric. Most officials agree that tests tell only part of what we should know about achievement. They concede that if the stakes attached to tests are too high, schools may distort curriculums to prepare for exams and little else. Policy makers recognize that it is more expensive to assess high standards than the basics—it costs more to score an essay than to scan bubble-in answers.

But in many states, testing ignores such complexity. Without adjustments, the push for higher standards may be stalled or even reversed.

Richard Rothstein
New York Times
May 30, 2001

When we wrote this book, our aim was to make the case for an idea, the idea that it is important to be clear about what we want students to achieve and then to commit ourselves unequivocally to making sure that they achieve it. It is, at bottom, a simple idea, but, like many simple ideas, it is very powerful. This is true in part because we posited that it is both possible and necessary for virtually all children to master a curriculum that is intellectually demanding. That idea is the antithesis of the idea that underlies the system that has been in place for the better part of a century, the idea that the proper function of the system is to sort out the vast majority of students who cannot and should not be expected to achieve more than an eighth-grade level of literacy from a much smaller number who should be selected to receive a curriculum that will fit them to become the managers and professionals who will run the country.

We set out not only to make the case for a revolution in expectations, driven by a new kind of academic achievement standards, but to show how it could be made to work in practice. We wanted to help teachers, school district central office staff, school board members, and state officials actually take the steps needed to create their own version of this revolution in their community and state.

Since *Standards for Our Schools* was published in 1998, it has enjoyed a wide readership across the country. No doubt this is because the standards movement itself has moved from the periphery to the very center of education policymaking in the United States. The rhetoric of standards and accountability pervaded the education platforms of both major party candidates in the presidential election of 2000. All but one state has adopted some form of statewide standards, and most have state tests that are more or less aligned with those standards. Many have imposed high school graduation standards based on scores made on the new statewide tests, and some have outlawed promotion for students who do not meet the state standards for entrance into the next grade. And with the passage of HR1, the omnibus education bill that President Bush signed in January 2002, the federal government heartily endorsed the idea of standards-based education and made it the law of the land. Almost everywhere and at every level, the idea appears to have taken hold that all students should be held to high standards and that educators should be held accountable for getting them there.

One would think that we, the authors of this book, would, therefore, be celebrating our success. But celebration is clearly premature.

The quotation at the beginning of this preface tells the story. In many states, the standards themselves are narrow, poorly written, and sometimes just plain wrong. In others, the tests used to measure student progress are only vaguely related to the standards, measure only a small part of what is worth teaching and knowing, are poorly constructed, and, for all these reasons, cannot bear the weight of the consequences that fall on students and teachers when scores are low.

Under great pressure to teach to such tests, some teachers, sometimes egged on by their principals, cheat by sharing test items with their students before the test is administered. Others, some of them very good teachers, furious that their teaching is so tightly constrained by tests that measure so little of what they think is worth teaching, boycott the tests or quit altogether. Groups that advocate for minority children denounce the system on the basis of the disproportionate number of minority children who are held back or who fail to get diplomas based on the new promotion and graduation standards. Parents of gifted children denounce the system with equal vehemence because they see the new system as focused on minimum standards for "slow" children rather than giving their children an opportunity to excel. Advocates for children from inner-city and poor rural schools decry the imposition of tough standards and accountability without allocation of the additional resources needed to enable students at such schools to reach the new standards.

These criticisms have real merit, in our judgment. None of them, singly or together, as we see it, constitute a reason to abandon the course on which the nation is now set, but they constitute an agenda of problems that need to be confronted and addressed honestly. The problem lies not in the underlying principles but in the way those principles have been implemented in policy and practice.

This is not the place for a detailed response to the critics. Our purpose here is to set this new edition of our book in its current context. To do that, it is important to connect some of the critiques to the material presented in the body of the book.

Take, for example, the frustration of some teachers with the narrow scope of some of the statewide accountability tests and with the pressure they are under to teach to those tests. In the opening chapters of this book, we introduce the reader to the idea of performance standards and exams that are truly referenced to high-quality standards. We describe a kind of examination that some of the best teachers in the nation think is worth teaching to. We describe a kind of test that can be prepared for, not by teaching the answers to specific questions expected to be on the test, but only by mastering a rich curriculum that requires a deep understanding of the material studied.

Many critics of the standards and accountability movement would have the public believe that emphasis on rote memory and automatic execution of learned procedures is a universal property of all tests. Anyone familiar with the College Board's Advanced Placement tests knows that is not so.

Nor is it true that standards and accountability systems must necessarily depend solely on statewide, externally administered tests. The examination system developed by Cambridge University and now in use worldwide provides a score for the course that is based in part on a subscore for what is called "coursework" and in part on the score given for performance on the end-of-course examination. Cambridge provides guidelines for teachers on assignments for students as well as guidance for grading those assignments. The grades given by the teachers are then checked by Cambridge graders and, if necessary, corrected, to make sure that all students are graded against the same standards.

The Advanced Placement tests and the Cambridge examinations, as well as the New Standards reference examinations with which we have been associated, show that it is possible to construct tests and examinations that are not subject to the widespread criticisms of the tests currently in use. But these examinations are not cheap, and, with the exception of the Advanced Placement tests, Americans are not used to paying very much for their tests. With tests, as with other things, you get what you pay for.

The same point can be made about the standards in place in many states. We agree that many are far too narrow; insufficiently focused on thinking skills; not well balanced among skills, concepts, and applications; cannot be covered in the time available; do not constitute a coherent whole; and do not describe a curriculum framework that makes any sense. Not least important, almost none provide examples of the kind of student work that meets the standards. All of these criticisms are true, but not necessarily immutably true. We provide in this book examples of standards that actually meet the criteria implicit in this list and show how such standards can be constructed. Once again, the problem is not that such standards cannot be built and used; it is that they have not yet been widely put in place.

The idea that the standards movement will hold back minority students who would otherwise succeed is utterly misguided. We begin this book with a portrait of a student we have called Jeff. His story shows how the lack of explicit standards in our schools has operated to deprive students of whom little is expected of any chance of success. The world in which we live is full of standards. Harvard University does not admit everyone who wishes to go to their college. Neither Merrill Lynch nor Marriott offers employment to everyone who wants to become an investment banker or a hotel desk clerk. They all have standards. Our society is ceaselessly sorting out those who are well educated and trained from those who are not. The greatest favor we can do for low-achieving students is to make the implicit standards explicit, so they will know, often for the first time, what they have to do to succeed.

Nor it is true that "standards" really means minimum standards and that the standards movement is therefore a threat to anyone committed to high achievement. In this book, we show how to construct standards and exams that will stretch anyone and provide incentives for students who are doing very well against world-class standards to do even better.

Even less is it true that it is wrong to implement a standards-based system until inner-city and poor rural areas have all the resources that wealthy suburbs have to educate their children. At the end of this book, we have added an afterword, which describes the work of our America's Choice School Design program, a program that we put into operation just as the hardcover edition of this book was being published. The America's Choice School Design is our answer to the question, "How would you design schools to reflect in detail your vision of how a standards-based system ought to work?" The America's Choice School Designs for elementary, K–8, middle schools, and high schools are based on the principles laid out in this book, as well as our visits to nineteen countries, our own experience with school reform, and the growing body of research on school effectiveness. It has become one of the fastest-growing comprehensive school reform programs offering technical assistance and professional development in the nation. America's Choice designs are now used by schools and districts all over the country.

Some suburban schools that were already functioning at a high level have adopted the designs and have improved their performance. But most of the schools in our network serve low-income students. The only resources they have are those that are typically available to such schools almost everywhere. The independent evaluation from the Consortium for Policy Research in Education shows that when America's Choice schools are compared with schools serving similar student bodies that are not in the program, students in the America's Choice schools make substantially greater gains on their state accountability tests, in terms of the proportion of students meeting the standard. If there were no state accountability program, the performance of most of these students would still be in the basement. Whether they are well or poorly implemented, these systems are focusing attention and resources on low-performing schools and creating uniquely powerful incentives to improve the performance of students in those schools.

We hope that you are reading this book because you, too, believe that it is both possible and necessary for all of our students to achieve at much higher levels than they do now. We hope that, when you have read it, we will have convinced you that the basic ideas behind the standards movement are absolutely sound. And we hope, too, that we will have helped you acquire the tools and techniques you will need to implement those ideas in a way that is no less sound.

Washington, D.C.   MARC S. TUCKER
July 2002   JUDY B. CODDING

For Jeff, and all the others of whom we have expected so little and to whom we owe so much

Acknowledgments

This book is a distillation of the ideas and experience of the rather large family of people who are and have been connected with the National Center on Education and the Economy and its programs—New Standards, the National Alliance, and the Workforce Development Program—and the people in states, school districts, and local communities in which we have been working over the past nine years. Though you will see those ideas and that experience refracted through our own lenses, we are very conscious of our debt to more people than we can possibly acknowledge here.

Much of the work on standards, assessments, the Certificate of Initial Mastery, and curriculum that is described here has gone forward under the direction of Harold Asturias, Ann Borthwick, Vince Breglio, Phil Daro, Sally Hampton, Sally Mentor Hay, Andy Plattner, Bob Rothman, Ann Shannon, Elizabeth Stage, David Wiley, and Michael Young. Lauren Resnick, codirector, with Marc Tucker, of New Standards, has played a crucial leadership role in the national conversation about standards and assessment while shaping New Standards with Marc and contributing significantly to the work of the National Alliance. What we say here about teaching to the standards and leading and managing schools owes a debt to Loretta Johnson, Tom Jones, David Marsh, Mary Anne Mays, David Mintz, Marge Sable, and Carol Solis. Our chapter on elementary and middle schools was improved by the contribution of Jacqueline Austin, and the chapter on the new high school could not have been written without the work of John Porter and Jackie Kraemer. The chapter on "central" and the issue of accountability owes a great deal to Merle Audette, Pat Harvey, and Mike Strembitsky.

The story we tell in the Prologue is in some ways the axis on which the book turns. Every word in it is true, though we were required to keep the identity of the school and community veiled by the terms of our agreement with the superintendent of schools. We are indebted to public opinion expert Vince Breglio of RSM Associates for selecting the focus group participants, assisting in the interviews, and providing transcripts and also, especially, to the many people who were willing to participate in a very intense evening and two days of nonstop interviews.

At several points in the book, we describe aspects of the Danish education system in some detail. We could not have done this without the unfailing hospitality and patient assistance on several occasions of Roland Østerlund, director of the vocational education department of the Danish Ministry of Education, and Lars Mahler, director of the Aalborg Technical College in Aalborg, Denmark, and his colleague, Karl Axel-Skjolstrup.

As is always the case with a book like this, many of the ideas here have origins that are very hard to trace. But that is not true of all of them. We are heavily indebted to David Hornbeck's seminal contributions on the incentives front, first in Kentucky and then in Philadelphia; to Paul Vallas, Gery Chico, and Pat Harvey for the razor-sharp outlines of the Chicago accountability plan; to John Murphy for his work on the Charlotte-Mecklenburg accountability design, and to Tim Barnicle for his contributions on workforce development; all of which have left a big print on our recommendations here. Eileen Shapiro and Trina Soske have made valuable contributions to our work in many ways, not least when they helped us create a planning system for schools and districts tied to student performance standards.

The work on which much of this book is based could not have been done at all had it not been funded. We will be forever grateful to Rebecca Rimel and Bob Schwartz of The Pew Charitable Trusts, David Hamburg and Vivien Stewart of Carnegie Corporation of New York, and Adele Simmons and Peter Gerber of the John D. and Catherine T. MacArthur Foundation of Chicago for their years of support for our work. We are deeply grateful to David Kearns for his support through the years, not least in his role as chairman of New American Schools, and to John Anderson, New American Schools' president. Tom Glennan, adviser to NAS, has helped us reflect on work in very useful ways. Over the years, The Boeing Company provided crucial support for our work, and for that we are deeply grateful to Frank Shrontz, former Boeing chairman, and Ronn Robinson, Boeing's director of education policy. Thanks, too, go to the nearly two score states and a dozen districts that supported New Standards and the National Alliance through thick and thin. Many chief state school officers and school superintendents made courageous bets on us. We can acknowledge here the support of only a few, but that list must include the chairs of the New Standards Governing Board and the National Alliance coordinating council—Delaine Eastin, Bill Lepley, Rick Mills, and Tom Sobol.

Through it all, we have felt and appreciated the steady support of our own board of trustees and especially our former chair, John Sculley, and our current chair, Ray Marshall.

To Carolyn Carey we express our gratitude for keeping track of the innumerable drafts and getting them straight.

From within the National Center, Bob Hochstein, Jackie Kraemer, David Mintz, Andy Plattner, Anthony Priest, Bob Rothman, Elizabeth Stage, and Mike Strembitsky took the time to comment on drafts and thereby improve them. Thank you.

Others, outside the organization, who were also good enough to respond to our request for comments included Jacqueline Austin, principal of the Kennedy Montessori Elementary School in Louisville, Kentucky; Tom Corcoran, codirector of the Consortium for Policy Research in Education, at the University of Pennsylvania; Rudolph F. Crew, chancellor of the Board of Education of the City of New York; Denis Doyle, senior fellow at the Hudson Institute; Chester E. Finn Jr., senior fellow at the Hudson Institute; Sherry King, superintendent of the Mamaroneck Union Free School District in Mamaroneck, New York; Richard Murnane of the Graduate School of Education at Harvard University; Lauren Resnick, director of the Learning Research and Development Center at the University of Pittsburgh (and codirector of New Standards and senior fellow of the National Center on Education and the Economy); and Tom Payzant, superintendent of the Boston Public Schools. The comments of many of these people on our first draft greatly improved the manuscript, an outcome for which we are profoundly grateful.

Our thanks, too, are extended to Bob Rothman for helping with arrangements for the interviews that became the Prologue, for compiling the glossary, and for providing steady encouragement and assistance all the way through the enterprise. And to Suzie Sullivan, for patient assistance with permissions and endnotes. Few authors can be as lucky as we in having as our editor Leslie Iura. Her enthusiasm and encouragement have been vital assets in this project.

For Judy, a great debt is owed to Ted Sizer for advice and encouragement, and to the Pasadena High School administrators, Kathy, Fred, Ruth, and Larry, who shared her challenges and joys, and to all the teachers, students, and parents in Pasadena from whom she learned so much. And a special thanks to Vera Vigness, superintendent of the Pasadena Unified School District, whose commitment has been a steady inspiration.

When it comes to support from the long-suffering, the honors must go to our families, who have given up what might otherwise have been perfectly enjoyable vacations, weekends, and evenings while we were toiling away. Many, many thanks for that.

The Authors

MARC S. TUCKER is president of the National Center on Education and the Economy. A former associate director of the National Institute of Education and coauthor of *Thinking for a Living: Education and the Wealth of Nations* (1992), Tucker was the primary author of the 1986 Carnegie report *A Nation Prepared*, a principal author of *America's Choice*, the report of the Commission on the Skills of the American Workforce, and designer of the National Board for Professional Teaching Standards. He is codirector of New Standards and head of the Policy Committee of the National Skill Standards Board.

JUDY B. CODDING is vice president of programs for the National Center on Education and the Economy and director of the National Alliance on Restructuring Education, a program of the NCEE. Before assuming her present position, she was principal of Pasadena High School in California, a large urban comprehensive high school serving predominantly low-income African American and Latino students. Previously, she was a teacher and principal of Bronxville High School and Scarsdale High School, both in New York, suburban high schools serving mainly high-income Anglo students. In addition, she has been an elementary and middle school teacher. She served as a charter principal of the Coalition of Essential Schools, a national high school reform effort.

Prologue
The View from the Plains

Walk up to a map of the United States. Eyeball the middle of this great landmass, and your glance is as likely as not to fall on the plains states—breadbasket of America, fattener of our beef, gateway to the American West. French and Spanish explorers were there a century before Lewis and Clark mapped the land, making their way through the buffalo hunted by nomadic native American tribes. In 1849, little villages exploded into boomtowns as people from all over the world flooded through the area on their way to the gold rush. As the Civil War faded into history, the plains were carved up by the transcontinental railroads and their spurs, connecting east and west through this land of endless grass. Soon some of the little towns became railway hubs, bustling with switching yards, repair and maintenance shops, warehouses, grain elevators, and feedlots. As the economy swelled, workers' bungalows spread out in the flats and handsome homes sprouted on the heights above, where the managers and owners lived. From the heights, one could see forever across the high plains.

Then, in the latter half of the twentieth century, as the airplane and long-haul tractor trailer took much of the freight business from the railroads, the bustle went out of the local economy. Today, one passes one former switching yard after another, dust blowing across rusty tracks, the paint peeling from the disused freight warehouses. It is a working-class community now, half its working population commuting every day to jobs in the insurance offices, financial industry back offices, and distribution and telemarketing establishments, the other half laboring in the slaughterhouses, making frozen dinners that will be sold in supermarkets all over the United States, or staffing local manufacturing firms. Like countless other cities and towns in the United States, this town has made the transition from the old economy to the new with a certain grace. And it is doing fine, thank you. The unemployment rate is down to a little over 3 percent. Employers looking to fill no-skill, dead-end jobs find that they have to pay at least $7.25 an hour to get anyone who is able to fog a glass when they breathe. The citizens of this town have money in their pockets and are reasonably confident about the future.

We came here to Plainsville to get a picture of what the world looks like to a typical teenager about to graduate from high school in a typical working-class community. We eventually focused on a young man we'll call Jeff. What does he want to do with his life? How well did his school prepare him to do it? What are his employment prospects? What sort of technical skills does he have? How did he acquire them? What do typical employers here look for in new employees? Does this young man have what they are looking for? What opportunities are available to get more education? More training? We figured that this young person would have a lot going for him, seeing that year after year, his state compares well with the schools of other states on almost any dimension.

Our first impression of Jeff was that he should be scheduled for a Hollywood screen test. He was a handsome young man with one of the most winning smiles you ever saw. And he was smart, too, the kind of smart that one thinks of as quintessentially American— level-headed, practical, commonsense smart . . . street smart. Jeff is engaging. It comes as no surprise to learn that he has lots of friends, is at ease with people, and is pretty self-confident. In all these ways, he really does have a lot going for him.

Jeff is in his last year at Walt Whitman High School, "WW," as everyone calls it (this is not the real name of the school). Built in the 1920s, WW has a handsome granite facade, a classical look about it. Beside the school is the parking lot, full of student cars and some belonging to the faculty.

As the school day begins, the students stream from the parking lot into the school in clumps, in animated conversation. They strike one as very well behaved and rather all-American. Just beyond the school grounds, on both sides of the street, the scene is rather seedy. But here, on campus, there are no graffiti anywhere. The school is spotless. Everything points to a school in which the students take a lot of pride.

As we talk to the administrators, faculty, students, and parents, a fuller picture emerges. One-third of the faculty are WW graduates. This is one community that has escaped the turmoil experienced by many others—the interracial tension that has raked much of urban America, the social class divisions that have turned many comprehensive high schools into umbrellas over camps so separate that they might as well be on different planets and others into places where there are open hostilities between faculty and students. Not here. When teachers look at the kids in this high school, they see youngsters who might be their own, who share their values and aspirations and are experiencing the same problems their own kids are facing. This is a school where the students feel welcome and wanted, where their accomplishments are celebrated and their ambitions are shared. So Jeff has all of that going for him, too.

Bill Stanley (not his real name) has been WW's principal for two years. He cares a lot about this school and the people in it. A prominent figure in a highly regarded organization of professional educators, he has led his high school into a pioneering role with respect to new academic standards and new forms of performance assessment. He is a risk taker, more knowledgeable about new developments in education than most and more likely to take an active leadership position than many principals we have met. WW, we think, is lucky to have him.

But as the circle of our conversations broadens and the days go on, it becomes clear that this school system has failed Jeff badly. More accurately, the larger system of which the Plainsville (not its real name) schools are a part has failed Jeff badly.

Jeff's mom and dad are both forty. His dad, whose name he has, grew up in Plainsville, like his father before him. Jeff's paternal grandparents live just down the street; so does his girlfriend. Jeff told us he wants to live in Plainsville all his life.

His dad runs a construction company, and his mom is a respiratory therapist. Both graduated from high school. His dad was briefly in college but, as he tells it, woke up one day and said, "Why am I here?" and left. His mom finished two years of college. Jeff has two younger brothers. Here's how Jeff described his brothers, Johnny and Rusty: "Johnny had absolutely no mechanical ability at all and took welding because it's in my family and I do it. And he took welding and now he's good at something. So now he thinks he's good at everything, and now he attempts things—before he wouldn't even try. My brother Rusty is really, really smart. He's like in his own little world. He's into animals and bugs and books, and he has the exact same behavior problems I had when I was in fourth grade or fifth grade. You know, being goofy, just doing little stupid things."

Jeff has fond memories of elementary school. He remembers loving history, social studies, and science—especially science, because it was "hands-on." Reading was easy for him and fun. It still is. When we asked whether he reads a newspaper, he told us that he reads two newspapers every day.

When he got to junior high school, he became a "screw-up." Got himself kicked out of class regularly for "throwing paper, . . . making goofy weird noises, tapping [my] pen, kicking the desk, little things." By the middle of seventh grade, though, he had stopped worrying so much about being popular and settled down.

At the beginning of junior high, Jeff's grades were very good. "Then, in eighth, ninth, and tenth I got like D's and C's and then I did really, really good the first semester of eleventh grade, and then after that I had enough credits to where I only had to go a half a day and I just . . ."

"Coasted?"

"Yeah."

A quick look at Jeff's transcript is revealing. There is little doubt that Jeff is capable—A's and B's in honors world history in tenth grade, an A in zoology that same year and another in biology, A's in art and computer technology in the eighth grade. But these are the exceptions. Generally, Jeff has done just enough to get by. His record is studded with C– and D grades. Now, in his senior year, Jeff is taking only two courses, just enough to complete the forty-four credits he needs to graduate. As he admitted to us, he is coasting to a finish.

Jeff knows he can do really well at academic work when he puts his mind to it, but he doesn't see the point. We asked him why he didn't take physics, chemistry, and algebra II.

"I don't know. . . . I don't really care because . . . my little brother's in precalculus and I look at what he's doing and I have no idea what that stuff means and so to me it doesn't mean anything." He told us that he took no geometry because he had no idea how he would use it. But it was important to Jeff to graduate—and also, he knew, very important to his parents.

So we asked Bill Stanley, Jeff's principal, what it takes to get a diploma from WW.

His answer: "They must earn forty-four credits." This must include four years of English, two and a half years of social studies, two years of math, two years of science, and four years of physical education. Nothing is said about the content of the math and science courses.

"Does it matter what grades they get in their courses?"

"No, a passing grade will get you there. . . . D– or above will get you the credit."

We asked both the students and the teachers what the kids had to do to get a D– in a course. They both told the same story: just come to school most of the time, don't cause too much trouble, and turn in most of your assignments. The quality of the work on the assignments doesn't matter much, just as long as something gets turned in to the teacher.

On the whole, though, the grades at WW are surprisingly high. Surprising because the scores on the standardized tests of basic skills are very low. We asked Bill if he could explain how 33.4 percent of the students were getting A's in their classes when the standardized test scores were so low. He had apparently not thought about these two sets of data in relation to one another but began to speculate about the answer.

"It says that there is an underlying concern among the teachers to say, 'I don't expect what I did before. I'm not asking the same things I was asking five years ago or ten years.' It's like there's a push back when they say they want the kids to do the following things. So that begins to lead to a feeling about what's worth fighting for and what's not. . . . I think that may have some effect on grades." It isn't just the students that "push back." The parents, too, put a lot of heat on Bill and the rest of the faculty when the failure rate gets to be significant.

Bill worries about the lack of any real standards in the school. He has begun instituting a program to do something about it. The idea is to have the faculty develop a set of 'performance tasks' that the kids will have to pass to graduate. The performance tasks are to be problems that incorporate real-life challenges and require knowledge from several disciplines for their solution.

But Bill and the staff are in a quandary about how to set the passing standard for these performance tasks. Knowing that there is very little support among the parents and faculty for standards that

might make it more difficult to graduate from WW, they are thinking of setting the limit for passing the performance tasks at a fairly
modest level, at least initially.

We asked Bill about the kids like Jeff, who are just sliding by, the
ones who complete high school, often without a solid program, go
to community college or directly to work, and then drift into the
community college (and, often, out of community college) a few
years later.

"There are a lot of students who will leave an academic program.
They haven't done a lot of industrial technology or vocational
work. Their grades are average, and they can survive in a high
school environment. . . . My feeling is, knowing the students here,
that there needs to be a lot more talking with them, their parents,
and the staff about some kind of a career focus. Someone to say,
'What is the picture in your mind once you leave school?' . . . A lot
of them have a picture, but most do not."

It is clear that Bill Stanley cares a lot about these kids. Virtually
everyone we met on the faculty does. After we talked to Bill, we
walked down the hall to talk to the senior guidance counselor at
WW. She shared Bill's concern about the low standards at the
school but worried that there were a lot of kids at the school who
would drop out if the standards for graduation were any higher.

She said, "Half the kids don't leave the school with the skills
they need to support a family. . . . They do the minimum to get a
diploma." She told us that out of a student body of 1,400, only 21
are enrolled in calculus and 119 in algebra II. No Advanced Placement courses are offered, she said, because the administration does
not think that the students would do well in them and so the school
sends its better students to the local community college to take
courses for which the state university system will give equivalency
credit instead. It was not easy for her to give us quick answers to
some fairly straightforward questions about how many students were

taking certain key courses and subjects. To get the answers, she had to do the runs by hand, adding up numbers manually from a bunch of different forms. We got the impression that data of this kind are not used much in the routine of school planning.

Everyone told us that one of the biggest problems facing the school is attendance. The faculty have been struggling with this problem, mainly because suspending the kids as a disciplinary measure seems more a reward than a punishment. It struck us that the attendance problem, while both real and important, was a symptom of the larger problem—hundreds of kids like Jeff for whom school was important mainly as a social setting, a place to spend time with their friends while waiting for life to begin.

Conversations about attendance led naturally to the topic of the dropout rate, which Bill had told us was about 5 to 6 percent. At first that seemed inconsistent with a very high truancy rate. So we added up the numbers. A school of this size would graduate about 350 students a year, if no one dropped out. But it was actually graduating only about 230.

As we put the data together with what we were learning in our conversations with Bill and his faculty, a picture was emerging of a student body, a very large fraction of which was bored, drifting, and largely uneducated. When, we wondered, did this begin—in high school or before?

Bill told us that "in too many cases, we deal with students who are not prepared to do some of the things like comprehend what they read. . . . When I talk to teachers who teach kindergarten in the district, they tell me that students are coming to kindergarten with the language skills of a two- or three-year-old. And apparently that just keeps going and works its way through . . . the grades."

"Do you see a difference between the reading level of your students and the math level?" we asked.

"No—they're comparable. . . . [But] math tends to arrange the world in levels more than the rest of the curriculum. . . . Once a determination is made as to what level [a student is placed in], it's not real flexible. . . . If you're not in algebra in your first year, you may not get there."

"When do you think the tracking begins?"

"Coming out of elementary school," he replied.

Again and again, Jeff tells us that he is happiest when he can work "hands-on," and he gets restless when he has to stay put. He didn't take any foreign languages, he said, because he decided to take welding and machine shop and auto mechanics and other technical subjects instead. But Jeff knows that the school doesn't have enough money to get modern equipment for these shop classes.

We talked to Jeff's wood shop teacher about the industrial technology program. He is a very discouraged man.

"If you go out in industry and you look at some of the things that they are doing out there, . . . we are way behind as far as teaching these kids. I went out and looked at . . . Bridgeton Pipe [not its real name] to see what is expected, and they are doing a lot of high-tech stuff compared to what we are trying to teach these kids." But he has no resources to do what he knows needs to be done. What resources there are go into the college-prep program. "The type of kids that we get are a lot of the lower kids. . . . The better kids all go into your college-prep-type classes."

We asked him how many of the students are in the industrial technology program because they have a genuine interest in pursuing a vocational program leading to a career, as opposed to the proportion there because their counselors did not know where else to put them. "I would say about 20 percent. . . . And another 20 percent are in there because they are interested in . . . hobby-type work. And the [others] are there just because. . . ."

Then we asked about the academic skills of the students in the vocational program. "I would have to say 25 percent don't have a clue about math skills at all. I got kids who don't know one end of the ruler from the other. It's really hard for them to do anything

[like] measuring or to get ready to make any kind of project when they can't even measure. Figuring fractions, subtracting and dividing fractions is an example. For example, you have to take a one by six and rip it down the center and have two equal pieces—they don't have a clue." So he has to do his best to teach these kids arithmetic and fractions in his wood shop classes. "Some of the kids come in here and say, 'I didn't come here for math,' and I say, 'Yes, but you have to know math in order to be here. How are you going to measure this board and cut it if you don't know that?' 'Well,' [they say], 'I never thought of that.'"

We assumed that the people who employ these youngsters when they graduate would be very concerned about the lack of these most basic skills in the pool of young people from which they must recruit their new employees. The employer group we talked to included representatives of a credit card processing company, a commercial print shop, a farm supplies store, a flower and gift shop, a dental lab that makes dentures and crowns, a masonry contractor, a card shop, and a bank. We were in for a surprise.

By far the biggest concern among the employers was work ethic. They wanted young people who would show up for work regularly, be on time, and do what they were told. Their biggest complaint was that their young workers rarely showed up on time and sometimes just failed to come in at all if it was inconvenient for them to do so. They repeatedly lamented the fact that the supply of young people from rural farm communities—kids who had just the kind of work ethic they were looking for—had dried up. Again and again in our conversation, they returned to the theme that things had taken a turn for the worse when the courts had made it impossible for teachers to deliver old-fashioned discipline to the kids—with the rod, if necessary.

Every time we raised the issue of the academic and technical skills young people were acquiring in school, this group of employers said that if the kids had the right work ethic, they would teach the kids everything else they needed to know. The employers had clearly given up on the schools.

Surely, we thought, the vice president of the masonry contracting firm would want young people who had enough math to be able to measure a wall or a brick. We asked whether masons needed this kind of math.

"You have to be able to measure, add, subtract, divide. Just basic math."

So we told him what the wood shop teacher had said about the inability of his students to handle simple fractions and asked whether the high school graduates he was hiring could do such math.

"They have similar problems. They can't take hold. . . . I would say the biggest problem is more than with fractions. It is a matter of adding whole numbers. A good percentage of them [get] frustrated, [can't] come up with the right answer."

"Is this a problem for you?

"Not really. If they are interested in working, I can teach them mathematics."

"Do you think that you ought to be doing that?"

"At the moment, I would be glad to do that if I could find qualified people."

But surely, if the high school was not producing young people with the academic and technical skills to power one of the most advanced economies in the industrialized world, there must be some other institution that was filling the void. We discovered that there was another part of the school system, a vocational center, to which the comprehensive high school sent some of the non-college-bound students. But virtually everyone we talked to seemed to regard this institution as even more of a dumping ground than the industrial technology (vocational) program in the comprehensive high school. That left the community college. We found a student counselor and adviser at the local community college, a very thoughtful, experienced educator, who told us what we needed to know.

It turns out that the community college has some very good two-year technical programs leading to careers with starting salaries of $30,000 a year or more in fields like civil engineering and computer programming. But these programs are in real trouble, greatly undersubscribed and experiencing falling enrollments. The fastest-growing division of the college is "general studies," in which about 60 percent of the student body is enrolled.

So we asked about employer interest in general studies graduates.

"There are not a lot of jobs for the general studies degree, and we tell them that."

"If there are not really good employment prospects for somebody with that particular degree, why do you think it's the fastest-growing program?"

"I think there's a bias against vocational-technical kinds of training. For example, we just dropped our welding program. There are tons of jobs out there in welding, but we can't convince anybody that it's a good thing to go into. . . . [Kids] don't grow up dreaming that they want to be a welder. The students who were in a program like that for the most part were males who came back in their thirties and got retrained. . . . [But] we have other programs, [like] architecture; to succeed in those, they have to have very good math ability. Our programmers with a two-year technical degree start for twenty-nine thousand dollars . . . which is better than most people are going to make with a four-year degree. And five years out, these people can project in the thirties, forties, and some of them in the fifties."

"But these programs are not oversubscribed?"

"No. The programs are so difficult that students put in forty to fifty hours a week in these programs. And they need very good math and analytical skills coming in."

So some of the strong programs with good pay and career prospects are experiencing declining enrollments because they are perceived as blue-collar and therefore low-status. But others that are perceived as white-collar and high-status are also in decline. The counselor told us that the students who enroll in these programs, often after some time in the workforce, typically have no idea that they require strong academic skills and are quickly discouraged when they find out they can't do the work. The civil engineering major, which could handle thirty or forty people, has only seven enrolled. The construction industry, he says, is begging for graduates from this program.

Given what we had learned about the quality of the vocational offerings at WW, we asked whether it might make sense for the high school students to come to the community college for their vocational courses while they are still in high school, instead of taking the vocational courses in the high school. He told us that there is a system for doing this already. "A kid would be going into his senior year. If he has already met all of his graduation requirements, he could go into a program called Select Senior. Basically, it is a full-time vocational or technical program. The state or the district pays; it doesn't come out of the kid's pocket." But, he said, "the districts see it as a major expenditure if too many kids are counseled into it." The result is that very few kids even know that they have that option. When we asked Jeff about it, he told us he had never heard about it.

We were almost done. There was time for one last question.

"What do you think the prospects are for the kids who don't go to four-year colleges and don't go to your school?"

"Most of them will struggle with finding a job that will pay enough. They are setting themselves up to struggle with life. It's a never-ending cycle that they will have a tough time breaking. It's sad that we can't reach more people."

We asked Jeff when he first started thinking about what he wanted to do when he got out of high school. "I don't know," he said. "Ever since I was a kid, I messed with mechanical things. I had a motorcycle when I was six, and I tore it apart, and I could fix it and everything else. And I had a minibike and go-carts and motorcycles; then I got cars. My car's all jacked up; it's got nice tires on it and everything. I've got two cars. My girlfriend bought one, but I fixed it. I started working for my dad when I was thirteen so that I could make money. . . . I liked what he did."

"What will you do when you graduate?" we asked.

He said something about maybe going to college after his girl-friend graduates from high school. But then he said, "I want to work for a while. I don't know if I want to go to college. . . . I just want to wait it out. Maybe I don't want to be a mechanic. Maybe I'd get tired of laying on my back all day long. . . . I don't know."

We asked Jeff's dad about what his son was like as a mechanic in his shop.

"He is my best help. He really likes to do what he is doing. He likes to tinker with things. He likes to weld. He likes to fix things. He is real good at figuring things out and solving problems. He doesn't give up."

"Do you think there is anything that you or his mother could have done to motivate Jeff to take tougher courses and work harder in school?"

"I think I should have put my foot down and demanded better grades."

"What made you not do that?"

"First kid. I am just learning. I will make a [great] grandparent."

"Is there anything that you would like to see changed at WW?"

"The entire school system has a problem, in my opinion, with its athletic department. Winning isn't everything, obviously, but their basketball team, for instance, has three wins and fifteen losses. It has been like this for the last ten years. Football is the same way."

Which statistic will Jeff be? Of those who graduate from WW, about one-quarter go to four-year colleges, an equal number go to the community college, and the rest go mostly into the workforce and the military. Judging by the national averages, somewhere between half and three-quarters of those who go to the four-year colleges and the community colleges with the intention of getting some form of degree or certificate will not get one within five years of the time they first enrolled. Around half of those who go right into the workforce will enroll at a community college later on. But, as we learned, when they do, they are most likely to find that they lack the academic qualifications to enroll in demanding programs leading to strong technical careers and most likely, therefore, will enroll in general academics majors that lead, for the most part, nowhere. More than half of our young people, it seems, are firmly on the road to nowhere.

Introduction

Failure Is Not an Option

Perhaps American educators have a right to be angry. On the one hand, there is solid evidence that the performance of the public schools has been steadily improving over the years. A strong case can be made that this slow but steady improvement is a remarkable achievement, given the realities with which the schools are now contending: more time of more parents spent at the workplace and less at home with their children, almost a quarter of American schoolchildren slipping into poverty now, and the nation in the midst of its greatest wave of immigration ever.

On the other hand, there is Jeff, the young man whose story you read in the Prologue. (Throughout this book, we have changed names of students and teachers in vignettes.) A couple of generations back, there would have been nothing but pride at his getting his high school diploma. There were plenty of jobs around for youngsters like Jeff that paid pretty well. Not anymore. Even if Jeff gets a two-year degree in general studies, he is not likely to do as well as someone who got a high school diploma and went right to work in the 1950s or '60s.

Jeff's story is deeply troubling to us because we know things are different now, because we do not need an economist to tell us that Jeff is likely to face a future of struggle and disappointment if he does not greatly improve his skills. Our sense of failure here comes not from knowing that he knows less than he would have known if he had graduated forty years ago—he doesn't—but rather because those skills are no longer good enough and because we know that we can do better—have to do better.

There are millions of youngsters like Jeff in America's schools and many millions more who do not do as well, whose prospects are, if anything, worse. When they leave school, they swell the ranks of poorly educated young adults competing for a declining number of jobs requiring relatively low skills. The prospects for these students—perhaps a majority of our young people—are getting worse every day.

That is why the gains in achievement that might once have earned accolades are no longer good enough to earn grudging acceptance. The price the public is now demanding for continued support for the public schools is major improvements in student achievement across the board at little or no increase in cost.

To most educators, this seems unreasonable. Knowing that the schools have had to bear burdens greater than they have ever had to bear before, being asked to produce much higher achievement at no increase in cost seems like a crude joke.

But that is what is being demanded. Increasingly, the public does not believe that the people who govern, manage, and staff our schools can or will deliver. Hence the attraction of schools run for profit, schools run by churches, schools run by parent and teacher groups that do not have to deal with teachers unions and are accountable to no one—in short, tax-supported schools run by anyone but the public school system.

If we thought these silver bullets would work, we would embrace them instantly. But we don't.

We think there should be much more real competition among public schools than there is, but that is not what any of these alternatives are really about.

What is most likely to happen if they are pursued is the progressive abandonment of the public schools, in the sense of common schools, schools for everyone, and that is too high a price for a democratic country to pay. Too high, that is, if there is a practical alternative. An alternative is practical in the current situation only if it will plausibly lead most American students to do as well in school as their counterparts in countries where performance is highest.

That is what this book is about—describing that alternative. Unlike many of public education's critics, we think that American educators are hungry for a way to make their schools work, but they find themselves trapped in a century-old system that routinely defeats and frustrates the most capable and caring of school people. If that describes you, if you believe that we owe it to Jeff and the millions like him to do better, to give them the education they need and deserve, if you think that your schools could do it, then this is your book.

Our aim has been to write a practical guide to changing that system so that the good people in our schools can do for the Jeffs of the world what they entered teaching to do in the first place.

We describe many of the gritty, frustrating realities of life inside the system that make it so hard for dedicated educators to make the difference they want to make. But we also describe real things that real people have done and can do to triumph over the system and, much more important, to change the system itself.

We know that the public schools can deliver because we have seen them deliver. One of us has been the principal of a school in which inner-city children from all over the globe, whose only common characteristic was poverty, achieved standards that few experts thought possible; the other has studied entire countries in which public schooling is routinely superb.

Together, we run one of the nation's largest school reform networks, applying what we have learned to the needs of school districts and states eager to show that public education can meet the challenge. Our technical assistance teams are at work in urban centers like New York City, San Diego, Pittsburgh, Rochester, Louisville, and White Plains; in rural communities in Arkansas,

Pennsylvania, and Kentucky; in suburban communities in the states of Washington, Massachusetts, and New York; and in very diverse communities in California. Our largest technical assistance program is in Chicago, in America's second largest school district, where we are working closely with the central office team and with seventeen schools that were, when we began our work with them, among the worst-performing schools in the district.

We and our colleagues have worked with thousands of teachers, school administrators, state officials, student advocates, and education researchers to develop student performance standards and performance assessments that are used in many parts of the nation. In some places, we are helping big-city districts design whole new accountability structures; devolve budget, staffing, and program authority to the schools; and create new incentive structures for both students and staff. In others, we are providing large-scale staff development resources. Sometimes the focus is linking local standards to national standards; sometimes it is matching curriculum to standards; sometimes it is leadership training; sometimes it is working with parents and public. But everywhere we work, the bottom line is results—defining them, measuring them, and producing them.

We have worked hard over the past ten years to examine the way education works in other parts of the world, to find nations that have consistently produced good results overall or in particular domains. And we have encouraged the educators we work with to analyze what these nations have done to get those results. You will find that we will ask the same of you, too.

This book, then, is grounded in the work we and our colleagues and our partners are doing—in our hopes, our collective experience, our mistakes, and our successes. We hope it connects with your own experience, helps you avoid some of our mistakes, and makes possible some successes you would not otherwise have had.

The fulcrum of this book is performance standards—standards for academic achievement that are as high as any in the world and so clearly described that virtually any youngster can look at them and say, "Ah, I understand now—I can do *that*." In Chapter One, we explain how we came to see standards as a key lever that could lead to broad improvements in student achievement and how we think such standards should be designed. And we also describe how performance assessments can be designed to match such standards, assessments that are worth teaching to.

Much of the current writing on standards ends right there, as if the introduction of high standards and the use of matching assessment systems could by themselves produce vast changes in student achievement. It simply is not so.

The fact is that the introduction of standards is full of hazards. Some educators will use standards as a kind of whip to hold youngsters back in the grades, as if holding them back would by itself cause them to be educated. In the same spirit, some will use standards simply to deny graduation and a diploma to youngsters who would otherwise have graduated, as if denying such youngsters the diploma would by itself ensure that more youngsters would do well enough to meet the new standards. Some will use new standards to narrow the curriculum into a little cleft in the rock of drill and practice in computation and grammar, as if this were all there is to a good education.

Even when all of these pitfalls are avoided, relying on standards and assessments alone to change student performance is tantamount to believing that a more sophisticated measure of student failure will by itself turn failure into success. It will not.

The most casual reader of this book will quickly come to see that standards-based education means an obsession with *results*, with reaching predetermined levels of student achievement. This requires an unrelenting determination to get virtually all students to high achievement levels, whatever that takes.

Our purpose is to define what that takes as clearly as we can. A whole body of research on effective schools can be caricatured as saying that what it takes is great leaders. It does take good leadership, but if it takes *rare* leadership, then by definition, we will only rarely get great schools. If this country is to have uniformly high achievement, we must make it possible for ordinary people to produce routinely what we currently regard as extraordinary levels of achievement. How can that be done?

The answer lies in changing the system, in creating a system of public education that is designed not, as this one is, to sort students into categories and educate only those deemed to be most capable but rather to bring everyone to high standards regardless of where they start.

What would that system look like? Obviously, it would have to have clear performance standards, set at attainably high levels, and assessments to match. But it would also have to have powerful curriculum materials and instructional techniques available to the teachers that are explicitly designed to get all kinds of students to the standards. It would need instructional technology to support that curriculum. The system would have to provide reliable, continuous feedback to teachers on student performance against the standards so that the teachers could change course quickly if students are not making good progress. A system that has long regarded getting out of high school into a four-year college as the benchmark of success and treated everyone who didn't as losers will have to be redesigned to provide numerous highly valued paths out of high school that lead to good careers and worthwhile lives. Our schools and school districts—whose highest values have been to tend school, protect the system, and maintain loyalty to those in charge—will have to be redesigned to replace all of these with a different value: getting as many students as possible to the new high standards. That will take a revolution in governance, organization, and management extending from the school board to the classroom. It will require great changes in school organization, the master schedule, and the incentives that operate on the students and the professionals alike, to name only a few of the changes that will have to be made.

We will describe these and many other changes in public education that are essential if it is to survive. They are all encompassed in our definition of standards-based education. That is because they are all needed to make sure that the students can actually reach the standards.

What we are proposing here is that the American education system, under the banner of standards, abandon immediately the idea that we are doing our job by sorting youngsters into winners and losers and instead dedicate ourselves to the idea that all students can and must achieve at internationally benchmarked levels. Radical though it may be, this is an idea that can save the public schools—perhaps the only one that can save them.

Interlude:
What Do You Mean, Tiffany
Won't Get Credit for Algebra I?

Judy B. Codding, Pasadena High School

The most important problem we faced at Pasadena High was the academic performance of our students. It was miserable across the board. When I joined the staff, half of the students were getting D's and F's in the core subjects. Thirty percent were dropping out, and another 30 percent would not graduate when they reached their senior year. I knew that we could not do everything at once, that we would have to pick some place to begin, but that place had to be strategic.

I was in luck. That was the year the College Board came out with its big Educational Equality Project report. It said pretty clearly that the single most important predictor for further education success was a student's performance in math through at least geometry. That was it. We were going to focus on math!

The faculty and I began poring over the data. We started analyzing our highest-performing math students, the ones who were in Advanced Placement calculus. The data showed that these students came to Pasadena High School without the knowledge or skills they needed to succeed in geometry or algebra II. Then why were they placed in AP calculus? The answer reveals the underbelly of the problem that our school—and schools like us all over the United States—faced.

Pressure had been put on the middle schools to offer algebra to as many students as possible. The middle schools had selected their better-performing math students and put them in an algebra class, whether or not they were actually well enough prepared to have a decent chance of success in algebra. These students took the course, were given passing grades, and were then sent to Pasadena High with credit for high school algebra. But the fact is that they did not have the foundation required for prealgebra! Not until we did a careful analysis of the "best-performing" math students did we begin to fully understand the math performance nightmare.

Then we went to look at the middle school recommendations for ninth-grade math placement for the coming school year. Our worst fears were realized. Our feeder middle schools were recommending that about one-third of the incoming ninth-grade class be placed in geometry or algebra II because they had successfully completed algebra I or geometry, another third should be placed in algebra I, and the remaining third should be placed in a low-level math class. The evidence we had accumulated of massive rates of failure in mathematics for these students' predecessors gave us no confidence at all in these recommendations, but we had no direct evidence that would enable us to challenge them. But evidence or not, we explained our reservations to the middle schools and asked them to look at the data we had accumulated in our effort to explain the high rate of failures we were experiencing in our high school math program.

You can imagine how well that was received by the middle school teachers and administrators! If we would just care more about the kids and do a better job teaching the subject, they said, we would not have such a high failure rate. The one did not necessarily follow the other. Yes, we should care more and should teach better, but it was clear to me that if both were done and we kept feeding unprepared kids into high school–level math classes, we would still have a disaster on our hands.

We would call a class "geometry" or "algebra II," but because of the lack of knowledge and skills of the students in those classes, the corresponding content would not be taught. The best of the students would continue to be passed up to the next course, whether they were ready for it or not. And so it went until they got into AP calculus. There, for the first time, the content and performance requirements were not left up to the whims of our school system and the faculty of the schools. The students in this course had to take the same national exam that all students in the country had to take. The results were appalling. We rarely had a student score above 3—on a scale of 1 to 5—on the AP calculus exam; 80 percent of our students scored 1 or 2, and many who were in the course did not even sit for the exam.

Clearly, we had to find a way to determine the mathematics knowledge and skills of the students coming from our feeder middle schools, yet it was futile to try to derive an accurate picture from middle school grades or course credits. I recalled reading about prealgebra and algebra diagnostic and achievement tests that were available through UCLA. After much discussion with members of the Pasadena High math faculty, we decided to ask UCLA to test all incoming ninth-grade students who were recommended for algebra I, geometry, or algebra II. I called the two feeder middle school principals and requested permission to administer the appropriate California State University/University of California mathematics test to the eighth-grade students that the middle schools were recommending for algebra I, geometry, and algebra II, and to score the tests.

Both principals were outraged that we refused to continue to accept their recommendations and that we wanted additional information on which to base our math class placement. The principals and their teachers interpreted our request as an attack on the quality of the preparation the students had received. They saw it as questioning their knowledge, their teaching skills, even their integrity. They pointed out to me that the students who were being recommended for geometry and algebra II had already received high school and University of California system credit for the mathematics course, which by definition entitled them to proceed to the next course in the math sequence. If that credit was withdrawn and the students had to repeat the courses for which that credit had been given, both the students and their parents would be furious.

I explained that however true that might be, the fact was that by national standards, the mathematics performance of their best students was miserable, and we needed to figure out why and do something about it—together.

Unable to get the informal agreement of the middle schools to wproceed with the testing, I made a formal recommendation to the super-

intendent of schools that we test the middle school students who were recommended for algebra I, geometry, or algebra II and use the guidelines recommended to us by the UCLA staff for high school math placement. Students who scored below the 80 percent level would not be placed in either geometry or in algebra II because they do not have the proper foundation and should receive additional math instruction before proceeding. I also said to the superintendent that if we were not permitted to test the students in May, we would test them when they became our students in September. If we found out when we administered the test that student placement would have to be changed, it would cause massive scheduling problems in the fall. After much heated discussion, the superintendent reluctantly agreed that we should go ahead and do the testing.

Suddenly, the middle school principals had second thoughts. As soon as the superintendent had decided that the testing should go forward, the middle school teachers reviewed the recommendations they had made for ninth-grade math placement and took seventy students off the list of those who would be recommended for algebra I, geometry, and algebra II. We gave the students either the Algebra Readiness Test or the Elementary Algebra Diagnostic Test, depending on the class for which they were recommended.

I don't think any of us expected the horrendous results we received. Of the 110 students who took the test, only two scored above the 80 percent level, the level at which they were eligible to go on to geometry or algebra II. Fully 85 percent of the students who took the test scored below the 50th percentile. Our worst nightmare had become a reality: only two entering students were prepared to take high school–level math. The others didn't have the knowledge or the skills they needed to succeed in high school mathematics, and most did not even have the basic computational skills required for middle school math! Even more appalling was the realization that the five hundred students who had not taken the test were having trouble with basic arithmetic.

I kept asking myself how we could have gotten into this mess—and why? California's curriculum frameworks—which provided general guid-

ance on what should be taught and learned by students as they progress through California schools—were among the most admired in the United States. Were they just being ignored? Or were they missing something?

It dawned on me that curriculum frameworks were not enough, not nearly enough. There were no clear standards for what a student should be able to do by the end of middle school, in math or any other subject. Even if the frameworks had been crystal clear on that point, it would not have done much good without assessment instruments that could accurately determine whether an individual student met the standard.

Plainly, it was no longer enough to let each school faculty determine for themselves what constituted acceptable performance by their students. When I had asked the middle schools to let us test their eighth graders, some said that these minority kids had so many problems that we should just give the best of them a chance and move them along. But it was clear to me that there is nothing more damaging to poor and minority youngsters than pretending that they have mastered what they clearly have not. I had a different problem with the parents of the white children, who thought that because their children had been placed in more advanced courses, they should just move on. In both cases, the kids think they have done the work when they receive credit for the math course and assume that the credit gives them an automatic right to move on. The schools give their parents and guardians every reason to believe the same thing. But the students actually don't know the stuff, and they won't if we just keep passing them along. We just set them up for a terrible fall when the day of reckoning comes. I was upset for the kids, angry and embarrassed about what had happened, and convinced that it could not be up to the faculty of each school to set their own standards and develop their own assessment system. That was not working. There must be a better way.

1

Setting High Standards for Everyone

The story you just read is true. It is one of a number of stories we will tell that comes out of Judy Codding's experiences at Pasadena High School in Los Angeles. Some of what Judy describes in these stories is no longer there. Which leads to one of the most important things we have learned: there can be no sustained improvements in schools unless the systems of which they are a part are themselves substantially redesigned. As this book was being written, the Pasadena Unified School District was beginning to make those changes.

Judy became principal of Pasadena High in August 1988. PHS was home to some of the poorest city kids in California. A higher proportion of its students were in the foster care system than in any other high school in the state. Average per-pupil expenditure was around $3,500. About a third of the students were Anglo. The rest were every color of the rainbow. Educators will recognize this description. They know that most of these kids did not stand a chance—in school or later in life.

In the spring of 1989, the school administered the Stanford Achievement Tests in mathematics, reading, and language to all ninth-grade students. The average school performance for that year was in the 33rd percentile in mathematics. By the 1994 administration of the same tests, the average for the ninth graders had risen to the 57th percentile. What is even more interesting than this comparison is the fact that 1994's ninth graders—the ones who had measured in at the 57th percentile after only one year at Pasadena High—had had an average performance at the 26th percentile at the end of the seventh grade in the middle schools from which they had come.

These young people, who had been dealt the cruelest cards in America, were performing considerably better than the average American high school student! If you take the 5 percent at the bottom who rarely showed up for class out of the averages, the performance of the remaining 95 percent was truly astonishing.

We will share with you later in this book how this happened. The first point we want to make here is that it *can* happen, that these kids can perform at such levels—and much higher levels still.

Before Judy came to Pasadena High, she had served as principal only in very wealthy communities in the East. So when she became principal at PHS, it should have surprised no one that she shared the view of her colleagues in the Coalition of Essential Schools and in many elite high schools that the standards that drive high achievement have to come from the faculty of each school, that the process of defining these standards, school by school, lies at the very core of what it means to be a professional educator. This was before her experience at Pasadena made it clear what those standards would actually be if they were set by the faculty of each school. Clearly, the standards would be a function of the staff's expectations for the students, and as we all know, the expectations for students everywhere reflect nothing so much as their racial and economic background.

The Route to Standards: The Tragedy of Low Expectations

One of the most striking features of countries that are more successful than we in educating their students to high standards is the assumption made by parents, teachers, and the students themselves that the students can do it. By contrast, the single most important obstacle to high student achievement in the United States is our low expectations for students—not just students who are poor and come from minority backgrounds but, as Jeff's case poignantly shows, most of our students. Why is this so?

The answer lies in our history. Shortly after the turn of the twentieth century, the challenge facing teachers and school administrators was to produce a population of students entering the workforce that met the needs of the burgeoning factories and offices in which they would work. The mass production system was being introduced on a wide scale, and it was greatly reducing the need for skilled craftspeople. Only a small technical and managerial elite required serious academic preparation. Almost all of the rest, the vast mass of the American workforce, could do quite well with only a seventh- or eighth-grade level of literacy. The system they built met that requirement handsomely, year after year.

Then American psychologists announced a "finding" that cloaked this system in science and improved its efficiency substantially. Academic achievement, they said, is substantially determined by intelligence. And intelligence is a function of genetic endowment. Since intelligence is distributed along a normal curve, they said, it follows that the potential for academic achievement is distributed on the same bell curve. They went on to say that only the most intelligent of our young people—about the top 15 percent or so—are capable of serious academic work.

The word went out to America's schools, teachers, parents, and students. Pretty soon, teachers took the view that it would be damaging to the kids to ask more of them than they were capable of. For those in the bottom half of the distribution, the decent thing to do would be to give them high marks for making an effort—coming to school, turning in their homework, and behaving themselves— most of the time.

From this time on, much effort was put into deciding when youngsters first entered school, in kindergarten or first grade, what their intellectual potential was and then assigning them to an ability group based on that judgment. Since then, rare indeed is a student who escaped the fate that followed from that first assignment.

Now and then, an error was made when a student was passed from grade to grade. A student who had been thought to have little potential was misassigned to a group of "high-ability" kids and performed admirably. But few practitioners or policymakers noticed or cared. And so almost nothing was expected of millions and millions of young people who could easily have achieved at far higher levels than they did.

Most of the rest of the world was rather skeptical of our psychologists' findings and chose to disregard them. In much of northern Europe, it is illegal to group children by ability until they are at least fourteen years old, and in other countries it is simply not done.

In the United States, however, when young people first enter school, they are assigned to ability groups based on their teachers' estimates of their native ability. These estimates have closely matched the income and educational background of their parents. What we have actually had is a vast sorting system based largely on social class and racial background, with the outcome determined for many children before the game began.

The power of the idea of the system as a sorting machine runs deep. Look at who gets into the Advanced Placement courses in our high schools. Students who in middle-class and lower-middle-class communities are put into AP courses would never be encouraged to take them in wealthy communities. Conversely, students in wealthy communities who are counseled out of AP courses could easily get into them in less wealthy communities. Wherever we are, it seems, there has to be a "spread." The unspoken agreement is that AP is for the "elite" in our communities, though the actual achievement levels of those elites vary widely.

When most jobs required little skill and less education, maybe it did not matter that we expected far less of our students than parents and teachers expected of students in other countries. Now it matters very much. Today more than ever, what you will earn will be a function of what you know and can do. The only job security in contemporary America is the job security of being highly skilled in an area of high demand and being able to learn complex new things very quickly.

One obvious response to having very low implicit standards for the majority of our students is to have high explicit standards for all of them.

The Route to Standards: The Problem of Unmotivated Students

But low expectations is not the only problem that standards will have to solve. Another factor affecting student performance is no less important: weak motivation to take tough courses and to work hard in school.

In the fall of 1989, the National Center on Education and the Economy assembled a large research team for the Commission on the Skills of the American Workforce and sent it to Europe and Asia. During that trip, some of us found ourselves at the massive Daimler-Benz factory in Stuttgart, Germany, looking out from an observation deck at a hall the size of a football field. It was the center of the facility that Mercedes-Benz uses to train teenage apprentices to be machinists and auto mechanics. The young men and women on the floor were all dressed in white lab coats. Some were sitting at computers loaded with AutoCAD software, designing parts and learning how the software could be used to control the metalworking machines that make auto parts. Others were operating the numerically controlled machines that actually make the parts. Some were learning how to perform precise measurements on newly manufactured parts. And still others were learning how to operate diagnostic equipment that could detect faults in the digital circuits that control the vital functions of modern automobiles.

The chairman of Daimler-Benz had retired just before we arrived. We were astonished to learn that he had come up the ranks

from the apprenticeship program—astonished because it was incon-
ceivable to us that the chairman of, say, General Motors or AT&T
would rise to the top of the organization from an American vocational school. Then we learned that the chairman of Deutsche
Bank, who had retired in the same year, had also come up through
the apprenticeship program.

All over Germany, young people enroll in apprenticeship programs at age sixteen to become machinists and auto mechanics,
among other occupations. But clearly there is a great advantage in
becoming an apprentice at Daimler. So we asked our hosts what it
takes to be accepted in the Daimler program. The answer was, "It
depends on the courses you take, the grades you get, how you do on
your exams, and the recommendations of your teachers."

A few months later, we found ourselves in Toyota City, Japan,
the home of the Toyota Motor Corporation. We walked through
the areas where rolls of steel are stamped and formed into car bodies and from there into the assembly area. Properly speaking, the
workers there do not build the car bodies; computer-programmed
machines do. The workers mind the machines, as many as six or
eight of them at a time. When we probed into the skills required to
do this, we discovered that young people joining the line at age
eighteen are expected to become part of a work team that sets a certain amount of time aside each week for study. At those sessions,
the supervisor gives the team members texts to take home and read
so that they can participate in the group study sessions. These texts,
it turns out, are on digital electronics and mechanics. The workers,
all of them, are expected to have had high school courses in Japanese, mathematics, physics, and chemistry that will prepare them to
do college-level work in engineering on their own and as a member of the work team when they get to Toyota. As the line gets ever
more efficient at the Toyota production facility, Toyota management
reassigns the line workers to the computer programming department, work they can do because, some years ago, Toyota decided
that everyone on the line should have the qualifications that junior
engineers have in the United States.

Compare this requirement to the requirements that Jeff faced in his high school. Or think about it in relation to the fate of the computer programming course at the local community college, endangered because the American high school graduates who apply for that program cannot handle the English and mathematics the program requires.

As at Daimler-Benz, positions at Toyota are mostly filled by people who first came to the firm in entry-level jobs, so one can go to the top from the factory floor. Therefore the benefits of getting an entry-level job at Toyota are very attractive. We asked how a young Japanese person gets such a job.

It turns out that there is no apprenticeship program in Japan. Like most other large employers, Toyota has contract relationships with certain high schools. Year after year, it goes back to those high schools to get the number of young people it needs to fill new openings. Entrance to high schools is competitive in Japan. Having a contract with a firm like Toyota is a plum. So it is very important for a Japanese high school principal who has such a contract to keep it. It is therefore imperative for that principal to recommend only students who have what it takes to succeed in the firm.

So we asked Japanese high school principals what it takes to get on the list of students recommended to Toyota. The answer: it depends on the courses you take, the grades you get, how you do on your exams, and the recommendations of your teachers.

The systems in Germany and Japan could not be more different, but the result is exactly the same. Whether you want to be a brain surgeon or an auto mechanic, it pays to take tough courses and work hard in school.

What about the United States? You will remember that we asked Jeff whether he saw any relationship between how he did in high school and what he wanted for himself when he left school. Somewhat surprised at the question, he said that there must be some relationship but he had never thought about it.

The vast majority of American students, unlike their counterparts in Europe and Asia, have very little incentive to take tough courses or study hard, especially in high school. Students who have little hope of getting a diploma or who do not expect to get more than a dead-end, minimum-wage job when they leave high school typically become dropouts, heading for the door as soon as the law allows. The ones, like Jeff, who choose to stay in high school beyond the age of sixteen know that they can go from high school to community college and many four-year colleges with only a high school diploma. Since they already have the level of literacy needed to get the diploma, the only other requirement to get their diploma is to show up most of time and stay out of trouble. They would be foolish to take a tough course or study hard: they might fail a tough course, and studying hard for an easy course would buy them nothing, since neither the employer nor the nonselective college is particularly interested in their grades as long as they have the diploma.

Only the students who plan to go to a selective college—a very small percentage of all students—have any incentive to take tough courses and study hard for the rest of their high school career.

European and Asian youngsters, including those bound for work at the age of sixteen or eighteen, take tough courses and work hard in school because failure to do so might mean that they do not get to go to college at all or get a good job. Americans are typically appalled to hear this. If one believes that most youngsters are not capable of serious academic work, it seems unfair to set up a system that assumes that anyone can succeed academically who works at it hard enough.

There are many reasons why the performance of American youngsters in secondary school lags behind that of their European and Asian counterparts. But we would not be surprised to find that weak incentives for the students to make a serious effort to learn explain more than half of the difference. It is hardly clear how the performance of American students can meet or exceed the performance of Asian and European youngsters when they leave high school if their students are highly motivated to achieve and ours are not.

The Idea of an Internationally Benchmarked Certificate Standard: The CIM

The idea of the Certificate of Initial Mastery (CIM) was first proposed by the Commission on the Skills of the American Workforce in its landmark 1990 report, *America's Choice: high skills or low wages!*[1] Designed to address the dual problems of low expectations and lack of motivation, it is a simple proposal: find out which countries do the best job of educating their young people in mathematics, science, their native language, and applied learning (the generic skills required to be successful in the modern workplace); find out what they expect of most of their young people at the age of sixteen; create a certificate here in the United States set to that standard; and offer it to anyone who passes an assessment matched to that standard.

Anyone, at any age, could get the certificate. It would never be too late. People seeking the certificate could take the examination portion of the assessment as often as they liked. School districts would be expected to make sure that almost all the students in their care receive the certificate before they reach the age at which they can no longer attend a high school free of charge.

Alternative education programs for out-of-school youth and adults would have to be redesigned to enable them to reach the same certificate standard, and more resources would have to be made available for this purpose because the standard would be more demanding than the high school equivalency standards now in place.

This idea of a certificate standard is very different from the idea behind the high school diploma. Where we now award a diploma for time spent in school, we would instead award a certificate for reaching a predetermined—high—level of measured achievement. All educators believe that youngsters learn at different rates. If that is true, it follows that not all students will earn this new certificate in any given grade or at any given age. It is in the essence of the idea that some will earn it earlier and some will earn it later than others.

If the fundamental goal of public schooling becomes getting all students to a high, internationally benchmarked standard, doesn't it make sense to specify that standard and then award a certificate to everyone who meets it?

What led us to the idea of the certificate standard was the observation that two of the most important impediments to widespread high achievement are low expectations and low student motivation to take tough courses and work hard. How would the certificate standard change that?

First, the certificate standard would end the practice of setting different expectations for different groups of students. The common mantra "All kids can learn" would finally become policy, and what they would be expected to learn would for the first time be explicit. Second, students in the United States would quickly discover that employers that offered jobs leading to good careers and most colleges would demand the certificate. So for the first time, most American students would have a reason to take tough courses and work hard in school.

Later, when we describe our proposals for redesigning the high school, we will explain how the Certificate of Initial Mastery can relate to the high school diploma and college entrance examinations and can be used to restructure opportunities for young people. What is important here is the potential for a high certificate standard to serve as the fulcrum for comprehensive school reform. All students should be expected to achieve it. All schools should understand that their job is to get every student there. All parents should expect their children to get the certificate and their schools to get them there. The certificate standard becomes the gold standard, the universal goal, the standard that counts.

The American Standards Movement

This idea of a universal certificate standard does not exist in a vacuum. The United States is in the midst of a movement to use standards as the rallying principle for the improvement of academic achievement in the schools. To the extent that any such movement can be said to have a beginning, this movement began in 1989, when President George Bush invited the state governors to join him in Charlottesville, Virginia, at the first national summit on education. That meeting produced agreement among the participants on the need for national education goals. A few months later, the governors and the president agreed on a set of goals, and not long after that, they agreed on establishment of the National Education Goals Panel, an unofficial but very high level group of governors and administration officials who would take responsibility for monitoring the nation's progress toward the goals.

Governor Roy Romer of Colorado, who served as the first chair of the Goals Panel, concluded early on that goals would be a far less powerful instrument for improving American education than standards would be, and he undertook a one-person crusade to persuade the American people that this country needed explicit education standards and new forms of assessment to go with them. In the meantime, the Bush administration, in the person of Diane Ravitch, then assistant secretary of education for research and improvement, provided funds to a number of national subject-matter organizations of educators to begin the process of developing national standards for their disciplines.

Al Shanker, then president of the American Federation of Teachers (AFT), became a powerful voice for the standards movement among teachers, a voice that carried well beyond his constituency into the counsels of business and government at every level. And the staff of the AFT, through its study of the development and use of standards in other countries and its thoughtful analysis of the development of standards in the United States, earned the respect of the nation for its "standards for standards."

Bob Schwartz, director of education programs at The Pew Charitable Trusts in Philadelphia, provided funds to the Council for Basic Education to help states develop their own standards and to other organizations that were beginning, each in its own way, to make their own unique contributions. Eva Baker, Chris Cross, Denis Doyle, Chester Finn Jr., Linda Darling-Hammond, Robert Linn, John Murphy, Diane Ravitch, Lauren Resnick, Grant Wiggins, Dennie Palmer Wolf, and others[2] also contributed to the development of the ideas that informed the gathering movement through their writings and consulting practices. The National Board for Professional Teaching Standards' work to develop standards for teachers inevitably contributed to the growing discussion about standards for students.

One by one, the national disciplinary societies, from the National Council of Teachers of Mathematics to the National Council of Teachers of English, and others, like the National Science Board and the American Association for the Advancement of Science, produced standards for their disciplines. At the same time, state after state was gathering its citizens together to build a statewide consensus on the right standards for that state, drawing on the work of the disciplinary societies, the experts in the field, and our own program, New Standards, which we will describe in a moment.

The business community threw its weight behind the standards movement when Lou Gerstner of IBM joined Frank Shrontz of Boeing, John Clendenin of Bell South, George Fisher of Eastman Kodak, other business leaders, several governors, and the leadership of the National Governors' Association to sponsor the Second National Education Summit, at the IBM Palisades Conference Center in New York. The outcome of that meeting was a formal commitment from the governors to produce standards for their states within two years. The organizers of the summit also committed to the formation of a new organization, Achieve, to assist the states in producing high, internationally benchmarked standards.

Perhaps the crowning moment in this phase of the national march toward standards came in President Clinton's second State of the Union message, when he called for national but not federal standards and announced his initiative to develop two national examinations, one in reading at the fourth-grade level and one in mathematics at the eighth-grade level, to be based on the general assessment design and curriculum frameworks embodied in the National Assessment of Educational Progress (NAEP).

What is remarkable about this story is the speed with which it all took place. In the brief moment between 1989 and the first days of 1997, the nation came within a hair's breadth of committing itself to national academic standards for the schools, something that would have been unthinkable through our whole prior history.

Standards: The State of Play

Where does all this activity leave the nation? The answer depends on what the goal is.

If the goal is to make sure that the states have standards, victory is at hand. If it is to make sure that the states have high, internationally competitive standards, however, it is a different story. When Mark Musick, the highly regarded head of the Southern Regional Education Board, compared the performance of students on the National Assessment of Educational Progress to the performance of the same students on their state assessments, he found that many states' students who scored very high on their state assessments scored very low on NAEP. They may have standards, but, thanks to Mark Musick[3], it is now clear that these standards vary widely in rigor.

A detailed assessment of the standards produced by the disciplinary societies and the standards offered by the president's education initiative requires clear guidelines against which to judge them. The judges need standards for the standards.

What should those standards be? We have already explained our feelings on the certificate standard. Beyond that, we believe standards should serve as an antidote to the tracking system, to the strong press for classifying students into ability groups that simply reflect and then reinforce low expectations for those students. Standards should be used to set a very high foundation requirement for all students, reflecting high expectations for everyone. Thus our view implies that a standard is not a cut point on a curve but rather a clear target for everyone to shoot at, a target that almost all students can achieve if they work hard and long enough.

Standards should be usable by students, in the sense that a student should be able to look at the standards and know instantly what topics have to be mastered, what knowledge has to be gained, and what kind of work he or she has to produce to meet the standard. By the same token, standards should be usable by teachers, in the sense that teachers should be able to look at the standards and know what topics they have to teach, what the students need to know, and what kind of work their students have to do to meet the standards. In other words, it should be possible to teach to the standards. This is what we mean by performance standards— the standard should incorporate examples of the kinds of performance that meet the standard. For an example, see the New Standards performance standards in Resource B.

Standards should be expressed in a way that enables them to be used to motivate students to take tough courses and to study hard. The clearest and most easily understood example of such a standard is the certificate. One either gets the certificate or does not, depending on whether the standard has been met. The bar exam, the medical boards, and architectural registration boards are all examples of this sort of standard.

Standards should actually require that students know the things that lie at the heart of the core subjects in the curriculum, but knowledge by itself is not enough. They must also master the core concepts in the disciplines because conceptual mastery is the key to being able to learn more. And it is no less essential for students to be able to apply what they know to real-world problems. Book knowledge is essential, but book knowledge without the ability to put that knowledge to work is of little value. Both the standards and the assessments that go with them should mirror the requirements of life outside the school as much as possible.

Standards, to be successful, must have broad support among

teachers and the general public. Teachers who do not support them will not teach to them. And if they do not have broad support among the public, they will not last long.

Standards should be competitive, in the sense that they should be at least as high as the standards to which students in other countries are held in the same subjects at the same grade or age levels.

Last, standards should be as universal as possible. Standards have a lot in common with telephone companies. A telephone company that can connect you only to telephones on your block is not worth much. A company that can connect you to millions of other telephones around the country is worth a great deal more. In this highly mobile society, a certificate that says you have met a standard that is honored everywhere in the United States is worth a lot more than one that is honored only in your state or community.

Here is how we see the initiatives we just described in relation to these admittedly demanding standards for standards.

Few of the standards being produced by the professional societies or the states were referenced to what was expected of students in other countries.

The professional societies that developed the subject-matter standards were understandably concerned about the way their subjects were being taught in the schools and wanted to take a tough stand in their standards against what they saw as a limited vision of the subject. Leaders in English language arts were concerned, for example, about the reduction of English to the teaching of grammar and diction, mathematics leaders about the teaching of mathematics as little more than arithmetic computation. The result, though, was that when the public looked for these topics in the standards, they were hard to find. From the public's point of view, that simply defied common sense. Some state standards presented another problem. Reflecting many teachers' concern that young people grow up as sensitive, caring adults with what they believe to be good values, they made sure that their state standards commissions put statements in their standards documents reflecting these views.

Many parents who had no objection to state standards for arithmetic, geometry, and physics had a lot of trouble with standards that suggested that the schools should teach values with which they did not agree and wondered whether the schools should in any case be taking over from the family the role of teaching values to young people or should adopt standards that would give schools a license to pry into the details of family relationships at home.

Because the professional societies were not making the hard choices as to what was most important to teach in the subject, their recommendations, if acted on by teachers, would require much more time to teach than was actually available in the school day, week, and year. And because these societies were working independently of one another, the resulting standards were framed in very different ways, making it hard for teachers to grasp what a standard really is and how to teach to it. To be truly useful, the standards would have to be clear, specific, and expressed in a common framework across the disciplines. And they would have to reflect some hard choices as to what was most important in each discipline.

Perhaps most serious from the standpoint of the needs of school people, the standards that the states and professional societies were producing were not performance standards. They specified content—"A student should know . . . and be able to . . ."—but did not convey with any vividness what kind of work would actually meet the content standard. But if students were going to work toward a standard, if teachers were to judge student progress toward a standard and parents were to help their children at home, it would have to be crystal clear what the standard is. One would have to be able to look at a particular piece of student work and say whether or not it meets the standard. Equally important, the only way to break the back of the sorting system is to make the standards clear enough so they would truly be the same for everyone.

This book is about standards-based reform of public education, and there can be no standards-based reform without assessments matched to the standards. Teachers cannot improve teaching and curriculum unless they know how their students are doing against the standards. Students will have no reason to take tough courses and work hard unless something that they care about depends on how well they do on exams matched to the standards. The voters cannot hold the schools accountable unless they have some measure of how well the students are doing. But the professional societies had no plans to develop assessments to match their standards. And the states were finding out that even for the wealthiest, developing examinations that would accurately measure the required range and depth of student learning was extremely expensive.

The New Standards Performance Standards and Assessment System

Following release of the report of the Commission on the Skills of the American Workforce in the fall of 1990, one of the authors of this book, Marc Tucker, asked Lauren Resnick, who had been a commission member, if she and the institution she directs, the Learning Research and Development Center at the University of Pittsburgh, would be willing to join with him and the National Center on Education and the Economy to build the system of standards and assessments that would be needed to make the Certificate of Initial Mastery a reality.

She agreed, and thus was born New Standards. Eventually, seventeen states, six school districts, the American Association for the Advancement of Science, the National Council of Teachers of English, and the University of California joined the coalition. Directed by Resnick and Tucker, New Standards has been funded mainly by large grants from The Pew Charitable Trusts, the MacArthur Foundation, and partnership dues of the states and districts.

Resnick and Tucker's original design for New Standards assumed that the standards that would drive its performance assessments would come from the national standards development projects started by the Bush administration. But for all the reasons just described, that did not work. So New Standards staff, working closely with key members of the professional societies that had created the standards supported by the Bush administration, built a set of standards designed to reflect the "standards for standards" we just described. The objective was to produce a comprehensive, unified set of performance standards for English language arts, mathematics, science, and applied learning for elementary schools, middle schools, and high schools that actually met the standards for standards. The standards development work was led by Ann Borthwick, and the assessment development work was led by Phil Daro of the New Standards staff.

The New Standards governing board, many of whose members were the chief state school officers and superintendents of the participating states and school districts, approved the standards, the final version of which came back from the printer at the beginning of December 1996. Here is what we learned about the challenges involved.

Building Good Standards

The job of creating standards that are usable by teachers and students begins with making tough choices about what is most important to teach and learn. The disciplinary societies had a hard time with this because their members, collectively, believe that everything encompassed by the discipline is important. The states had a hard time with this because the educators who served on the committees typically wanted to include what they teach in their classrooms. Add all the teachers on the statewide committee and all the teachers who lobby them, and the standards quickly become a mile wide and an inch deep. Someone has to lead the process who is empowered to make sure that the standards do not cover more territory in one year than a classroom teacher can cover in one year. This very rarely happens.

Far too many standards documents include statements like "The student shall develop an appreciation of literature," and far too few include statements along the lines of the New Standards requirement that students read twenty-five books a year. It is very hard to measure or even define "an appreciation of literature," and so it becomes a pious wish, but it is quite possible to create a book list and require students to read twenty-five items on that list. Students are unlikely to develop an appreciation of literature without reading some of it.

E. D. Hirsch is right when he says that American educators have become so caught up in the trendy observation that one cannot expect students to learn in school everything they will need to know in life that knowledge itself gets devalued.[4] There are very important things—facts and procedures—that students *can* be taught and *do* have to know, and those things must be clearly specified.

But it is also true that facts unhinged from mastery of essential concepts lead to learning quickly lost and that conceptual mastery that is not applied to real-world problems is arid and useless. Good standards respond to these requirements using examples of student work to show how knowledge, conceptual mastery, and application of what one knows to real-world problems can be combined in a single piece of student work that meets the standards.

The idea of including examples of student work in the standards is the key to making the standards usable by teachers, students, and parents. This format for standards has three essential parts: performance descriptions, samples of student work, and commentaries on the student work. Let us look at each in turn.

1. *Performance Descriptions.* A performance description is a succinct narrative statement of what students are expected to know and be able to do that describes what is most essential to learn in each discipline and is confined to things that can actually be assessed (which leaves out, for example, such things as "love of learning"). Our performance descriptions build directly on the work of professional associations in the disciplines (for example, the National Council of Teachers of Mathematics).

2. *Samples of Student Work.* Examples of actual student work are matched to the performance descriptions to provide a vivid image of what it actually takes to meet the standard.

3. *Commentaries on the Student Work.* These commentaries draw attention to the features of the student work that meet the standard and provide reasons why the expert graders made that judgment. In this way, the reader comes to understand exactly what it takes to meet the standard.

Two examples of performance standards, both from the *New Standards Performance Standards*, appear on the following pages, one from the elementary school math standards and another from the high school English language arts standards (see also Resource B).

In Exhibit 1.1, "Sharing 25," we find all the basic elements of the performance standards. We are told just how the task was presented to the students, that the task was designed to assess performance against two of the mathematics standards ("arithmetic and number concepts" and "mathematical skills and tools") with a reminder of the text for those standards and what the circumstances were in which the task was administered to the students. Then we are shown a piece of student work produced in response to the task the students were given, accompanied by a commentary that compares the work to the performance descriptions.

In the margins of the standards document, the reader is referred to the full statement of the standards for this age and subject, and the appendix shows how these standards are related to other standards for the same subject and grade level and to other subjects at other grade levels.

All of the same elements are present in Exhibit 1.2, "School Bond Levy." Here the subject is English rather than mathematics, and it is set at the high school rather than the elementary school level. The object is to assess the student against two standards, the "writing" standard and the standard for "conventions, grammar, and usage of the English language." The performance descriptions for

Exhibit 1.1. Sharing 25: An Example of an Elementary School Mathematics Task

The Task

In each situation below, four friends want to "share 25" as equally as possible. Show or explain how to "share 25" in each situation.

1. Four friends shared 25 balloons as equally as possible.
2. Four friends shared $25 as equally as possible.
3. Four friends shared 25 cookies as equally as possible.

Students were given five minutes to complete this task.

Sharing 25...

In each situation below, four friends want to "share 25" as equally as possible. Show or explain how to "share 25" in each situation.

1. Four friends shared 25 balloons as equally as possible.

A --➤ 3 people get 6 and one person got 7

2. Four friends shared $25 as equally as possible.

B --➤ Each person gets $6.25

3. Four friends shared 25 cookies as equally as possible.

C --➤ Each person gets 6 and a quarter

Reprinted from Writing in Math Class pp.76–78 © 1995 Math Solutions. Used by permission.

Note: 'A,' 'B,' and 'C' refer to the commentary that follows.

Exhibit 1.1. Continued

Performance Descriptions Assessed by This Task

- Arithmetic and Number Concepts: Add, subtract, multiply, and divide whole numbers.
- Arithmetic and Number Concepts: Estimate, approximate, round off, use landmark numbers, or use exact numbers in calculations.
- Arithmetic and Number Concepts: Describe and compare quantities by using simple fractions.
- Arithmetic and Number Concepts: Describe and compare quantities by using simple decimals.
- Mathematical Skills and Tools: Add, subtract, multiply, and divide whole numbers correctly.
- Mathematical Skills and Tools: Compute time and money.
- Mathematical Skills and Tools: Use $+$, $-$, $\times$, $\div$, $/$, $\overline{)}$, \$, ¢, %, and . (decimal point) correctly in number sentences and expressions.

Commentary: What the Work Shows

Ⓐ Ⓑ Ⓒ The student demonstrated conceptual understanding by applying arithmetic skills differently, and appropriately, in a variety of situations.

Ⓐ Ⓑ Ⓒ The correct answers demonstrate rounding off or use of exact number, as appropriate, in each situation.

Exhibit 1.2. School Bond Levy: An Example of a High School English Language Arts Task

The Task

Students were asked to write a persuasive essay based on research. Students worked on this task individually and had the opportunity to make revisions.

Performance Descriptions Assessed by This Task

- Writing: Produce a persuasive essay.
- Conventions: Demonstrate an understanding of the rules of the English language.

Exhibit 1.2. Continued

School Bond Levy

(A) The _____ School Board has recently proposed a bond levy to add new facilities as well as conduct some major repairs to the school. The bond includes building a new gymnasium, a new science room and lab, a new Media Center/Library, new Chapter 1 and Special Education classrooms, and other facilities such as more parking space, an increase in storage area, and new locker rooms. Along with new construction, the board is proposing to remodel facilities such as the drama/music areas, the entire roof, the heating system, the school kitchen, and present gym as well. This bond allowing _____ School to add more facilities should be passed in order for young students to be provided with a better education.

(C) Several arguments have been brought up concerning the levy since it failed in the March election. Some say that the school doesn't need to have brand new facilities and better classrooms, but it does. Just this year the school had to shut down for days at a time as a result of a malfunction of the heating system. The roof of the library also had a leaking problem all winter long. The leaking has actually caused the ceiling tiles to rot to the point where they are having to be removed. It isn't safe to sit underneath them because, in fact, they have fallen to tables where students had been working only minutes before.

(B) Another issue that people may be concerned with is the money that taxpayers have to put up for the building. The cost of the project in its entirety will be 2.9 million dollars, meaning that for the next 25 years, taxpayers would pay 40 cents more per thousand dollars in property tax than they do this year. The project does cost a significant amount of money, but the school needs it. If something isn't done now, then the facilities such as the library, the science room and others will continue to grow steadily worse. The construction and remodeling needs to be done eventually, so why not

Exhibit 1.2. Continued

D now, when interest rates are low and expenses are also low. Super-intendent _____ commented that it would cost the taxpayers much less money now than ten years from now. Another reason that this is a good time to pass this bond is that the results of Ballot Measure 5 are going into effect at the same time as the levy. As it stands now, property tax rates will go down another $2.50 by next year; however, if taxpayers don't mind paying what they do now and can handle a 40 cent increase, then the school can be that much better.

Many other good reasons exist for funding this construction now. For one, better facilities will be made available to everyone: staff members, students, and community members. The new gym will allow student athletes to have earlier practices and more time for homework. With only one gym in a K–12 school system, the junior high has to practice in the morning before school, starting at

E 6:30 A.M., meaning that both the girls and boys teams had to prac-tice at the same time, with half of the court for the girls half for the boys. After school, the high school girls would practice from 3:30 to 5:30 P.M. The varsity boys would then start at 5:30 or 6:00 and go until 7:30. After that, the junior varsity boys would come in for an hour and a half. It's absurd to think that student athletes cam make good use of their time with a schedule like that. If the bond were to pass, both the new gym and the present gym would be used for practices and athletes wouldn't have to wait so long to practice every day.

Another reason that the gym should be built is that it is no longer adequate. The bleachers are too close to the court and so there is no room to walk by without getting in the way during a game. The gym also poses a problem for the cheerleaders. As it is now, there is no room for them to cheer. The have to stand on one of the ends which, of course, is right in the way of people walking

Exhibit 1.2. Continued

by. If a new gym were built, enough room would be provided surrounding the court that there wouldn't be any of the problems there are now.

Another advantage to the bond proposal is that it would provide more space in the school. The school has always been small, which is in some ways nice, but it needs to expand. The lack of space is a problem because everyone is crammed into one little hallway trying to make it around from class to class. As it is, there isn't enough room for the library to just be a library or the kitchen to just be a kitchen. Students can't even go to the library when they need to because Health, Media, and other classes are held there. The Satellite Learning classroom, which shares a space with the kitchen, usually has a difficult learning atmosphere each day people prepare food for the hot lunch program. Another problem area is the current science room and lab. Lab facilities are outdated and cannot be replaced for a variety of reasons related to the plumbing and electrical systems. Both science teachers have said publicly that the chemical storage room is inadequate and unsafe. The science curriculum is a core part of students' education and they deserve good facilities.

It is clear then, that _____ School needs significant improvements in which case the bond must be passed. As a community, education is an essential part of the future. In the past, _____ has relied in the timber industry for employment, but times are changing and the younger generations need to be better prepared to meet the challenges that arise. For example, they need to able to take part in a variety of activities and be able to achieve in many different areas. If the school is inadequate, how can the younger generations be provided with the education and training they need to be successful in the future?

F

Exhibit 1.2. Continued

Commentary: What the Work Shows

Ⓐ The essay engages the reader by establishing the context of identifying the facilities that the bond levy will add or improve, and by taking a clear stand on the issue. The persona is that of a serious, reasonable individual willing to address opposing viewpoints.

Ⓑ The essay's organization takes into consideration its audience of adults concerned with accelerating tax levies. For example, paragraph three deals with costs by detailing the actual dollar amount needed, and by arguing that current low interest rates and expenses make additions and repairs more cost effective today than they would be in the future.

All of the information and arguments included are relevant to the purpose of the essay.

Ⓒ The student anticipated reader concerns about the need for repairs by recounting in detail the results of a heating system failure and the unsafe conditions in the library.

Ⓓ The arguments are supported with clear, detailed evidence in which the student provided an account of the total costs and the results of Ballot Measure 5.

Ⓔ The student cited scheduling difficulties resulting from having only one gym. The arguments are supported with effective illustrations showing why more space is needed.

Detailed information is included in an effort to persuade the audience, particularly those who voted against the initial bond initiative.

Ⓕ The student used an effective strategy in closing the argument with an emotional plea: "If the school is inadequate, how can the younger generations be provided with the education and training they need to be successful in the future?"

In almost error free writing, the student managed grammar, usage, spelling, punctuation, sentence construction, and paragraph structure.

both standards are spelled out. The commentary makes six concise points about the way the work compares to the writing standard and one key point about the way it relates to the standard for conventions, grammar, and usage. Here again, obviously, there is no one right answer, so we must rely on a close reading of the performance statement, the commentary, and the student work to arrive at a complete understanding of the standard.

Imagine sharing standards of this kind with parents. For the first time, they have a clear image of the kind of work that actually meets the school's standards and are in a position to compare their own son's or daughter's work with the standard to which that work will be held.

What is important about these performance standards? First, they are high and the same for all students. Second, they are rigorous and world-class. Third, they are useful, developing what is needed for citizenship, employment, and lifelong learning. Fourth, they are parsimonious and focus on what is most important in each discipline. Fifth, they take into account how much time there is to teach and learn the subject and how much time is available for assessment. Sixth, they are clear and usable. Seventh, they are also adaptable without sacrificing clarity, in these cases inviting responses that should give no particular advantage to students from any particular background. Last, they reflect a broad consensus on what is truly important, starting, in these cases, with the widely held view that the capacity to compute accurately and to use the conventions of English and demonstrate a command of good grammar and good diction are essential basics around which the rest of the standards must be built.

Note that the answers given in the first example of a performance standard are all mathematically correct but differ from one another. This is because the students are required by the task not just to compute but to make sense of the real world in mathematical terms. They are getting different answers because they have framed different problems. In many ways, this is the essence of what is required in a good standard—relating skills and knowledge of the subject to the real world, showing not just that you know but that you know how to do something practical with what you know.

The problems that modern life will present to the young people now in school when they are adults will be far more demanding than adding up restaurant checks and calculating tips. The standards for success in our democracy and our economy will be very high indeed. The voter deciding on the merits of competing arguments about the use of public lands, the parent deciding on the merits of different approaches to a serious medical problem for a sick child, and the worker in an electricity-generating station who must contribute as a team member to an instant life-or-death decision on how to deal with a nuclear emergency all need exceptional skills to cope.

What we see here is a welding together of two great streams of American curricular thought—the academic and the vocational— into one idea that represents the triumph of neither over the other but rather the best of both. The disciplines are very much present in the examples of standards you just saw, and the need to master the structures of knowledge that they represent is greater than ever. But they are not to be inert knowledge, mastered for its own sake. They are to achieve their ultimate justification in their active use, which has up to now been the domain of vocational education. These standards, then, are standards for a *useful* education. They marry head and hand. This is an old idea, going back in the United States at least to Alfred Whitehead's seminal essay, *The Aims of Education*, written in the early part of this century.[5] Its time has come.

We said earlier that no standards will work unless they are broadly supported by the public. Actually, it would be more accurate to say that no standards *should* work unless they are broadly sup-ported by the public. In the end, the question of what is worth study-ing and learning is a matter for the public to decide; in a democracy, the public is the final arbiter of such questions. To make sure that the public's views were strongly taken into account, we hired Vince

Breglio, one of the nation's leading public opinion experts, to run focus groups all the way through the standards-making process. Breglio's findings[6] were strongly confirmed by a study done independently by the Public Agenda Foundation.[7] The public—including self-described conservatives—is strongly behind standards of the kind we have described here, as long as they are founded on the basics. They want to be sure that the mathematics standards make it unambiguously clear that it is important to be able to add, subtract, multiply, and divide, with and without a calculator. They are equally insistent that students must be able to spell well, have good diction, and get the gist of what they read in the daily paper. Standards that do not start with these basics will sink without a trace in every part of the country and in every major group.

We said that standards must be competitive. Very few of the standards developed by the states or by the disciplinary groups have met this requirement. This is probably true in part because it is expensive to do so and because the target keeps moving. There is no international registry of national academic standards to which one can turn. It is not even clear what constitutes a national standard. Is it the document issued by the ministry of education that specifies the topics to be studied in each subject at each grade level? Is it the national exams, with their cut points? Is it the textbooks in widest use? Is it the actual accomplishments of the students as measured by some common measure? Or is it some combination of all of these things?

New Standards addressed this problem in two ways. First, we did some research in several European and Asian countries on mathematics standards, taking the various definitions of a national standard into account. Second, when drafts of all our standards were done, we sent them to curriculum experts in countries around the world with high education performance and asked those experts to compare our standards to their standards and to call our attention to any case in which they believed our standards were below theirs so that we could improve them.

Exams Matched to the Standards

The New Standards assessment system was developed under the leadership of Phil Daro, now New Standards executive director, and his colleagues Harold Asturias, Sally Hampton, and Elizabeth Stage. It is based on reference examinations, called that because they are carefully referenced to the performance standards. At the end of 1996, the New Standards reference examinations were available in English language arts and mathematics at grades 4, 8, and 10. The mathematics exam is available in Spanish as well as English. With funding from the National Science Foundation, New Standards is developing matching science examinations at the fourth- and eighth-grade levels. Assessments in applied learning will follow.

The typical exam in a given subject at a given grade level is designed to be administered during three forty-five-minute periods during a two-week window. It includes a number of fairly lengthy tasks of the kind illustrated in Exhibit 1.3, found on the next page, as well as a number of short tasks and multiple choice items that ask for the answers to rather straightforward questions.

The president's proposed national examinations in mathematics and English are to be applauded. The problem with them, however, is that they are not set to standards of the kind that we have described in this chapter. The standards will not be ones that teachers can teach to and students will not have examples of the kind of work that they have to produce, so the proposed exams will be very weak engines for improving student performance.

What to Do Right Now

You do not have to use our standards and assessments to engage in standards-based education and do it well. We have shared some of our work on New Standards with you because we are proud of it, and we are proud of it because it reflects our beliefs about what good standards should be. We have built a matching set of performance

Exhibit 1.3. Cubes: An Example of a Middle School and High School Mathematics Task

The Task

In this task students are first asked to figure the volume and the surface area of a cube with edges 3 cm. They are then asked to decide whether or not a given mathematical statement about the relationship between a cube's surface area and volume is mathematically accurate. Finally, they are asked to support their decision—show why the statement is or is not mathematically accurate.

This task is designed to assess conceptual understanding of volume and surface area as described in the Geometry and Measurement performance standard. It also assesses mathematical skills and mathematical communication, and has the potential to assess conceptual understanding as described in the Function and Algebra performance standard.

Students are given about fifteen minutes to complete the task. It is designed with the assumption that each student has a calculator, a ruler, and a pencil.

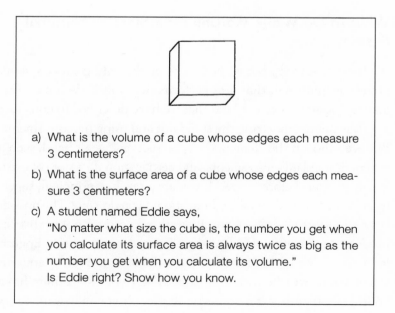

a) What is the volume of a cube whose edges each measure 3 centimeters?

b) What is the surface area of a cube whose edges each measure 3 centimeters?

c) A student named Eddie says,
   "No matter what size the cube is, the number you get when you calculate its surface area is always twice as big as the number you get when you calculate its volume."
   Is Eddie right? Show how you know.

Exhibit 1.3. Continued

Performance Descriptions Assessed by This Task

- Geometry and measurement concepts
- Function and algebra concepts
- Mathematical skills and tools
- Mathematical communication

---

examinations because standards without matching assessments are little more than window dressing.

This book assumes not that you are using our standards but rather that you are or will be using some form of performance standards that answers to many of the same design principles. The reality is that most states will have their own standards for years to come. It is possible to build good examinations that reflect those standards and have most or all of the characteristics that we believe make a high-quality examination.

What to Do While Waiting for a State or National System

We have described what we believe to be the right goal—a system, preferably national, that uses performance standards and performance assessments of the kind that we have described to construct a certificate incorporating the standards and using the assessments. But even though the elements to construct one are at hand, such a system of standards, assessments, and certification does not yet exist. It may be years before it does. If you are a teacher, principal, superintendent, or board member, what should you do *now?* The answer is simple: start where you are. Everything your school or district needs to implement a standards-based assessment system in English language arts and mathematics is available from New Standards today. More will be available shortly. Or your state may have another system that it prefers you to use. Or you may want to try something else. The crucial point is that the standards and assessments needed to begin a program of standards-based reform are at hand. You can use what is available until some form of national system emerges.

If Judy were starting out now at Pasadena High, she would not have to cast around to get some guidance on the standards her students should be meeting. She would not have to go to war with the faculty of the feeder schools over what should be expected in math from every graduating eighth grader. She would not have to do the research to find a way to assess accurately the skills of the eighth graders in relation to the standards. The parents and guardians of the students in the school would not have to find out that the mathematics credits their children had received were meaningless and courses they had taken in algebra had little or no algebra in them to learn. The superintendent would not have to make an agonized choice between the claims of a high school principal championing the needs of the kids and middle school principals whose professional integrity was being questioned.

None of those things would have to happen. Judy's target would be clear, and the means of measuring student progress toward it would be at hand, not just for algebra but for all of mathematics, reading, writing, and the rest of English language arts. The standards would be available not just for these subjects but for science and applied learning, too, with the assessments for those subjects soon to follow. It would be quite clear what the middle schools were supposed to accomplish and how it was to be measured.

That is a long way to have come in just a few years. These are powerful tools. Having them available makes it possible to ask the most important question: How can I get my students to the standards? That is the subject of the rest of this book.

Interlude:
But How Will We Actually Get
These Kids to Algebra II?

Judy B. Codding, Pasadena High School

I've told you how we established beyond doubt that most of the students who entered Pasadena High School in the ninth grade were illiterate in math and how we came to decide that we were going to do something about it. Figuring out what to do proved much more difficult than I had anticipated.

The school offered a two-year general math curriculum that was designed for students who would never take math again. We all knew that that sort of math sequence should not be offered in any high school. Teachers did not like teaching the course because they felt it lacked substance (which was true—there was very little math in this math course). The kids hated it because they knew it was for the "dummies." Who wants to be categorized like that?

Enrolling 85 percent of our entering ninth-grade students in such a dead-end math sequence served no purpose except to give kids the opportunity to earn their two years of required math credit through seat time. The math they learned would prepare not one student to enter college or to hold any but a dead-end job. The general math sequence was a fraud, and everyone knew it.

Only 20 percent of our students graduated with credit (though there was no telling what they actually knew and learned) in algebra or geometry; the rest had credit only for general math. We set out to get at least 80 percent graduating with a good working knowledge of algebra and geometry. Not that that would be good enough, but it would be a mighty and worthwhile accomplishment. But we didn't want to rely solely on course credit to measure our success; we wanted to have some assurance that our students had actually mastered the content. I've already told you what had happened when we relied on course credit alone to place our students in a math program as they arrived in high school.

I asked the math department to recommend a curriculum that would ensure that at least 80 percent of our students would acquire the knowledge and skills they needed for upper-level high school math and science study. I say science because the poor math foundation of our students was dramatically affecting how they performed in their science classes. After much discussion, the math department recommended a new math series that was getting very high marks around the country. When I met with representatives from that program, it was very clear to me that although their program would be wonderful for that handful of students at Pasadena who had a strong math foundation, it would leave the rest in the dust. It assumed a computational and conceptual foundation that most of our students just didn't have.

I honestly did not know what to do. I asked the district math coordinator for some recommendations; he had nothing to offer but some standard textbook series. I wondered why the recommended math textbook series would help now when it hadn't worked in the past. I knew we had to have a program that would enable our kids to catch up to where they had to be in a rapid sprint. At best, following the textbook series as it was intended to be used would take years we did not have. At worst, they would fare no better in the standard series the second time around than they had the first time (which was actually the most likely outcome).

We needed a program that would not only give our kids the computational and conceptual foundation they needed but also provide them with the opportunity to succeed in math (for the first time, for most of them), to understand the purpose of studying math by seeing how it could be applied to their own lives, and to provide both teachers and students with the support and structure needed for high achievement. The standard textbook series did none of these things.

Fortunately, the school district had a very energetic director of high schools. We agreed that we had to seek out something that was specially designed to meet the needs of our student population but would not "dumb down" what the kids needed to know. We laid out a plan to talk with people all over the country to find what we were looking for.

And we finally found a program that filled the bill. Beginning in September 1991, we began to pilot the Comprehensive Math and Science Program (CMSP), a program directed by Dr. Gil Lopez and supported by the National Science Foundation. The program was based at Columbia University and Cooper Union. We started with around sixty randomly selected ninth-grade students. The following year we implemented the program for 85 percent—over five hundred—of the ninth-grade students. The year after that, the 1993–94 school year, we had approximately 85 percent of all ninth and tenth graders in CMSP.

Over time, the kids and many of the adults came to call the program "Ground Zero." That's because the curriculum had to go back to basic arithmetic before students could be exposed to prealgebra, algebra, and geometry topics. CMSP is designed to provide underachieving math students with a highly structured experience that has nine main elements:

1. A four-semester sequenced math curriculum is set up in which students take two different math classes every day, one focused on computational and conceptual understanding and the other on application. The courses are taught by two different teachers who use the topics in one course to complement and reinforce the topics in the other; 75 percent of the topics taught include verbal problems.

2. The school uses its Title I money to support in-class, after-school, and Saturday tutoring programs for students who need extra support to succeed.

3. Parents sign a contract with the school, pledging them to do all that is necessary to support their children as they reach for a high math standard, including guaranteeing that they will support their

children attending after-school and Saturday tutoring sessions if the students are falling behind.

4. The students are assessed frequently and given continual feedback so that they know at all times whether they are mastering the material.

5. A high standard of achievement is expected of all students, which means that students take weekly tests developed by CMSP. The only grades are A, B, and no credit. Gone are the days of gratuitous C's and D's.

6. A student who has not mastered the content has to attend an intensive summer program. Mastering the content is defined as getting at least a B for the year's work, including the final exam.

7. All teachers teaching CMSP have to attend an intensive one-week summer training program and monthly math seminars during the school year.

8. The school has to dedicate half the time of a math teacher to coordinating the CMSP math program in the school.

9. The school has to buy and use the CMSP materials.

This was an enormous commitment for Pasadena High. Juggling the master schedule to permit 85 percent of all ninth and tenth graders to take two periods of math with two different teachers was an absolute nightmare.

But the real agony came when we realized that we had to double the math faculty in order to permit almost half the students in the school to take two math classes a day. Doing this demanded excruciating trade-offs. Making our academic priorities prevail would test the resolve of everyone concerned.

Would we be willing to do what had to be done about our students' math competence if it meant that programs like wood shop, auto repair, and elective history and English classes would no longer be offered? Could we move away from being a "shopping mall high school" and focus on *student performance in the core curriculum? Would the student and parent community really support this effort when their favorite course or activity got cut? Would we be willing to set student achievement as our number one priority even if it meant that some teachers would lose their jobs? Would changing the use of Title I money ever be acceptable to the community when the jobs of some community residents were lost as a result? Could the district superintendent, the school board, and I stand the heat?*

Nothing about the implementation of CMSP was easy. I told you earlier about the nightmare of going to the middle schools, testing the students, and then having to inform the parents and guardians of those students who had received University of California credit for math that their children might have the credit but did not know anything and would have to do it all over again. I forgot to tell you that when we went through the redesign of the master schedule, we had to make sure that a teacher who taught a class in math computation and concepts had to have just the same students as the teacher who taught the applications side—further compounding the scheduling problem—so that they could coordinate their lessons and talk about the progress of each student.

But the really big problems were all to come. First and foremost was the problem of recruiting the math teachers we needed for the new program. What math teacher wants to teach ninth-grade students who have little math knowledge? And the teachers who would be doing this would be accountable for student performance in very different and more demanding ways than teachers or administrators anywhere had been used to. We would be using exams developed by CMSP over which we had no control. Were we willing to be accountable in the same ways we were asking the middle schools to be accountable?

A related problem was recruiting new math teachers to the school who knew enough mathematics and knew it well enough to teach what we needed to have taught. It's no secret that thoroughly prepared math teachers are in short supply. Even though the new teachers would be teaching in CMSP, they needed to know calculus in order to understand what students needed to know and be able to do when they got to the upper-level math classes. Too many teachers already at PHS did not have an adequate math background; I refused to add more.

The training of the math teachers in CMSP was another problem. We had to find the money needed for the intensive summer training and monthly seminars during the school year, which meant taking money from the existing school program, never a popular thing to do. What is sacred in the high school program has little to do with whether it is actually working.

To gain human, material, and financial resources, we closed most of the vocational education classes. They had become the dumping ground for nonachieving students, and everyone knew it. Because we lacked the money to keep up the equipment for the vocational education courses, the program was not only weak but also miseducative.

Shutting down these vocational courses meant that teachers who were certified only to teach those classes no longer had a job. Some had been at the school for thirty years. This was a very painful decision for me. Those teachers were good people, most of whom cared a lot about kids. They were unwilling to seek retraining at that stage in their careers. I could not blame them. My dilemma was to do what was best for the well-intentioned teachers who had put in many years of service but did not have the knowledge or skills that were now needed or to do what was best for the students.

Most of the teachers in the school understood why I was making the decision in favor of the students but found it personally difficult to support that decision because of their fondness for colleagues of long-standing.

Even after wiping out the entire vocational education department, we still did not have enough slots to hire all the teachers we needed for the new math program. I decided that we had to do the impossible. We had to cut down on many of the elective courses in the school and use the staff slots supporting those classes to support the staffing of CMSP.

But what was I going to do with those students who now would not have vocational education or other elective courses from which to choose? To accommodate these students, and fully aware that students in most urban high schools are not allowed to have unscheduled time for security reasons, we very reluctantly decided to create a massive study hall program at the end of the school day in the auditorium. It would have to accommodate six hundred students and be staffed by one teacher (the minimum required by law), teacher's aides, and security staff.

I don't think I have ever done anything that was so educationally wrong-minded. But we had to get the staffing slots to support CMSP, and they would not come from the district, so I had to find them in our current staffing allocation. Putting six hundred students with one teacher freed up four slots to support CMSP—enough to staff twenty sections of math.

Finding the staffing slots in the regular school day was not our only challenge. The program called for other resources we did not have unless we reprogrammed resources being used for other purposes.

For example, CMSP trained a cadre of our higher-performing high school math students to act as tutors during CMSP class time, after school, and on Saturdays. They received community service credit for the classroom tutoring they did and were paid $5 an hour for the after-school and Saturday tutoring. CMSP also trained Pasadena City College and Cal Tech students as tutors.

Then we had to offer an intensive summer school CMSP math academy to students who had not achieved at the 80th percentile or higher in order for those students to go on to the next level. The academy was taught by Pasadena High School CMSP teachers with extra in-class support provided by the tutors. The tutors were able to give students the kind of support and personalization we knew it would take for many of them to be able to achieve the standard we had set.

We found the money for all these things by raiding other items in our meager budget of $3,500 per child per year. Thank goodness, all the tough decisions and hard work by the teachers paid off! Student performance went up dramatically in a short period of time.

The 1991 pilot study reported that the CMSP students outscored their ninth-grade peers on the Stanford Achievement Test by 27.9 points. At the conclusion of the 1991–92 school year, 90.4 percent of CMSP students received a grade of A or B in math, as opposed to 18 percent of the other ninth-grade math students. Also, 71.4 percent of the CMSP ninth-grade students passed the math proficiency exam, compared with only 47.3 percent of the tenth-grade students.

In the Pasadena system, the math proficiency exam is taken for the first time in the tenth grade, and students have until they graduate to pass it. However, we decided to have all ninth-grade CMSP students take the test. The results were astounding. The combined evidence convinced me that I had to figure out a way to make CMSP available to all ninth-grade students who did not have the knowledge or skills to complete geometry or above before they completed high school. For PHS, this meant 85 percent of the incoming ninth-grade class in 1992 had to be in the CMSP program.

By the spring of 1993, PHS student math scores on the Stanford Achievement Test had jumped from the 26th percentile when those students took the test in middle school to the 54th percentile at the high school. The following year, PHS students scored in the 57th percentile. Two years after the program began, overall math student achievement soared and failures plummeted, from 47 percent receiving a D or F in math to only 22 percent. This was not yet good enough, but it was much better than it had been. PHS went from the worst-performing high school in the district on the math Stanford Achievement Test to the highest-performing school.

Our teachers, initially doubtful that their students could do much better than they had been doing, became the biggest advocates for high expectations for all students once they saw for themselves what these students could achieve. As for myself, I would never again underestimate what it would take to produce and implement a curriculum that was in fact matched to the standards we set for the students.

2

Teaching to the Standards

As the nineteenth century came to a close, the United States stood poised between two contending images of a desirable curriculum for American students. The Committee of Ten, convened by the National Education Association, offered a vision of a common and demanding curriculum, centered on the traditional academic subjects, for all high school students. They wanted students to put off occupational decisions until after graduation, feeling that if this were not done, children from poorer families would lose out. Twenty-five years later, the same organization, under different leadership, reversed course with the release of the Cardinal Principles of Secondary Education in 1918. The authors of this document maintained that high schools should look after the "nature and needs" of the heterogeneous body of students flooding into American high schools. They wanted a curriculum of great variety, much of it very practical, that would contain something for everyone, from which any individual (or an adviser) could chose what was appropriate, given that individual's background, intelligence, and probable occupational niche. They rejected the Committee of Ten's vision as an elitist ideal that was inappropriate for a democratic society.

Nearly a century has gone by since the Committee of Ten lost the argument. That argument, however farsighted, fell on the deaf ears of a society whose economy did not demand a highly educated population, whose citizens admired schooling but distrusted learning, and whose educators had their hands full coping with the needs of ever greater numbers of students. The educators responded by producing a great smorgasbord of a curriculum perceived to be nothing if not democratic. For almost a century, discussions about curriculum in this country have centered on which courses should be offered and which should be required for which students. Running very smoothly just under the slogan of democracy, the giant sorting engine was operating with a quiet hum for all those years.

A Sea Change in Thinking About Learning

But the Committee of Ten may have the last laugh, at least in the essentials. A rising chorus is calling for a return to the demands of the core disciplines and the idea that all students should meet a common high academic standard before going their separate ways.

This is not the only revolution under way in this arena. The United States has never had any standards at all—at least not standards of the kind described in this book. It has had tests, but the idea that one should teach to these tests has for years been repugnant to American teachers, who viewed the curriculum implicit in the most widely used tests as demeaning to them and to their students. Just a few years ago, many educators and some key policymakers moved to new ground by proposing that state curriculum frameworks might be instituted to guide practice in the classroom. Curriculum frameworks were seen as less intrusive than the introduction of explicit standards and statewide high-stakes tests but a considerable step from the hands-off attitude that had been taken toward local autonomy in curriculum matters.

But Judy was not alone in her realization at Pasadena High that curriculum frameworks are not enough. Now the idea that one should teach to both explicit standards and the test is gaining ground, provided, of course, that they are standards and exams worth teaching to. And many are beginning to wonder whether the standards that drive assessment and curriculum ought also to drive the initial preparation and licensing of teachers. So with remarkable speed, considering the historical record, the idea of alignment around standards is taking hold.

These revolutions—a return to insistence that everyone master a demanding common academic core; commitment to a high academic standard for everyone, irrespective of occupational choice or personal background; and acceptance of the idea that the curriculum and the preparation of teachers should be tied to explicit student performance standards and aligned with assessments that are also aligned with the standards—would be extraordinary by themselves after such a long commitment to principles and practices so deeply at odds with them.

But that is not all. Americans may be growing less suspicious of the truly educated person. For the first time in a century, there is evidence for growing support among many segments of the public, the education profession, and the business community for the idea that mastery of the underlying structure of the academic disciplines and their core content of knowledge matters very much, that it is far more important to understand a few things deeply than many things only superficially, and that the ability to reason well is not a luxury reserved for the rich and fortunate but a necessity for every member of society. If this is so, if there is a fundamental shift under way toward support for genuine intellectual effort in school, combined with an embracing of the idea that this intellectual effort should be not the arid scholasticism of the latter half of the nineteenth century but useful intellectual effort—thinking for real-world purposes—then the terms of the curriculum debate in the United States have shifted in a quite fundamental way.

In the something-for-everyone sorting world of the century now coming to a close, the emphasis was on what was taught, not what was learned; on coverage, not mastery; on remembering for the test, not learning for the long haul; on gaining students' interest, not educating for rigor.

The Third International Mathematics and Science Study (TIMSS) revealed the enormous price this country has paid for these preferences.[1] Lacking a ministry that could set a curriculum, we had our curriculum set for us by the textbook publishers. Because they could not afford to publish textbooks for only one jurisdiction, they combined the curriculum requests they received from many jurisdictions. The result was the largest and most expensive textbooks in the world, each one covering many more topics in a given subject than were covered in any one grade in other countries. Thus the United States achieved coverage at the expense of mastery.

Later on, we will share our ideas for a new approach to instructional materials. But before we do that, we want to present the principles of learning on which they are based.

The Principles of Learning

The answers to these questions must reflect the principles of learning to which one subscribes. So let us lay out the principles that we believe should guide schools as they design their curriculum. Adapted from a similar list developed by Lauren Resnick,[2] the principles presented here are meant to guide the process of building an environment for learning that will get your students to high standards. Each is supported by decades of educational research. Taken together, they are a powerful instrument for curriculum and instructional design. We briefly discuss each in turn here and then apply them when we propose specific steps for building an effective school learning environment.

1. *Student effort is a more important determinant of achievement than natural ability.* This may be the single most important statement in this book. The evidence for it is overwhelming. The American idea that the most important factor in explaining educational achievement is inherited ability is simply wrong; there are differences in natural intelligence that cannot be completely overcome by effort, education, and experience, but most students can achieve

at what most of us would regard as very high levels if they work hard enough at it. Asian peoples, especially the ethnic Chinese, Japanese, and Koreans, believe that effort counts for much more than inherited ability. They also have some of the highest levels of academic achievement in the world. This should tell us something. The whole education system must be redesigned to do everything possible to elicit and reward student effort.

2. *Getting all students to achieve at high levels depends on clear expectations that are the same for all students.* Students will not make the effort if the adults around them communicate the belief that no matter how much effort they put in, they do not have what it takes to achieve. And this is just what adults in the United States have done for decades for the majority of our students. The best way for this country to reverse that course is to set a high standard that is the same everywhere and for everyone and make it clear to all but the most severely handicapped that they are expected by all the adults in their lives to reach that standard. Period.

3. *All students need a thinking curriculum—one that provides a deep understanding of the subject and the ability to apply that understanding to the complex, real-world problems that the student will face as an adult.* Many educators have read these words or others like them recently to call for an "integrated" curriculum organized around themes of some kind. Such a curriculum might, for example, consist of three months of work for an entire class in which they study a particular historical place and time, using that exploration as the basis for all their work in English, math, science, history, and economics. Students often find such programs interesting and even engaging, and so do their teachers, but all too often the learning that students actually do in such situations is very shallow. It is essential that students develop a deep understanding of the structure of knowledge in the core disciplines and that they actually gain the knowledge that is essential in that discipline. "Applying what one knows" requires knowing something, but application is of equal importance—in nonroutine problems, problems that may have many right answers,

problems for which the knowledge needed to solve them may not lie readily at hand, problems that may require conflicting criteria for their solution, and problems that have no predetermined path for their solution. Interdisciplinary projects organized around themes may have their place in such a curriculum, but much more is required to realize this principle in practice.

4. *Students of all ages learn best in two types of circumstances: when they are seeking and using knowledge and skills to address problems that challenge and engage them and when they are teaching others.* Decades of cognitive research show that listening to lectures, doing the typical homework at the end of the chapter, and remembering this lifeless material long enough to pass the quiz or take the exam at the end of the semester typically results in learning that neither goes very deep nor lasts very long. We learn well when we are hanging the new knowledge on something we already know, when we see the connections to things we know and care about, when we can use the new knowledge or skill to do something that we need or want to do. We really understand when we have tested what we have learned against what we thought we knew already and integrated the new knowledge into the framework we have built to hold and explain what we already knew. No one knows whether they understand what they learned in a book or class about carpentry until they actually build something. What does it mean to know how to do arithmetic and fractions if one cannot add up the items in a restaurant check and calculate the tip or measure a two-by-four and cut it in half? Does one really understand the geology text if one cannot even begin to describe the history of the rocks at a particular road cut in the highway? What do we make of the history student who can perfectly capture what the leading historians of the American Revolution have said about that era but are at a loss when asked to reason from their analysis to the implications for modern-day Russia? The first part of this principle stresses the importance of a curriculum at the heart of which is knowledge that

is not "inert," in Alfred North Whitehead's terms, but is "alive," connected with a student's experience, and built into the student's personal repertoire of knowledge and skills by active use.

The second point here is narrower but very important. A mountain of research, as well as the common store of experience, confirms what we all know: we often learn best by teaching something we thought we knew to others. In the context of public education, it is now clear that organizing our schools so that older children routinely teach younger children has powerful positive effects on the younger children that are dwarfed by the positive effects on the learning of the older children.

The two points embraced by this principle are obviously related. One of the reasons that people learn so much from teaching others is that they are put in a position in which they are forced to find out whether they really know what they think they know by the questions they are asked by the learner. They don't like it when they have to bluff their way through the answers. It is very like the participant in the carpentry class who must now go out and frame a house.

5. *People learn well when working beside an expert who models skilled practice and encourages and guides learners as they create products or performances for audiences whose reactions really matter.* If the house falls down, someone may be hurt, and many are sure to be angry. It matters a lot whether or not it was framed well. But most of the work that students do is not like that at all. It all seems like make-work, of interest only to the teacher and the student, instantly forgotten after it is graded. Carpentry students that get good enough to frame a house that will remain standing do not acquire those skills by reading the right chapters in the text and doing their homework problems on time. They are taught by teachers who look at their carpentry and critique it, in an ordered way, so that as each skill is actually acquired and made good by use, another new challenge is presented, and the teacher shows the apprentice how to

meet it. The student once again tries to emulate the teacher and the teacher critiques the work, on and on until the student acquires enough expertise to do the job independently.

Writing is just as much of a craft as carpentry, but consider what we do. We ask a student to write a paper. We grade it. We may put some comments on it and then hand out another assignment. This house will never stand. If we were as serious about student writing as we are about the carpenter-to-be, we would ask a student to write a paper, give the student extensive comments on the paper, and ask the student to write it again and again until it meets a high standard for a paper of that type—and then do it again with a more complex and ambitious assignment. This is what happens when a carpentry student is required first to reach mastery level framing a standard wall section and then, much later, framing a complex dormer in which many roof planes intersect at many angles.

In both cases, the expert is leading the apprentice up a carefully stepped ladder of challenges, each of which builds on the expertise gained at earlier stages. Writing does not stand alone. Much of what we want students to learn in school has some or all of this apprentice-like character, with respect to both the way in which it is learned and the need to be sure that the product of the effort means something important to adults whose opinion the student values.

We said earlier that a revolution is taking place on the curriculum front, that a discussion about what courses to offer has turned into a discussion about what content and performance standards students should meet and how to get them to the standards. This shift in orientation has not resolved many issues of long-standing, and it has raised many new ones. The principles we just described do not address all of these issues, nor will they serve as infallible guides to those they do address. But they have been helpful to us, and in the pages that follow, you will see how they have informed our view of the most important things schools can do to improve the learning environment for their students.

What You Can Do: Deciding on Your Own Standards

We described the standards that have been developed by the New Standards organization in Chapter One. We are very proud of them. We believe that they represent a major advance in American thinking about what standards should be and how they should be expressed. We think they are both visionary and practical, in the sense that they represent high aspirations for students, but they also make it possible to devise a curriculum for students that will enable them to learn what is called for in the standards in the time that is available in the school year.

But we do not think that these standards—or state standards that are cast in the same mold—are all that a state, a district, or a school needs. There are other subjects that are no less important than English language arts, mathematics, science, and applied learning, among them history, the arts, geography, economics, foreign languages, and personal health and fitness. You will need standards for those subjects and for others you regard as equally important. If you are making policy at the state or district level, though, you need to ask yourself whether there is actually enough time in the school day, week, and year to enable real teachers in real schools to teach the material addressed by the standards, properly and thoroughly, and whether teachers will have sufficient time remaining for the next lower level—the district or the school—to add standards of their own that reflect what they hold most dear. If the answer to any of these things is no, go back to the drawing board. This is very hard work.

But assume for the moment that you have written acceptable standards. You are still not done. What we want for our young people cannot simply be framed subject by subject. There are those who say that the schools should be responsible for academics and nothing else, in particular nothing having to do with values. But that is nonsense. Schools teach values every minute of every day, whether they intend to or not, by virtue of what they do.

Young people are very acute observers of adults and the discrepancies between what they say and what they actually do. Few parents want the teachers of their sons and daughters to be indifferent to lying and cheating or to refrain from disciplining the bully or praising the teenager who volunteers to help the less fortunate. There are moral positions that constitute the moral bedrock of our lives together, and we expect the schools to articulate and reinforce them whenever possible.

And there is more. We all know that success in high school is a good predictor of success in college but is not very well correlated with success in life. The race, at the end of the day, often goes to the one who is better at reading people and situations, who can get along with other people, who has leadership qualities, who is determined, who has the inner resources to weather a crisis when others would fall apart, and so on. Conversely, the student who feels that he or she has no chance in life is not likely to be a good student. What's the point if I'm going to fail anyway?

Not long ago, many teachers took this line of reasoning to arrive at the conclusion that students' "self-image"—how they feel about themselves—is more important than academic achievement. Coaches often argue that the leadership and teamwork skills developed in competitive sports are more important than the academic skills developed in the classroom. Our view is simple. The academic and work-related skills embodied in the New Standards performance standards are the essentials. Most of the weight of the judgment as to whether a school is doing its job should be based on measures of progress against these standards. But the other qualities should not be ignored, and each state, district, and school will have to come to its own conclusion as to the right balance. The discussion as to what you are about, especially at the school level, will be repaid, if it is seriously undertaken and frequently renewed in an honest way, by a growing consensus that will serve the students well as they develop in a moral environment that nourishes and leavens their intellectual growth.

Not all of the standards a school or district sets will be directly measurable for individual students. But that does not mean that they are wholly unmeasurable. Take honesty, for example, or the capacity for becoming responsible for one's own behavior. A school can keep a record of the documented cases of cheating in a given period and pay attention to the trend lines revealed by these data. It can ask students to fill in questionnaires anonymously that provide data on the number of instances of cheating that they have either participated in or know about other students participating in. When the data are in, the school leaders can ask students and staff to develop and enforce an honor code related to cheating that is based on the analysis of the data.

It is possible to find out what students as a group think about such matters as whether the adults in the school act fairly or simply reward the most obedient and whether students who do the right thing are reinforced by the staff or hung out to dry, ignored. If there are qualities you really want to develop in youngsters as they are growing up, you can in fact find out how you are doing with techniques such as these.

The main point here is that you need to think hard about what you want for the students, state the result clearly, and then find a creative way to measure student and school progress against the standards. Start with the standards you are committed to, or whatever standards your state requires, and branch out from there. Aim for parsimony—it is far better to have only a few things identified as terribly important than to have so many goals that it becomes impossible to set priorities. Consider everything—and then make the tough choices. And find an objective way to measure your progress toward as many of your standards as possible.

When you have decided on the standards and the measures you will use, the hard work—deciding on the curriculum, the materials, and the instructional strategies you will use to get the students to the standards—still lies ahead.

What Schools Can Do: Building Standards-Based Classrooms

One of our colleagues, Sally Hampton, has described the ways in which classrooms might be changed by the existence of performance standards of the kind that New Standards has developed.[3] Sally's field is English language arts, so the examples that follow are from the English language arts curriculum.

The standards are everywhere, and the materials in the classroom are selected to match them. Imagine, as you enter the standards-based school, that you look up at the walls. Everywhere you look, you see posters with performance statements from the standards. Peering into the homerooms, you see folders in which the students are accumulating the work that they are doing to demonstrate at year's end that they can meet the standards for that grade. On the shelves, you find familiar textbooks and collections of works of literature. But the texts have been carefully marked to indicate which topics, stories, and questions are to be read and which can be ignored, based on the teachers' assessment of the degree to which any individual section will help the students meet the standards. In addition to the usual texts and works of literature, there are also unfamiliar items in profusion—selected sections from computer manuals and other technical works, newspaper and magazine articles, instructions for playing computer games, memos written by people in the central office to explain a policy or a procedure. There might be instructions for planting a vegetable garden and doing routine maintenance on a lawn mower. Clearly, the definition of English incorporates literature but goes beyond it to encompass the many genres in which we use the language to communicate with one another, from the sublime to the most practical, all of which are described in the standards.

A glance around the school, in short, makes it clear that the materials that students are expected to use have been very carefully selected in the light of their match to the standards.

The year-by-year curriculum is planned backward from the benchmarks. As we talk with the teachers, we find that they spend a lot of time planning together, working backward from the benchmark standards at grades 4, 8, and 10 to produce a set of expectations for each of the grades leading up to and going beyond the benchmark grades. In writing, for example, they do this for each of the genres specified in the standards. Then, at each grade, they work together to come to a consensus on a set of pieces of student work that meets the standards for that grade level, accumulating sets of student work that cover the standards they have developed for that grade.

The detailed curriculum is based on analysis of students' strengths and weaknesses against the standards. At the beginning of the school year, the teachers agree on a set of assignments that they will give the students to assess where they stand in relation to the standards developed for that grade, genre by genre. Then they collect the work the students do and sit down with a stack of two-by-three-inch note sheets. They divide these little sheets into three sections. In one section, marked "+," the teachers note the features specified by the standards that the student has successfully incorporated into the work. In the next section, marked "−," the teachers record elements specified by the standards that the student left out. And in the last section, marked "X," the teachers mark habitual error patterns, such as run-on sentences, spelling problems, and subject-verb irregularities.

After doing this, the teachers review the note sheets for the whole class. They use the notes to figure out what most of the students already know and thus need not be taught again, what the students do not know, and what kinds of errors they typically make. On the basis of that analysis, the teachers lay out a program of instruction designed to get their students to the performance standards they devised for that grade.

Extended lessons are based on analysis. The teachers get together to plan out a series of extended lessons for the year, each extended lesson pitched to a level of difficulty a little greater than the last one. Throughout the year, the teachers stop from time to time to focus attention on class members' work that is meeting the standards for that portion of the school course, engaging the class in a discussion of exactly what features of the work correspond to what the standards call for.

Drawing on a common feature of Japanese schools, a team of teachers develop each extended lesson. Then they assign one of their most capable team members to teach it. All the teachers watch that teacher in the classroom and then gather to critique the draft extended lesson in light of what they saw. Then the extended lesson is revised to reflect the critique. And this continues until the whole team is satisfied with the quality of the extended lesson. Sometimes it takes a whole year to develop one class-period extended lesson in this way, but when it is finished, it is first-rate, and all the teachers can take advantage of the work that went into it.

The faculty discussions of individual extended lessons are found to be valuable professional development experiences, and they become a regular feature of school life. No less important, this experience creates a whole new professional culture in the school. Teachers who are unsure of themselves, upon getting one of these extended lessons, want very much to look their best in front of their colleagues and often seek help as they develop their student extended lessons. The same peer pressure that has so often undermined student performance now contributes mightily to improved professional performance.

Students are expected to take responsibility for reaching the standards. In this whole process, Sally stresses the importance of the students themselves internalizing the standards and adopting them as their own. Only when the students fully understand what the standard is and take responsibility for achieving it can real progress be made. There is nothing magic about this. We see examples of it all about us when the subject is sports rather than academics. The youngster who accomplishes much on the baseball diamond or the football field has learned the rules of the game, set a target for personal accomplishment, and does not rest until it is achieved.

Because this kind of personal responsibility is the goal, it is essential that students be able to make reliable judgments about the quality of their own work. The key is good rubrics that will be used by both students and teachers to judge the quality of student work against the standards. By "rubrics" we mean detailed guides for scoring or grading student work.

The standards-based classroom surrounds the students with indicators of quality. Our colleague Phil Daro has conceptualized this as a sort of "quality triangle," the three points of which are defined as "course content," "student products," and "student process." At the first point, the standards are used to define the content of instruction—what the student should know and be able to do. At the second point, the standards define the quality of work the students must produce and are therefore used to assess the quality of student work. At the third point, the standards are used to define the process of production of student work, letting the student know what categories of work are wanted and providing the basis of the feedback they get as they produce it. In this sense, the standards-based classroom is actually a quality-based classroom.

What Teachers Need: Alternatives to Today's Textbooks

There is a reason that the use of textbooks is so prevalent in American schools. Making high-quality instructional materials is demanding, time-consuming, and expensive work. Although we just described a process by which classroom teachers might develop their own assignments, the reality is that teaching is a full-time job, and it is very unlikely that full-time teachers can also develop all the high-quality curriculum materials they will need, any more than full-time practicing physicians are likely to come up with all the procedures, equipment, and medications they need.

Led by Sally Hampton, Phil Daro, and Sally Mentor Hay, the National Center on Education and the Economy has conceptualized

the standards-driven instructional system of the future to consist of
concept books, extended lesson books, and *courses of study.*

1. *Concept books.* We pointed out earlier that American textbooks are concept-poor. But there is no real understanding
   without a good grasp of the concepts that underlie the disciplines. We believe that every student should be given a concept book for every core subject in the curriculum covering
   multiple years of concepts for each subject. These concept
   books should be in paperback form, given, not loaned, to
   the student, for that student to keep and share with his or
   her parents. Each book would contain the material needed
   for the student to study the conceptual underpinnings of the
   most important concepts to be introduced in that subject
   during each of the three years covered by the book.

2. *Extended lesson books.* Extended lesson books would contain
   a set of problems or extended lessons of the type described
   earlier. The set of extended lessons for each year would cover
   roughly half of a year's major extended lessons. They would be
   very carefully fashioned and fully field-tested, designed to represent the essentials for each of the standards to be covered
   during the period for which the book is prepared. Each book
   would contain, in addition to the extended lessons, the
   related rubrics required to assess the work produced by the
   students, examples of student work that meet the standards
   assessed by the extended lesson, and a commentary on that
   work, indicating in detail what features of the student work
   examples meet which parts of the standards.

3. *Courses of study.* These are a new kind of teacher's guide,
   one that lays out a program or course of study for a year that
   will enable the students to reach the standards for that year
   in a particular subject. It would be best to have many
   courses of study for each set of standards, rather than just
   one, because we believe that there will be many ways to

get to the standards, and teachers should be able to choose the approach that they feel most comfortable with. Each course of study should reference the standards and show how the lessons in the extended lesson book can be combined with literature texts, commercial software, commercially available texts, and other supplementary material to get students to the standards. The courses of study should clearly describe a small number of topics to be covered in a particular year or grade and the sequence in which they should be covered. Each of these topics would get treated in-depth but would not be covered in subsequent years. This is in direct contrast to current practice, which gives the student superficial exposure to the same topics year after year. In this system, students will have the opportunity to really master each major topic in the discipline before going on to the next, and the topics will be sequenced in a way that follows the underlying logic of the discipline. They should help the teacher anticipate problems that may crop up as the students work on the extended lessons and deal with those problems, contain material related to the lessons to be taught, and provide suggestions on alternate materials that can be integrated into the class.

Over time, as development proceeds on this plan, the instructional materials industry in the United States, which has always been highly responsive to its market, will produce and market materials that reflect what is learned from the development process. The standards-based classroom is unlikely to flourish until this happens.

The National Center on Education and the Economy has initiated a development program based on these principles. The first materials produced by this program were field tested beginning in the spring of 1997.

But it will take years before materials of the kind we just described are widely available. So what can you do now?

First, you can conduct an audit of your curriculum to determine the fit between your current curriculum and the standards you have selected and then do a systematic analysis to determine what commercially available materials are most closely aligned with your standards. You might want to focus this analysis by converting the standards into curriculum frameworks. The purpose of the frameworks is to provide a developmental sequence into which the standards can be placed, from which a guide can be constructed showing the sequence in which the material in the standards is typically mastered.

In all likelihood, this analysis will reveal that substantial segments of your curriculum and much of your current repertoire of materials are not well aligned with either the standards or the framework. The next step is to identify materials currently available on the market that are better aligned with your standards than the ones you are using.

But for all the reasons we suggested earlier, it is unlikely that you will be able to address all of your standards adequately using commercially available materials. So you may have to produce your own custom units of study to fill in these holes.

A while back, our colleague Marge Sable developed a hugely popular workshop that addressed this question of what you can do head on. Later, another colleague, Sally Mentor Hay, and others crafted a multimedia module based on Marge's work. The module involves a four-step process to be used by a group of teachers developing standards-driven units of instruction. Here is how it goes.[4]

1. *Identify the main components of the extended student work unit.* The teacher begins by identifying the relevant academic and applied learning standards. The extended student work is described and the criteria for evaluating the work developed. A core question that focuses the student work is also developed. Finally, a culminating event is devised to showcase the student's work.

2. *Write the student assignment.* Using the components just
   described, the teacher writes up the unit as an extended lesson. Then the teacher writes up the evaluation criteria. Then
   the extended student work and culminating event are broken
   down into a series of discrete tasks for the students, and,
   finally, the whole unit is pulled together.

3. *Produce teacher notes.* Here the teacher engages in some
   reflection on the kind of classroom environment that will
   be needed if this approach to instruction is to succeed,
   identifies needed resources, and considers methods of
   getting students engaged in the unit.

4. *Reflect and revise.* In which the teachers review, revise, and
   edit their extended lessons.

In many cases, people who participate in this process focus
mainly on producing units of study. But in many other cases, the
product of the effort is a much deeper appreciation of what it means
to have a standards-based curriculum and instructional program.
This understanding of the requirements of a standards-based curriculum then often becomes the basis for intensive analysis of a
school's or district's current curriculum against the criteria produced
by this training.

Analyzing your current curriculum against your standards and
devising your own instructional units to fill in the blanks is not your
only alternative. A number of the national reform networks, including E. D. Hirsch's elementary school network, the design teams
sponsored by New American Schools, and programs sponsored by
the National Science Foundation (like Gil Lopez's CMSP program)
have standards, curriculum frameworks, and sometimes their own
curriculum materials.[5] Our message to you here is that it is very
important to look at any such program and analyze it just as you
would your own current curriculum against the standards you think
your student should meet. Pick the program with the best initial
match, and adapt it as much as necessary.

What Schools Can Do: Examining Effective Instructional Practice

Materials, of course, are simply a resource for teachers and students. Much depends on the way teachers choose to teach. American teaching styles have been geared to the mass production system of sorting we described earlier. That is not our ideology, but it is the reality. The question is how we might alter our teaching styles to bring our style of instruction into line with the idea of a thinking curriculum and the commitment to bring virtually all students up to a high standard of achievement.

Harold Stevenson and Jim Stigler, authors of *The Learning Gap*, have found a most intriguing approach in Japan.[6] Ask American teachers what single change would contribute most to improved student performance, and they typically say reduced class size. This is true whether their current class size is large or small and whether the district in which they work is wealthy or poor. When Japanese teachers are told this, they cannot understand it. Class sizes in Japan are typically much larger than in the United States (though overall ratios of teachers to students are about the same). In Japan, teachers believe that large classes, not small ones, are the key to success. What is going on here?

The way Americans think about it is quite straightforward. Assuming mixed abilities in the classroom, if the class is pitched to the students on top, the middle will struggle and the bottom will get left out altogether. If it is pitched to the middle, the top will be bored and the bottom will be struggling to keep up. There is no question of pitching to the bottom.

That is not how the Japanese think about it at all. To illustrate the point, we will describe a typical Japanese math class. The teacher presents a problem at the beginning of the class and asks the students to work at the problem at their desks. The teacher circles the classroom with a clipboard, making notes on the different strategies the students are using to solve the problem. What she is looking for is an array of strategies that reflect different levels of sophistication. After she has collected what she believes to be a sufficiently varied set of strategies, she calls a halt to the individual work and begins to ask individual students, one at a time, to come to the chalkboard and share with the rest of the class the strategy he or she devised for solving the problem. Rarely does the teacher announce that the result or the strategy is wrong, even if it is patently wrong. To the contrary, the teacher is working hard to build student understanding of the reasoning underlying good solutions by exploring many different ways of getting both good and not so good answers. Everyone in the classroom knows—and does not need to be told—that a particular answer is wrong or right.

Because the teacher deliberately brings to the board students whose approaches represent different levels of sophistication, every student in the classroom has a chance to see someone using a strategy very like the one that he or she used. Thus the instruction is highly individualized, because each student gets to see the whole class discuss the strategy that student used. But unlike our approach to individualization, all the students are engaged all the time in the work of the whole class. Throughout, the emphasis is on understanding the concepts employed and on real mastery by all the students of each concept. It is education for thinking, the very opposite of the American stereotype of Japanese education.

Jim Stigler has made extensive videotapes of both American and Japanese classroom teaching that vividly illustrate these points. We strongly recommend that you obtain these videos through the Web site established to support the Third International Mathematics and Science Study, which can be ordered through the U.S. Department of Education's Web site (www.ed.gov/NCES/timss/index.html).

Interestingly, Japanese students overwhelm American students in comparative studies of educational achievement. So they know how to get right answers even though the way their classes are organized, unlike ours, does not focus directly on right answers.

For the Japanese teacher, disaster consists in not having enough examples of different types of reasoning among her students. Large class size is more likely to produce a wider range of examples of different student strategies for solving the problem than small ones. The Japanese teacher is not particularly worried about boring the swift or leaving the slow behind because both can get quite a lot out of the instructional technique we have just described. The swift are not bored and the slow are not often left bewildered—despite the fact that there is no ability grouping!

For the record, we are not here advocating increasing the size of American classes. What we are advocating is attention to a method of whole class instruction that can be used to get many of the benefits of individualized instruction without creating a situation in which many students are left without any teacher attention while the teacher is attending to one or only a few students.

The boredom and bewilderment so common in American classrooms are the direct result of our style of pedagogy. We depend much more than the Japanese on lectures at the beginning of class to convey the concepts and skills the students are supposed to master. In the American classroom, help is given to individuals while other students are left on their own (whereas in the Japanese classroom, everyone gets the coaching, not just one student). We emphasize how to do something, while the Japanese emphasize how to understand something.

Because the Japanese concentrate on understanding in their pedagogy, their students learn more, and they learn it better. Because they spend most of their class time on analyzing mistakes students make as they work problems through rather than on lecturing to students, they can engage virtually all the students all of the time without fear of boring the quick or leaving the slow behind. There is a lot of food for thought here.

What Schools Can Do: Aligning Instructional Technology with the Standards

Once you have aligned your assessment system, curriculum, materials, and instructional methods with the new standards we are using, the next step is to do the same thing with the instructional technologies you are using in the classroom.

When the phrase "instructional technology" comes up, the image it conjures up for most people is software that does what the teacher is supposed to do—deliver instruction. Most of the software sold to schools since the advent of the personal computer has been software of this kind, and most of that software has been used to support student drill and practice in the basic skills. Nothing could be more emblematic of the mass production classroom than the glassy-eyed stare of young people sitting in ordered rows of desks behind their computers doing the same drill-and-practice exercises that they used to do in the workbook.

There is, of course, another kind of instructional software, software that more closely resembles the "productivity software" used in business. In the business environment, this is software that makes workers more productive. It does not instruct them; it does what the steam shovel did for the day laborer—takes the shovel out of the hands of the day laborer and puts him in the cab of the steam shovel, enabling him to move far more earth in a day.

Think of the humble word processor. Earlier in this chapter, we pointed out that writing is a craft that one gets better at when one has to do the same writing task repeatedly and is critiqued and coached between tries by a more experienced writer and editor (in this case, one's teacher). No tool could be more brilliantly conceived to support this process than the word processor. Whereas before, the student had to laboriously write out by hand a new copy of an edited text to produce a clean copy of the draft of a paper, now one simply makes the necessary changes on the text stored in the computer and hits "print." The computer does the rest. The physical task of editing and printing the text has been made effortless, leaving only the intellectual task of improving the quality of the writing. Enhancements have been made to word processors to give them bells and whistles that augment their effectiveness in a learning environment, but these enhancements do not turn them into devices for delivering instruction. They are still productivity tools for students, and very powerful ones at that.

Or take another example, *Measurement in Motion,* a CD-ROM made by Learning in Motion.[7] This software is very different from the word processor in that it was specifically designed for use in educational settings, but it is still productivity software in that it does not teach but rather makes the student a more productive learner. *Measurement in Motion* comes with brief film clips of natural phenomena that have mathematical properties—a Ferris wheel in an amusement park, horses changing their gaits from walk to trot to canter and then gallop, a candle burning down. It comes with templates that the user can place on a still shot in the sequence being analyzed. The user can then specify relationships among points on the templates. When the motion resumes, the software analyzes the changing relationships among the changing variables. These relationships can then be graphically represented in many different ways. For example, with the burning candle, the user can mark the point of the top of the candle just below the flame and the bottom of the candle. When the full motion starts and the candle burns down to the bottom, the program will record the rate at which the candle burns. Is the rate constant, or does it change as the candle burns down? The candle can be marked in segments, and the program will create a table showing the burn rate for each segment of the candle. The burn rates (which are different) can then be displayed as a bar chart, a pie chart, a graph arrayed in two dimensions, and so on. A car on the Ferris wheel can be marked, and so can the Ferris wheel's axle. The speed of rotation can be recorded, as well as the angle of arc traveled in any given time span, and so on. The hooves of the horses can be marked so that changes in such things as the length of stride for any given gait can be measured and compared across gaits. What's more, the user can put other video sequences into the computer's memory and conduct the same kinds of analyses and have available the full range of types of visual display for the results. It is hard to imagine a more powerful tool for helping students develop an intuitive feel for the mathematical content of real-world phenomena and for the mathematical analysis of those phenomena. Just as with the word processor, there is no didactic teaching here, just a very powerful tool for learning and using mathematics. We said earlier that the boundary between learning and using may be virtually nonexistent, that only through using what we know do we actually come to know it. *Measurement in Motion* is a perfect example of a technology-based tool that incorporates this principle in a powerful way. It is perfectly matched to both the learning principles we advocate and the standards we have developed.

Quite a different kind of tool is the *3–D World Atlas*, another CD-ROM.[8] It is the old world atlas come alive and made far more useful as a result. It contains, of course, maps galore and a great deal of statistical information, some of it historical, on a great variety of jurisdictions of all kinds. It also contains satellite photos and full-motion video shots made from aerial flybys of selected locations, mainly big cities. The satellite photos are arranged in a nested way so that it is possible to "zoom in" from a very wide shot of an area of the planet to many much smaller ones. One can stop the flybys to linger on a particular view of a city in which one is especially interested. The data on the various locations is arranged in tables and can be selected by fields for computer analysis. The student can then use the data on the commodities produced by a selected group of countries over time to do an analysis of the relationships among inflation, national income, and commodity prices in countries that are heavily dependent on international trade in commodities as opposed to countries that are not so dependent on trade in commodities. Or the student could do a study of population growth in relation to infant health and mortality or of average per capita income in relation to the nature of national political systems. The program's makers are now considering adding historical maps and data to augment the mostly current and recent data that it now contains. Whether or not these enhancements are added, one does not have to work hard to grasp the enormous power of the *3–D World Atlas* as a research tool for students of all ages.

Our last example comes from the work of Seymour Papert and his colleagues at MIT's media lab. Some years ago, we found ourselves at a middle school in Boston that served as a lab for Seymour's LEGO-Logo program.[9] Most of the students were out of the school that day, but we found an eighth grader in a red dress working in the lab, around which was scattered various constructions made from LEGO pieces. Each had one or more little motors and sensors attached, and wires ran from the motors and sensors back to Apple computers loaded with the Logo programming language that Seymour developed for the schools some years before.

We asked the girl if she could tell us how one such construction worked. She did not make it herself, she said, but if we had a minute, she could read the program the other student had written and tell us how it worked. She turned on the computer, read the program, and told us that it was a vehicle that had been programmed to follow the wavy path of a piece of white adhesive tape on the floor. Then she turned it on and showed us how it worked.

We asked about a very elaborate construction sitting on the workbench. She said the whole class had worked on that one. It was intended to imitate the great walking war machines in the *Star Wars* films. She hooked it up and turned on the computer. It wobbled forward in the most menacing way, to her great delight. A few minutes later, we encountered one of the math teachers in the school, who told us that the students had come to her some months before for some help with the mathematics required to build this warfighting machine. It seemed that the wobble required them to build something that would rotate on an eccentric, and the design therefore required some mathematics that most people would not learn until graduate school. But they happily learned it. The students' interest in and mastery of mathematics, she said, had soared with the advent of the LEGO-Logo lab.

Nothing could be a better fit with the part of the New Standards applied learning standards that calls for the development of design skills, than the program we have just described. The girl in the red dress was well on her way toward the development of an engineering way of thinking and real facility for engineering design.

But this story illustrates another point. We believe that the image of these technologies as a substitute for the teacher, delivering direct instruction to the student, is misleading and destructive. These technologies are in fact poor teachers, mainly because of their primitiveness: only crudely can they respond in a way that reflects differences in how much a student knows, how the student has structured that knowledge, and the mental scaffolding available on which to build new knowledge. But if one considers how powerful these technologies can be when approached as productivity tools in ways we have described here, their full potential becomes apparent.

Only if these applications are carefully integrated into a curriculum designed to enable your students to reach the standards you have set for them will this potential be tapped. All too often teachers and others, captivated by the power of these applications and the excitement of students who get access to them, make applications like these available to students as a break from the regular curriculum, something of a treat. That is a disservice to both the students and the technology. In education, every minute counts, and everything one does should be tested against one criterion: whether it is more likely than anything else you could do in that minute to get your students to the standards. This applies with special force to technology, because of its expense as well as its power.

What is new here is the marriage of the idea of alignment to the idea that virtually all students can achieve at high levels. Marrying those ideas changes not only the nature of the standards, assessments, materials, instruction, and instructional technology that are aligned with each other, but also the way they combine to create a learning environment in the school. It changes everything.

Interlude:
Upset Victory: Student
Achievement 1, Everything Else 0

Judy B. Codding, Pasadena High School

When I became principal of Pasadena High School in Los Angeles, I was astonished to discover the role that interscholastic sports play in the life of high schools in California.

It is customary all over the state to schedule all varsity athletes and as many junior varsity and freshman athletes as possible—and their coaches, too—for a sports class the last period of the official school day. The coaches, of course, do not teach just physical education but English, history, math, science, and second languages as well. These arrangements have serious consequences.

Consider the implications for the scheduling of classes. There are a wide variety of classes, from certain second-language math classes to Advanced Placement physics, for which demand would not justify more than one class a day. None of those classes could be scheduled for last period. In a school like Pasadena High, with about a quarter of the students involved in interscholastic sports, the effect was like shortening the school day by a whole period, not just for the students involved in sports, but for virtually everyone.

The worst aspect of this situation was that it forced me to change the master schedule in the middle of the school year to accommodate the athletes involved in a spring sport who had not gone out for a fall sport. The entire school had to be reprogrammed twice a year: once for the fall semester and again for the spring semester. The problem was not the work required to reschedule but the devastating effect on instruction.

Take the example of José. In the first semester, he was taking English 11 with Ms. Jones during the last period of the day. This semester, he is taking advanced chemistry (offered only two periods), Spanish V (offered only one period), precalculus (offered three periods), and AP American history (offered three periods). Obviously, there is very little flexibility in his schedule. But he is on the baseball team. So, given customary practice in California, he must be in last-period sports for the second semester. Therefore, his English 11 class with Ms. Jones must be dropped. Ms. Jones does not teach a section of English 11 when José can fit the class into his schedule. So in the middle of the year, he must change English teachers just when the teacher is getting to know him and reach him as a student. The only English 11 class that will fit into José's schedule is third period, which already has thirty-seven students enrolled. To accommodate José in third-period English 11, another student's schedule must be changed. And the scheduling nightmare goes on.

That school and thousands like it place a higher priority on baseball than on English—and everyone knows it. Not only are the athletes affected, but so are the 75 percent of the students who do not participate in sports. All are deprived of the opportunity to get to know their teachers and for their teachers to know them. Many teachers feel that it is pointless to work hard with their students in these circumstances because they can't make much of a dent in a semester; some other teacher will take over and go in some other direction. The consequences for student achievement are serious and pervasive.

Then there is the English teacher who is also a coach—actually a coach who is also a teacher. English teachers in California typically teach five periods a day with at least thirty-six students in each class for a daily load of 180 students—far too many. But if an English teacher is a coach, he will teach only four classes of English, and his fifth assignment, for which he is paid one-fifth of his salary, is to coach, say, swimming. But the high school is not allocated any more teachers to cover for the coaching assignments. So what happens to the thirty-six students he would have had for last-period English?

You guessed it—the size of the English classes is increased so that the teacher can coach swimming, and his thirty-six students are distributed to the other English teachers. Now the eleventh-grade English teachers have forty students in their English 11 classes while the coach has twenty to work with in swimming.

Because coaching is so demanding—unlike English, of course—the coach has to have time to prepare, time that is not available to the teachers of academic subjects. All varsity coaches demand—and get—the period before last period as an unscheduled period, not because they need to give special attention to their English students, but because they need to prepare for their sports class—get the equipment ready, deal with hurt athletes, have a coaches' meeting, call game officials, and so on. So a teacher who teaches four periods of English and one sports class will have a teaching schedule that ends before lunch so that the remainder of the day can be devoted to the athletes. Pity the poor kid who wants to find his English teacher for help on an essay. That teacher has become a coach who is giving help where it really counts—to his athletes.

There is more. A typical large high school in California might have fifteen sports teams, most of which have both girls' and boys' teams with freshman, junior varsity, and varsity squads. Many have multiple coaches. At Pasadena High, we had eight to ten coaches for the eighty to one hundred kids on the football team. Wouldn't it be great if we had teacher-pupil ratios like that in the classroom!

During any school year, we would field twenty to twenty-five teams, each requiring multiple coaches. Coaches earned a stipend, which, if they were on the professional staff, was over and above their regular pay. They also had the sports class as part of their official teaching assignment. That and the equipment, uniforms, upkeep of fields, game officials, athletic director, assistant athletic director—all this had to come out of the school's regular budget. A school of 2,200 students will spend somewhere between $300,000 and $500,000 on its athletic program. All the money for this and for the academic program comes from the same $3,500 annual per-pupil expenditure pot.

Most California schools have a woefully inadequate budget for supplies, textbooks, and libraries. At Pasadena High, the school received approximately $21 per student for textbooks, less than enough for one new textbook per year per pupil. The sports budget of $300,000 was seven times my textbook budget.

I am not arguing against sports. All three of my children have been varsity athletes in competitive interscholastic sports. My children, my husband, and I all take great pride in their accomplishments on the field.

But when I arrived at Pasadena, I was appalled at the low achievement of the students. If achievement was going to improve, we would have to give it the highest possible priority because there were no additional resources available. The most precious resources we could redeploy were time—of both teachers and students—and money, especially the money spent on the faculty, which is the single biggest expenditure item in the schools. Something had to give, and that something, as I saw it, was the primary claim that the interscholastic sports program had on the time, budget, and personnel of Pasadena High.

I decided in the fall of the 1990–91 school year that the master schedule would be "rolled over" for the spring semester so that the students would remain in the same classes for the whole year. The effect of this decision was to make interscholastic sports an after-school activity. I made this decision in consultation with others—the student government, athletic director, assistant principals, and parents. The more discussions I had, the more apparent it was that few would support the decision. The priority for sports was deeply ingrained in the culture of the community and the state. But I felt that I had the responsibility to do what was best for the kids.

I did get the reluctant support of all my school administrators and of the superintendent, a man who understood the negative impact on the kids of constantly changing the master schedule to accommodate the athletes.

When I finally announced my decision, it precipitated a three-day walkout on the part of about half the student body and many of the coaches and teachers. The athletic booster parents—mostly white, middle-class parents—were vehemently against my decision. They knew how to ensure that their children got what they needed under the old system of revolving master schedules. One striking student, speaking for others, complained that doing sports after school made for a longer school day. He and others worried that Pasadena's competitive standing in inter-scholastic sports would suffer, and he opined that the school administration wanted to change the sports policy "because it was lazy." Under the glare of TV lights and in the face of constant questions from the media, I met continually over the next three days with various faculty, parent, and student groups.

We reached a compromise: we would roll over the master schedule so that nonathletes would not be forced to change their schedules, but we would hand-schedule as many athletes as possible into the last period of the day. Also, coaches would not be scheduled into the last period of the day, so their regular teaching schedules would not be disrupted and the class sizes of the students not on the field would not be inflated. Coaching would be in addition to their five-period teaching assignments unless they were physical education teachers, who could have a sports class as their fifth PE assignment. I held to the principle of keeping the kids with the same teachers and classes and not allocating any part of a full-time teaching position away from the core curriculum for coaching while agreeing to hand-schedule as many athletes as could be accommodated into the last-period sports class if it did not interrupt any other student's schedule.

What we did at Pasadena was actually very simple. We defined what we meant by good results in academic achievement, and we vowed that getting those results was our highest priority. We were fortunate at Pasadena High to have an athletic director and a lot of coaches who really cared a lot about the kids, not just about winning. These were people I liked and admired. There were no good guys and bad guys. But we had to make a choice, and in the end, we opted in favor of academic achievement.

3

Leading and Managing for Success

M any writers on education would have us think that all of education reform is contained in new ideas for instructional practice. It is true that student achievement will not improve without the kinds of changes we advocated in Chapter Two. But as the interlude you just read should make plain, much depends on how the school is led and managed.

Leading and managing are not the same thing. We associate leadership with people who show the way, guide us to a higher level, exert a moral force on us, and help us clarify our collective vision. Committing the school to a priority for student achievement over sports is a matter of leadership, not management. But figuring out how to get there requires managers who will use their good judgment, organizational ability, and interpersonal skills to help the organization achieve that vision.

Schools need leadership more than most organizations because of the function that these institutions serve and the kinds of people who are attracted to serve in them. People come to teaching out of a deep commitment or calling. They look to their leaders for the same commitment and something more. Both the teachers and the students look for someone who can inspire them, who can be a kind of moral touchstone. They want someone who will stand up for what is right, who will know how to compromise when compromise is wise but will make the hard decisions for the right reasons, who will stand tall and never trade away what is best for the students when the expedient thing is to duck.

Clearly, leading and managing are two halves of one whole. We have all met good managers who are not leaders. And we have also met inspired leaders who are hopeless managers. The first will make sure that everything runs smoothly, but to no purpose. The second will inspire but make no progress toward the goal. Whether circumstances give rise to great leaders or great leaders create their own circumstances is one of the oldest arguments in history, but it is certainly easier to provide guidance to help people manage more effectively than to teach them to lead more effectively.

For that reason, we will have more to say in this chapter about management than about leadership. But that is not because we think management more important than leadership. Indeed, throughout this book, we have tried to present examples of leadership at every point. But in this chapter, we set out what we think schools can and should do about school leadership, management, and organization to get better results.

What Schools Can Do: Leadership and Management

As a practical matter, a principal who lacks the capacity to manage the school effectively will accomplish nothing. The principal is where the buck stops, the person ultimately accountable. But even a principal who is a good manager will not achieve much alone. Before anything can happen, the principal must build a team to share the responsibility for leading the school, which means building a broad consensus around goals and plans, as well as managing the execution of the plan once it is decided on. We will call this team the "leadership and management team."

Many schools have "site-based teams" now, but they conceive of their job as governing the school. They are often composed of people selected not by the principal but according to rules set by others outside the school to make sure that the views of various constituencies are taken into account when policy decisions affecting the school are made. As the school board is to the district, so this body is to the school.

But there is a world of difference between governance on the one hand and management and leadership on the other, and both can be done without providing much real leadership. Governance means setting goals and making rules. Management means taking responsibility for producing results. The principal must have a team on whom he or she can rely to make sure that the work of the school gets done and gets done effectively, within whatever policy constraints exist, set by whatever authority sets them. (In Chapter Six, we will return to the issues of governance, school councils, and responsibility; in this chapter, we will assume that the principal is in charge and that the question before the principal is how to lead, organize, and manage for results.)

Two kinds of leadership and management structure are needed. First, in Chapter Five, we will talk about the need to break our large schools down into manageable areas. The point with respect to organization and management is simply that each unit within the school will need a head. Second, on the theory that only those things get done for which someone is responsible, each major task to be accomplished needs someone to drive it. As a first approximation, we would build a leadership and management team around the following tasks, assigning one person to each as its leader:

- Standards and assessment
- English language arts
- Mathematics
- Science
- School-to-work transition (especially in secondary schools)
- Instructional technology
- Community services and supports
- Professional development

- Budget, staffing, and procurement
- Data analysis, benchmarking, and strategic planning
- Parent involvement and public engagement
- School climate

You may have other priorities that you would add to these. But the number should be low, probably no more than a dozen. Teachers in smaller schools may have to double up.

The leaders will usually be teachers or other professional staff members. However, in some cases, particularly community supports and services, school-to-work transition, and public engagement, the principal might want to appoint a social worker, employer, or parent who is a journalist to these posts. At the secondary level, a student might be asked to lead the school climate team.

Slots on the leadership and management team should be positions to which teachers aspire, positions that enable a teacher to advance in the system without giving up teaching.

In any case, the people on the leadership and management team should not regard themselves as anointed to act alone. Their job is to get many others in the school and the wider community involved in their assignment, which is to help define the work, find benchmarking targets (details of this follow), conduct diagnostic surveys, lay out a plan, set milestones for what they want to accomplish, and get the work done, meeting the targets they have set. Everyone in the school should be involved in these activities and associated with at least one of these tasks.

The work of the leadership and management team members is to lead the work of their own group and to join the other leaders at the team table, over which the principal presides to make sure that the school is operating as a unified entity.

The principal could, of course, just pick whomever he or she wishes for these key leadership posts. But it will be an uphill battle to make the system work if the people picked do not have the confidence of the staff as a whole. There is therefore much merit in involving the staff in the choice of its leaders. Our own experience is that when this is done, the staff is much more likely to accept the leaders who are chosen and, even more important, much more likely to lead the charge in removing leaders who are not getting the job done effectively.

What Schools Can Do: Making Your School Safe and Orderly

The second prerequisite is a school that is safe and orderly. This is not a matter of valuing safety and orderliness for their own sake but rather of providing an environment in which students can focus on learning and teachers on teaching. If your school already meets this test—if it is free of drugs, students do not roam the halls when they should be in class, outsiders do not cause trouble on campus, and students do not swear at their teachers or cut the tires on their cars—then jump ahead to the next section. Otherwise, read on.

In some schools, safety and orderliness are such problems that the schools are practically out of control. Although you may not work in a school like this, you might find that some of the things we suggest would be useful where you do work.

Imagine a school where drive-by shootings are not unknown, outsiders come to the campus at the lunch hour looking for members of opposing gangs on whom to visit retribution, your students leave the campus to do the same in other schools, young people— your students and outsiders who do not belong at your school— roam the halls at all times, the lockers are as likely to contain drugs as books, graffiti deface many surfaces, students carry weapons to defend themselves, and students fight frequently. The teachers in this school blame the administrators for the lack of discipline, and the administrators complain that if only the teachers would teach classes that students wanted to be in, they would have a fighting chance of producing some discipline. What to do?

The best place to begin might be for the leadership and management team to get together with the students to make some rules and come to some agreements as to who is responsible for what.

Why students? Because rules the students help make are more likely to work than those handed down from above, and, perhaps surprisingly, the students are much more likely to impose tough rules than the adults are. This approach is especially useful in secondary schools, but we have also seen it carried out very effectively in elementary schools.

Let's get down to specifics. First, it is important to do whatever is necessary to keep outsiders away from the campus. You might have to put up a fence or hire security guards—do what you need to do. During class time, the only students allowed in the halls or between buildings should be students with a pass. It should be a very large pass that must be carried out in the open. That way, teachers and administrators do not have to challenge everyone, only individuals without a pass. Teachers should let only one student out of class with a pass at a time. Ideally, the staff should know each student by face and name (we will expand on this when we discuss organizing small internal units). It might be necessary to board up the lockers if that is the only way to keep drugs and weapons out of them.

Try to keep the rules few and simple with fair, appropriate, clear, and consistent consequences, and never flinch from administering them, whatever the temptation. One set we like goes like this: Any student caught with a weapon is immediately suspended and brought up for expulsion; the same goes for drug dealers—no exceptions. Students caught using drugs are also suspended but are immediately put into counseling and a support program rather than expelled. Students who are disrespectful in class are suspended, and before they can reenter the school, they and their parents have to have a face-to-face meeting with the teacher. Students caught painting graffiti on the school are suspended and then required to pay the out-of-pocket costs of fixing the damage and to participate personally in painting over their work or making other needed restorations, under the direction of the custodian; these students cannot return to school until they have come in with their parents for a conference with the principal, who will explain to both parents and students the seriousness of the infraction. Any student caught fighting is immediately suspended along with the others involved in the fight; these students will be readmitted only after they and their parents have met with the school administrators. That is not a complete set of rules, but it is a good start.

When we say that a safe and orderly school is a prerequisite for effective learning and teaching, do not conclude that we mean that this problem has to be licked before the school can take action in other areas to create an effective learning environment. In fact, one of the best ways to increase safety and make a school more orderly is to improve the instructional program so that the students want to come to school, take pride in their school, and are therefore motivated to contribute to making their school safe and orderly.

What Schools Can Do: Connecting with Your Students and Being There for Them

The necessary complement to the toughness and discipline required to make a school safe and orderly is the love and caring that makes students feel that they count.

Getting rid of the graffiti, for example, is important not just to send a message to students who disfigure their school but also because it is hard for the other students to take pride in a school that the adults involved do not care enough about to keep clean. Clearing off the graffiti within twenty-four hours of its application can be expensive but worthwhile. Finding a way to feed poor kids a midmorning meal will make a world of difference. So will providing some music they like (and the adults can tolerate) at lunch. These are the types of things that a caring leadership and management team can do, things that make it clear that the adults in the school do care.

Gestures like these are easy to make. But much more is needed if the faculty in most schools is going to really connect with the students. Young people who feel that no one cares whether they succeed or fail are not going to learn much in school. Students who do not feel important in school are likely to seek a sense of importance in a gang or may simply disengage emotionally and mentally from the educational process. An adequate response in most of our large, anonymous schools begins with breaking the student body, the staff, and the physical space in the school into small units in which the adults and the youngsters can get to know one another.

Much has been made in recent years of the need to create a more supportive environment for students by reducing the size of the schools they attend, schools in which they often feel that no adult knows them or cares much about them. Based on our experience, we think that the maximum size for an effective school is around four hundred students. Many—perhaps most—of our schools were designed to accommodate many more students than that. The problem can be solved by having one school in that building that is broken down into multiple "houses," each house being a unit of students and teachers that spend most of their time in school together while sharing a common administration, support services, and extracurricular program. Or it can be solved by locating genuinely separate schools in one building, with someone in charge of the physical facility. Either way, the arrangement in which a relatively small faculty group spends virtually all its time with a relatively small student body is certain to create an environment in which every member of the faculty gets to know almost every member of the student body over time and a genuine sense of community emerges. That sense of belonging and community can make all the difference, not just for the students, but also for the faculty.

When the young people in the school find that most of the adults they encounter in the school know them by name, know something about them, and care whether they do well or badly in school, there is a floor of care under the student upon which a house of accomplishment can be built.

Make occasions to build bonds between teachers and students at regular intervals in a student's career at school. A three-day retreat, taken together, can include serious study but also time to get to know one another better.

Try to celebrate student success as often as you can. One school we know holds regular awards assemblies. The students are asked to help decide what should be recognized. Among the ideas they have come up with are students with a perfect homework record or attendance record and the student whose grades went up the most in a given marking period. Students have asked the faculty to post the winners' names and achievements on bulletin boards and in display cases around the school. The students on the award committees have joined the teachers in approaching local stores for the donation of prizes to the winners, which the merchants were quite willing to give. Teachers—not the principal—hand out the awards and take enormous pride in their students' achievements.

It is impossible to overestimate the importance of these celebrations of student success. The purpose they serve is to constantly reinforce the unofficial credo of any school, its perpetual message to all of its inhabitants: "Effort produces achievement, and greater effort produces higher achievement. Anyone can do it, and the whole community rejoices when you succeed."

What Schools Can Do: Changing the Master Schedule

Recall what happened when Pasadena High decided that it wanted to bring all of its students up to a high algebra standard. Because so many of its students were poorly prepared in math, it became necessary to double the amount of time in the regular school day devoted to math. That meant that the time devoted to something else would have to be reduced by a comparable amount. One of the most compelling reasons to select Gil Lopez's math curriculum[1] was its attention to this point. Lopez assumed, as we do, that time is one of the most important assets a school has. How a school uses time is likely to spell the difference between success and failure.

It is important to begin, as Pasadena did, by analyzing student performance against the standards. We suggested some techniques you could use for this analysis in Chapter Two and in the section on planning in Chapter Four. Where are the students behind where they should be, and by how much? Are there some areas where they are behind that could explain deficiencies in other areas where they are also behind? Try to get to the root causes of the failures so that you can identify areas that, if worked on successfully, could lead to strong improved performance across the board. Do their problems doing fractions in the early grades explain their problems in related areas of math later on? Do their failures in math explain their problems in science? Do their problems in reading explain their low grades in math and all the other subjects that depend on reading?

Once you have identified the key problem areas, consider doing what Gil, Judy, and her staff did—providing much more time in the regular school day to master the crucial material for the students who need it. Judy eventually decided, as we have seen, to eliminate all the vocational shop courses and create a giant study hall to get the staff she needed to double the math faculty. Your solution will be different but might involve no less pain. How important, for example, is good writing to you? How big a student load do you think an English teacher can carry and still assign, read, and provide adequate feedback on writing assignments? If that number is much lower than the load your English teachers now carry, and you think it is very important that students leave school writing well, you will have to find the full-time equivalent positions somewhere to hire the additional English teachers required to reduce the load to the point you have decided is right (bearing in mind that although the teachers of all subjects should be concerned with good, clear writing, it is the special responsibility of the English teacher to provide systematic instruction in writing).

This is not to say that you must necessarily do this for English but rather that it is critical that you do this kind of analysis of what is most important for your students to know and be able to do, how those capabilities are related to one another, and what adjustments must be made in the allocation of time to subjects and student load for teachers. Do this analysis well, act on it, and you can be virtually certain to see substantial student achievement gains in key areas in a short time.

And there is no need to stop at the boundary of the regular school day. The most important feature of Gil's program is his recognition of the overriding importance of getting more class time in the afternoon, on Saturdays, and during the summer for the kids who need it.

For decades we have known that students from less advantaged backgrounds are likely to begin school in the fall having forgotten much of what they knew and were able to do when they left school the previous spring. The better-off kids, by contrast, are likely to know even more and be able to do even more when they start school in the fall than in the previous spring because their summer has been much richer in learning opportunities. We have also known that there is a simple cure for this problem, which is to require that the less advantaged students stay in school for much of the summer.

But we rarely do that because we have been running a sorting system. We have accepted as natural wide disparities in performance between the well-to-do and the not-so-well-off. Here lies one crucial test of our resolve. If we are in fact committed to bringing virtually all students up to a high standard, we have no choice but to make aggressive use of time as a weapon in our war. Specifically, this means not only redistributing time during the regular school day to provide more time for mastery of crucial skills, where that is needed, but it also means longer school days, Saturday academies, and summer school for students who are falling behind.

The money is there to do it, mostly in the form of federal and state funds for disadvantaged students. But instead of being spent on aides and hall monitors, it will have to be spent on more time with regular teachers outside the regular school day. Some adults will suffer if this happens, but the students can only benefit.

One reform that would go a long way toward leveling the playing field for students from low-income families is a school year consisting of four semesters of nine and one-half weeks each, with three weeks off between semesters. So far, the tourist industry has defeated all such proposals in state legislatures, but from an educational standpoint, the gains in terms of curtailing the learning now lost in the summer would be very substantial, and the quarterly periods between semesters would be ideal times to bring those who are behind up to speed.

The last point about time has to do with professional development. In Japan, the ratio of students to teachers overall is about the same as it is in the United States. But as we explained in Chapter Two, teachers in Japan spend about a third of their time in school planning, collaborating with other teachers, working one-on-one with individual students, and developing their professional knowledge and skills.

They get that time, you will recall, by having substantially larger classes than we do. But recall that the Japanese use large class sizes to get a positive learning result they could not get with smaller classes, individualizing instruction by focusing the attention of the whole class on the actual work of a few students and concentrating on how they went about getting a solution to the problem posed by the teacher. Getting time for professional development, then, turns out to be intimately related to the way a school is organized for student learning.

What Schools Can Do: Building a Highly Skilled and Knowledgeable Teaching Staff

The prevailing approach to professional development is well known: individual teachers take whatever courses they like that will enable them to advance in the ranks and increase their pay. Under the typical rules for advancement, the courses they take need not have anything to do with the agenda of the school in which they teach. At the same time, the district central office organizes district-provided professional development on topics of interest to the administration for a variety of reasons. These topics also rarely relate to the agenda of an individual school. In some districts, teachers' centers are available that offer a potpourri of courses on everything from multimedia to planning for retirement. Here, too, the chance that the course offerings will advance an individual school's agenda are essentially random.

A results-oriented school will have a strong professional development program that is keyed entirely to the agenda of that school. It is designed by the leadership and management team to help the staff gain the knowledge and skills needed to gather the data, analyze them, set the targets, do the benchmarking, devise the strategies, and correct course. Time is available, as we have just seen, for groups of teachers to discuss the work of individual students, analyze it, figure out what that student's problems are, and devise a response to those problems that will work. Time is also available for groups of teachers to research best practices related to the targets they have set for the school. For example, many high school principals view the master schedule challenge solely in terms of making it possible for the students to take the right courses in the right sequence they need to graduate, while maintaining a reasonable distribution of class loads for the teaching staff. These are important issues, but the point here is that the master schedule is a reflection of all the goals of the school, not just the goals we just mentioned.

The leadership and management team in a results-oriented school will set up the master schedule so that the teachers of a cohort of students that they are following through the years can meet together regularly for this sort of work. The schedule might be set up, for example, so that the students in a cluster all take their electives at one time so that the teachers of the core subjects can meet together. The schedule would also be set up so that the teachers in each discipline or subject can meet regularly to discuss the curriculum and instructional program in that subject.

In such a school, professional development is never an episodic, unconnected course or a workshop. Often it is not a course or workshop at all. The professional development program grows out of the long-term pursuit of a goal by the faculty of the school, out of asking, "What knowledge, skills, and information do we need to implement our school plan and get our students to the standards, and which of us needs to acquire that knowledge and those skills?" The never-ending analysis of student work might reveal a problem in the learning of English by students from certain countries or the need to find a better way to recover dropouts in a low-income community in which many students are the principal wage earners in their families. Who should be asked to lead the search for a solution, and when it is found, how should everyone else be given the skills and knowledge they need to make it work?

Two of the most powerful methods of improving school performance described in this book—analyzing student work and student performance and benchmarking best practices—are also among the most effective approaches to professional development for the instructional staff. The first requires teachers to examine their own practices very carefully in relation to the progress that their students are making against the standards; the second gets them into the mode of searching everywhere for the practices most likely to help them meet the student needs that the first activity reveals. It is in the very essence of benchmarking that one not only identifies best practices but comes to understand what it is about those practices that accounts for their effectiveness, as well as the nature of the changes that need to be made to accommodate your own circumstances.

We would suggest a third powerful tool to add to the school's professional development repertoire: apprenticing oneself to someone whose practice is exemplary. In the Middle Ages, a master took in an apprentice and provided instruction; the apprentice did as instructed, asked the master for feedback, and tried again and again until a high level of proficiency was reached. In the modern context of education, apprenticing might mean being away for a couple of days during the school year, visiting your master (or mentor), and then having your master visit your own classroom to provide guidance and feedback. Teaching is a craft, and apprenticeship is still the premier way to master a craft. There is, of course, no shame in an experienced teacher apprenticing. As we know from the movies, in Asia, the best of the best in many realms of sports and religion spend their lives finding someone just a little better than they are to apprentice themselves to.

Sometimes the master might be in the same district or even the same school. With respect to a particular subject, there is often more variation in average classroom performance within a school than there is in average school performance among districts. We think that a faculty would be richly rewarded if, when it is analyzing student performance within the school, it would look for variation by classroom and by teacher. The purpose is not to single out bad teachers but rather to identify those who consistently produce superior results. Having identified these "master teachers," the faculty could arrange for other teachers to visit the masters' classrooms to see if they can discern what specific aspects of those teachers' practice is producing the superior results.

This idea that professional development ought, at least in part, to be thought of as the search for information and competence that a faculty engages in to implement their school plan is a far cry from the idea of professional development as the taking of courses by individual teachers that others think they ought to take. But there is a major component of professional development, we believe, that need not be strongly connected to the school plan. Those of us in elementary and secondary education have long thought of professional development as a responsibility of the system, not the professionals themselves. Some years ago, David Tatel, now a federal judge, was attending a national meeting of prominent educators. The subject was professional development. He could not figure out what was going on. Finally, he blurted out, "Now I understand— this thing that you are all calling professional development and treating as a responsibility of the central administration to plan for, budget for, and allocate special time for is just a natural part of the continuing responsibility of the lawyer. We are expected to keep up with changing case law and development of new law. It is part of the job. It is built into our work. We would not be professionals if we did not accept that responsibility and take care of it constantly. The journals we subscribe to and the time we allocate to reading them at home at the end of the day are an integral part of it, just as is the legal research we do during the day and professional conversations we have with our colleagues."[2]

What Tatel said about lawyers is typically true in the other professions. Part of the solution to the professional development problem is the acceptance by teachers and administrators of their personal responsibility for keeping abreast of the profession. Development of a school culture that supports the never-ending search for better results will do a lot to support the development of personal responsibility for keeping up.

As we see it, the way educators think about professional development is intimately related to the question as to what is required to turn teaching into a true profession. True professionals in every field are involved in a process in which professional knowledge plays a crucial role in professional practice. That knowledge, as we have pointed out, can come from the research literature, benchmarking, or apprenticeship and can be conveyed by many means, formal and informal. Just as for the students, we favor active learning for education professionals wherever possible, but there is a big place, too, for *Education Week, Education Leadership, Phi Delta Kappan,* the publications of the American Educational Research Association, and the professional journals of the subject matter societies. The point is that much depends on teachers and school administrators doing the same kind and volume of professional reading and investigation and deliberate application of what they learn to their practice that lawyers and doctors do. Until that happens, teaching will continue to be more occupation than profession. How to foster this view of the educator's responsibility is a fit topic of discussion at meetings of school leadership and management teams and the superintendent's cabinet.

Some of you may at this point consider our view of the role of teachers idealized, a world away from the schools you know. Some staff members, you might say, are tired, played out, there only for the paycheck. If only we could get rid of the bad apples among the staff, we could do the right thing for the kids; but the system won't let us do that. Even full partners in law firms, if they are not producing, get eased out. Why not teachers?

People who cannot and will not perform should be eased out. But we know of schools where many people long thought of as nonperformers turned into top performers and those who couldn't or wouldn't simply left. They weren't removed by formal procedure. They just were no longer comfortable in an environment where everyone else was working hard toward common goals and had no time for those who preferred the old ways of doing things.

More than anything else, what it takes to produce that result is the realization that teachers need a lot of support and encouragement, that they need to be convinced that they really are regarded as essential members of the team, that their ideas count and their participation as full members of the team will be genuinely welcomed.

Using all the methods we have discussed, the leadership and management team has to convince the staff that success—their students' success and therefore their own success—is possible; that the leadership and management team welcomes their ideas, is fair, and will play no favorites; that the rules you see are the rules you get; and that everyone's successes will be celebrated, not just those of the leadership and management team. In such a school—where the faculty may be experiencing their first success in many years—there is a sense of real exhilaration. In an environment like that, virtually everyone wants to be part of the team and to do whatever it takes. In the relatively few cases in which teachers decide not to make the effort, it is their peers, not the leadership and management team members, who either help them get on board or convince them to seek other employment. We've seen such peer pressure and know it works.

The same vibrant atmosphere, of course, attracts capable people to the school who are prepared to work hard. Part of the leadership and management team's job is to work in a serious way to find the best recruits possible for the openings that come up and set up a rigorous screening and interview process for candidates. References should be checked. A team needs to watch the candidates teach and talk to them about why they taught the lesson the way they did and how they might have taught it differently to a different student body. It is important to make sure that the candidates understand what kind of school you are trying to create and are prepared to go the extra mile, can work in teams with other teachers, want to share in the management of the school, know how to engage students in active learning, and see the point in bringing parents into the school's orbit and spending time getting to know them. Find out how deeply they really understand the content and have mastered the intellectual framework of the subjects they will be teaching. Make sure that some combination of teachers will be available to teach after school, on weekends, and during the summer, if necessary. Find out how willing a candidate will be to do the often extensive research required to do a good job of benchmarking. Examine the standards of the National Board for Professional Teaching Standards and ask yourselves how you would use them to evaluate candidates for teaching positions in your school. Encourage the teachers on your leadership and management team to get board certification, and ask the board of education to help pay for their examining fees. Ask yourself whether the initial orientation process for new teachers is adequate. Nothing you do will be more important than hiring new staff. Make sure that you put the effort into it that the task deserves.

Last, we hope that you will consider deciding not to hire any more substitute teachers. Think about taking the money that you would otherwise spend on substitute teachers and putting it toward hiring however many full-time teachers (or fractions thereof) it will cover. Adopt the European class system (more about this in Chapter Four), where some or all of your teachers follow each cohort of students through the grades, and create teams for each grade.

Teachers on these teams can carry the extra load with help from some designated "floater" teachers on the staff. Your floater teachers will know the school, its students, and its routines far better than occasional substitutes. They can fill in not only when someone is sick but also when teachers are off benchmarking or attending a special meeting or conference off campus. Best of all, they are a part of your team and have a real investment in the success of your school.

What Schools Can Do: The Principal as Instructional Leader in the Standards-Based School

In this chapter, we shared Sally Hampton's image of a standards-based classroom. Clearly, such classrooms are not likely to be common practice in a school unless the principal plays a key role in bringing them into being and provides strong support for teachers who create such classrooms. In many places in this book, we describe other features of the standards-based school that are not likely to prevail without strong leadership from the principal, from careful and continuous analysis of student performance against the standards to the constant search for best practices that will address the problems revealed by that analysis and get the students to the standards.

What we want to focus on here is a point about the principal's leadership made eloquently by our colleague Phil Daro. Phil reminds us that the touchstone of a school focused on standards is a school focused on student work—it is only when the work produced by students is constantly analyzed with reference to work that meets the standard that the school can be said to be "standards-based."

And so we ask you to imagine a school in which the principal's in-box is always full of student work, and the principal is constantly making that work the centerpiece of his or her meetings with teachers and department heads. When visiting classrooms, the principal in this school not only sits in back of the class observing the teacher but also roams around the students' desks, asking to see the work they are producing and talking about it with them, asking what it took to produce the work, whether the student thinks it meets the standards and if so, why, and if not, why not. And the principal goes on to ask where the student gets the help needed to produce good work and whether that help is enough. While observing the classroom, the principal checks to see whether the relevant standards are posted around the room, the right rubrics are visible too, and student work that meets the standards has pride of place on the bulletin board.

Later, talking to the teacher, the principal asks for the teacher's views of how well the students are doing against the standards, talks about what he or she has seen that either corroborates the teacher's view or leads in some other direction, and helps the teacher to see how a penetrating view of the work students produce can lead to actions in the classroom that improve the chance that more students will meet the standards sooner.

In all these ways, the principal's personal leadership gets everyone to focus on the single most important question the school faces—whether students are producing work that meets the standards, and if they are not, what should be done about it.

These discussions about student work become a common reference point for all the other discussions that go on in the standards-based school, from those that focus on how to use the money available to the school to those that focus on how to use the available time, from discussions about curriculum materials to the things that the staff would like community organizations to do with respect to supporting the students and providing opportunities for them to practice and develop their basic skills. All through these discussions, the principal is bringing the faculty back to the standards and the quality of work that students are able to produce against those standards. It is a constant flow of discussion that never strays from the question of how we are doing and what we have to do to make sure that student performance improves. It is a discussion focused on the substance and the quality of instruction in and out of the classroom. It is a discussion led at all times by the principal of the school.

What Schools Can Do: Aligning Staff Incentives with Goals for Students

Being results-oriented means putting the results you value most first. Is it performance on the exams or performance on the athletic field? Here as elsewhere, actions speak louder than words. If your school routinely sends banal announcements over the public address system to ride right over whatever the teacher is saying in the classroom, if people are constantly walking into the classroom to interrupt what the teacher is saying or doing, or if your school drops the last period in the day (which just happens to be the science class) so that those students who want to can get on the bus for the football team's away game—if you do these things, you are sending messages that tell the students that almost anything is more important than academic achievement.

What is more important in your school, loyalty to the boss or helping kids succeed against great odds? Is it peace among the faculty or honoring those who made the greatest difference for the youngsters in the school? Everyone notices the answers to these questions and behaves accordingly.

Any system or institution rewards what it values, and what it values is noticed by everyone. A system that really cares about student achievement will provide all kinds of recognition and other kinds of rewards for students who achieve. And it will find countless ways to reward the teachers who contribute to that success. One of the most important challenges for the leadership team is finding appropriate ways to signal to students and faculty that the thing that you value most is the results you want for the students. You cannot just say it with words—you have to say it with action. The formal language for this imperative is "incentives and accountability." The leadership and management team is responsible for structuring the right incentives for students and faculty and for making sure that both are held accountable for their behavior.

In Chapter Six, we discuss ways that the state and the district can structure the formal incentives for teachers and other school staff. These include, among a great many other things, money—for the school and for its staff. If money is given to the school for the purpose of making incentive awards to the staff, the way this money is distributed will be watched very carefully to determine if the values that affect the distribution are the same as the stated values of the school.

But the same issues will arise even if there are no formal incentive payments. When the leadership and management team decides every year how the annual budget is to be apportioned, are the results determined by cronyism or by the strength of the competing proposals with respect to improving student performance? What happens to the first-rate teacher who always goes the extra mile for the students but who is also a thorn in the side of the principal? Will the teacher who worked heroically to make sure that last year's plan was a success be the one to go to the national conference, or will the slot go to the person who cast the deciding vote for the principal last week on the highly contested budget issue? Extra money in the paycheck is an incentive for everyone but is hardly the only incentive worth pursuing. All things that incite excellence are worth pursuing.

What Schools Can Do: Get Parents and Guardians Directly Involved

The education literature is full of tales of young people who were able to escape poverty because of a parent, grandparent, or guardian who, though poor in material resources, provided unending tough love and persisted through every adversity to support the child's pursuit of an education. Few of us can imagine the circumstances in which young people from any background can succeed in school over the long haul with no support at home.

It is also true that the time students spend outside of school affects their achievement in very direct ways. Most watch far too much television. Some work because their families depend on the income for food and shelter; many others work to support their car payments, buy fancy shoes, or wear gold necklaces. But most of these jobs contribute little to developing the general work or technical skills that these young people will need to pursue rewarding careers. Students should not be working more than ten hours per week if they can survive without doing so. In Asia, very few youngsters, whose achievement levels typically outstrip those of American children by wide margins, work after school. They do watch as much television as our young people, but they are allowed to watch only after they have finished their homework.

Much has been written and much less actually done on this theme in recent years. There are three concrete steps we think will make a difference.

1. *Make a contract with the parents and guardians of your students.* Like any contract, it will not work if it is one-sided. On the one hand, it could spell out what you will do for the students and the parents—for example, your commitment to getting all but the most severely handicapped to standards that are public and available to the parents and guardians; your readiness to brief the parents and guardians on those standards and how to read and understand the report cards that measure student progress against those standards; and your commitment to be available regularly at a time and place that is convenient for the parents for consultation about how the students are doing. It might also make clear that the school is prepared to provide, at no additional cost to students or families, additional class and tutoring time in the afternoons, on Saturdays, and during the summer to make sure that the students do not fall behind their classmates. On the other hand, the contract might also spell out what is expected of the parents—for example, that each

student be provided with a quiet place to do homework, that homework will always come before TV and other distractions, that the parent will check on the homework every day and make sure that it is done before the student is allowed to do something else, and that the parent will keep in touch with the student's "class teacher," described in Chapter Four, on a regular basis about problems that arise that need the teacher's attention. For elementary school students, the contract might also provide that the parents will read daily to their children and listen to the children reading to them.

The students should sign this contract, too. It should specify that the students agree to study first and only then watch television or do something else for recreation, to complete their assignments and take them to their parents for checking, and to cut back on paid work if it is interfering with their ability to perform well on homework assignments and in school.

2. *Start each year off with a home visit.* As each new school year is getting under way, the family of every student should get a visit from each student's "class teacher." The purpose is to help the teacher and the parents or guardians establish a personal bond, to enable the teacher to give the parents an idea of what the student will be expected to do over the next year, and to make some practical suggestions about how the parents might help that take the realities of their circumstances into account. Although it is very useful to have these visits in the student's home, to enable the teacher to get a feel for the home environment of each student, some parents will prefer to have these meetings somewhere else, and it is essential that you respect those wishes.

3. *Get out into the community and meet with the adults who interact with the kids.* Connecting with the community requires being out in it. The principal and other faculty members need to speak at the meetings of organizations like the Boys' Clubs, churches and their youth groups, the NAACP, the Urban League, La Raza, the Y, the Chamber of Commerce, and the Elks and other service clubs. If part of your student body comes from outside your neighborhood, it may

be especially important to get to their parts of town. All this takes time. But parents and other community members notice that you are doing this and understand that you have stuck your neck out to do so. As a result, when you need them, they are much more likely to be there for you. And in the process, you will find out a good deal about the circumstances that your students are growing up in, all of which they bring to school.

What Schools and Districts Can Do: Getting Help

We have tried to paint a picture of the many ways in which schools need to be transformed—from keeping school to a relentless search for better results, from an institution in which half the students are expected to be below grade level to one in which virtually all students are expected to succeed against high standards, from a textbook-based curriculum to a curriculum based on performance standards, from a something-for-everyone curriculum to a core curriculum, from an anonymous institution to a place where students feel a sense of belonging, from a place where teachers and students are never sure of their safety to a place where they feel secure, from a faculty expecting to be told what to do to a faculty that decides what to do, from a place where parents play a peripheral role to a place in which their role is central—and much more.

Few schools will be able to do all this without help, a lot of help. One way to get that help is to affiliate with a network of schools and educators that is structured to provide such assistance. For example, the Chicago public schools, with which we and our colleagues are working, decided to ask a number of school assistance networks based inside and outside Chicago to make themselves available to Chicago schools. The schools could choose which network they wanted to be affiliated with.

There are a number of such networks you might look to for help. We are associated with one such network, the National Alliance, which is a program of the National Center on Education and the

Economy. There are at least a dozen others with national reputations, including the eight Design Teams associated with New American Schools (of which our National Alliance is one), Success for All, The Galef Institute, the Coalition of Essential Schools, the Comer Schools, the Core Knowledge Network, Accelerated Schools, and others.[3] Some have highly developed capacities to provide technical assistance and professional development on a large scale; others do not. Few of these networks provide assistance in all the areas we have discussed here. Most work only with schools, not districts. Their philosophies differ widely.

Investigate them carefully, and pick one that you feel comfortable with. You are looking for a coach and some like-minded friends who can give you encouragement and honest advice, as well as powerful tools and structured feedback. You want a network that has access to resources you need and do not have and to people who, because they have been there before, can help you develop the capacity to do it yourself.

With this array of techniques in your toolbox, focus on the standards you have set for your students when they leave your school. If, for example, yours is a K–8 school, you will focus on the eighth-grade standards. Now, begin to plan backwards, setting year-by-year targets right back to kindergarten that your staff will buy. Now figure out what it will take to meet those targets. You're on your way.

Interlude:
The School Nobody Wanted

Jacqueline Austin, Kennedy Elementary School

I was in Louisville, Kentucky, in June 1987 and had just been made a principal. I was pretty excited. Everyone had told me that I would never make principal on the first try, that it typically took three or four tries. Especially since I was not a central office person but a third-grade teacher. Even so, I had done it on my first time out, and I was bursting with pride. And now Superintendent Ingwerson was asking me what school I wanted.

"Oh," I said, "you can set me up in a parking lot. I don't care which school you give me." It was only later that I learned that the other new principals cared a lot and, unlike me, they all knew enough to know that they did not want Kennedy. That was how I got it.

The John F. Kennedy Elementary School sits squarely between two public housing projects, publicly supported breeding grounds for poverty, drugs, and violent crime. In August, like new principals everywhere, I guess, I did what I thought I needed to do to get my school ready to open and to get my faculty up for the students who would shortly be crossing the streets from the projects into the school.

I was much too busy to pay any attention to the school board hearings that fall when a civil rights activist launched an attack on the board by reading data he had gotten from the districts' records using the public disclosure law. The data revealed appalling school performance for schools serving low-income students. To make his points, the attacker drew special attention to the performance of the Kennedy School. He demanded to know why Kennedy was failing its kids. How can you fail kindergarten? he wanted to know. But the records in fact showed large numbers of students in my school failing kindergarten and first grade, and the data got worse from there. The Kennedy School data were featured the next day on the front page of the Louisville Courier. Imagine how I felt when I opened my morning paper!

Later that day, I got the inevitable call to the superintendent's office. He was friendly but firm: he would do whatever he could to help, but the situation must improve. For the first time, yours truly, who had been wholly absorbed in getting my school opened successfully, started to look at the school's performance data, and I was truly appalled. The retention rates were only the tip of the iceberg. On indicator after indicator, I found that Kennedy came up the worst in the district. I was used to being first among equals, not last.

When I walked out of the superintendent's office, I thought, Well, I suppose I could just start crying and feeling sorry for myself because I got a bad school—or I can do something about it. People who know me know that I am not going to cry about it, so I might just as well do something about it.

But I didn't know what to do. Many people in the central office offered to help, but I didn't know what to ask for. Everything needed my attention at once, so I just ended up spending my time putting out fires.

Two months later, the superintendent called again, this time to ask if I wanted my school to be included in an application for a federal desegregation grant to create magnet schools in Louisville. I leaped at the chance.

I had been attracted to the Montessori idea for a long time, even before I discovered that Maria Montessori had originally developed her plan for low-income inner-city students. Montessori's program was aimed mainly at creating an environment that would provide the structures needed to help young people develop the social skills and basic cognitive skills that they would need for a lifetime of relating to others in constructive ways. I had noticed that the youngsters coming to school at ages five and six had the social skills normally expected of three-year-olds.

Ordinarily, even inner-city kids would have picked up some of these skills in a Head Start program, but very few of these kids had been in such a program. They did not know their colors, could not count, did not know their alphabet, and had no one reading to them outside of school. I thought the Montessori program would address all these problems head on.

No less important, I knew that Kennedy needed an overall vision and structure that could provide the foundation for building the confidence of the staff and hope for the future. I had my fingers crossed that the Montessori program could provide that vision and structure.

And very important to me, I knew that the American Montessori Program comes with a first-rate training program. It is possible to get Montessori training without getting certified, but we opted for setting up a school in which all the classroom teachers had to be certified. Certification requires two years of training, including a one-year internship. It is so demanding that successful completion of the program earns the participants a master's degree in education. Many of Kennedy's teachers, I discovered, did not have a master's degree.

So we used most of the magnet school funds we got to train twenty-five district teachers in the Montessori method. Most teachers at Kennedy just laughed at me when I offered them the training. Most were convinced that nothing good would ever happen to this school in the projects and so the training would be a waste of time. Only three Kennedy teachers were willing to sign up. So Superintendent Ingwerson offered the training to other district teachers. He got enough takers.

To my dismay, I found out that there is no authorized provider of Montessori training in all of Kentucky. So we persuaded the faculty of Xavier University in Cincinnati, Ohio, to come to Louisville to train our teachers and provide two days a week of internship supervision. When this was done, I went to my kindergarten teachers and told them that we were about to implement the Montessori program grade by grade at Kennedy. I told them that I was very sorry that they had not elected to participate, but I wished them well in whatever school they chose to transfer to. They were outraged, claiming that they had not decided to leave Kennedy and had no intention of transferring to another school.

But I had done my homework. Superintendent Ingwerson was behind me 100 percent, and the personnel director of the district had met with the union president, who agreed that if the program of the school was Montessori and Montessori required that the teachers be Montessori-certified, the teachers in that school had to be Montessori-certified. Both the superintendent and the union agreed that the teachers who had turned down the training had "volunteered" to transfer to another school. And they were transferred to those schools.

So year by year, the implementation of the program progressed grade by grade. Many of the Montessori-trained teachers in the district came to Kennedy. Some did not. So we began to recruit Montessori-certified teachers from all over the country. The original teachers who were not certified for the program were transferred to other schools as certified teachers came in. The teachers who had not been certified for Montessori were very jealous of the new teachers, mainly because I used most of my materials budget to purchase beautiful Montessori materials, while the other teachers mainly had to make do with what they had. But every now and then, I would buy some new materials that all the teachers in the school could use.

I felt all the way through that I was managing two schools, an old one that was being phased out, along with the teachers who inhabited that school, and the new one being added to grade by grade, year by year. It was, of course, especially hard on the teachers who had to leave a school in which they had been teaching many years. The reality that they never talk about in education school is that doing right by the students sometimes requires doing things that hurt the faculty. In most cases, as we all know, it is usually the faculty's interests that prevail when that conflict comes into play. But not at Kennedy.

Gradually, as we hired more and more Montessori teachers, the whole culture of the school changed, and the tension subsided.

Getting the parents on board was very important. One of the strategies we used was to offer a Montessori preschool program free of charge on a first-come, first-served basis—with a hitch. The hitch was that the parents had to come to school for two hours a week to help out. In this way, we got parents who were typically somewhat afraid of the school staff to come to the school and find out that we are OK people who really care about their children and are willing to listen respectfully to what they have to say. That worked pretty well. We basically scavenged the money to do this, but it was more than worthwhile.

Year by year, we implemented the program, and things improved. But I had known from the beginning that we would need much more than Montessori. The early mathematics curriculum in Montessori is very strong, but the reading program is primarily phonics-based, and the students were not understanding what they were reading well enough in the later grades. So we ended up eviscerating our Title I program with its specialist teachers and pull-out design and using the freed-up Title I funds to install instead a Reading Recovery program, which focuses on reading for understanding. But Reading Recovery is very expensive, and budget cuts in the district have forced us to cut it back.

I should mention that the Kentucky Education Reform Act (KERA) has made a big difference to Kennedy. It got everyone focused on results, and in particular on results as measured by Kentucky's new statewide assessment. The incentives in it have made a big impression on our staff.

Sometimes, I think, people look at us and see only Montessori. But the reality is very different. We actually live in the environment that KERA created: if there is a conflict between doing what Montessori would have us do and getting results, we go for the results. Most often, of course, it is not a question of conflict so much as what Montessori leaves out and what results require. In this connection, two features of KERA are particularly important to us.

First is the Family Resource Center. I cannot begin to convey how key it has been to have the center staff right here, working directly with the students and their parents. Whenever we have a problem with absentees, a center staff member will hop in a car and go to that student's home to get that student here. The city is tearing the housing projects down now, at last, but that is scattering our students all over. The Family Resource Center staff are tracking them down for us and arranging transportation for them back to the school. And center staff are constantly referring our kids to the county agencies that work with them and their families to make sure that all of us are doing everything we can to enable these children to come to school ready to learn. These centers have become indispensable.

The second crucial contribution of KERA, apart from the way it focuses the attention of the staff on results, is the Extended School Services provision of the act. This program provides funds that make it possible for the school to offer extra services to very low achieving students from 3:30 to 5:00 p.m. twice a week during the school year and all day from June 9 to June 20 every year.

But the biggest contribution of KERA, as I said earlier, is the focus on results. For me, the key to real leadership of an elementary school right now comes down to developing a strong shared vision among the staff and a relentless focus on results—being clear about the results we value, constantly measuring our progress toward them, and then being very hardheaded about doing what it takes to get our students to where they have to be.

We have come a long way. In the first few years, though we were working very hard, progress was terribly slow, but we stayed the course. By the fourth year, we began to see what we were looking for. Performance had tripled in reading and math, quadrupled in writing, and doubled in science and social studies from two years earlier. We had far exceeded our KERA performance targets, and our teachers were earning a performance bonus from the state of $2,300 each. Nine years after Superintendent Ingwerson summoned me to his office because of the appalling performance at Kennedy, the state commissioner came to our school to present me with the national Milken Foundation Award, given to outstanding elementary and secondary school principals.

But progress is not enough. I am constantly analyzing the results, and that analysis is now telling me that we have topped out. Our scores have leveled off. Our objective is for all of our students to hit the proficient mark on the state assessment. Now we have to develop a new strategy that will enable us to take the next step, so we can reach our goal. We won't rest until we get there.

4

Rethinking the Elementary and Middle Schools

In the interlude you just read, the angry citizen who put the Kennedy Elementary School on the front pages of the newspaper shortly after Jacque became its principal wanted to know how anyone could fail kindergarten. This raises an interesting question: What should Americans expect from the early years of education?

What Schools Can Do: Make Sure Every Student Acquires the Character, Social Skills, Self-Confidence, Sense of Personal Responsibility, and Love of Learning They Need

Some years ago, Marc Tucker found himself in a Japanese primary school. Expecting to see the American stereotype of the regimented Japanese classroom, he was astonished to find instead an environment that did more to honor the ideas of John Dewey than most American elementary schools. The children were happy and exuberant—laughing, playful, full of wonder, and clearly secure. They engaged in theater, dance, and art. The ancient tea ceremony had as important a place in the curriculum as the teaching of Japanese, mathematics, and science. The faculty explained that they felt the demands of the famous Japanese secondary schools as a palpable presence, as a world for which they had to prepare their students but also as a world from which they had to protect them at the same time. The attitude seemed to be that the rigors of the secondary school, with its competition, seriousness of purpose, and pressure, would come soon enough, and primary school could and should be the place and time for something else.

Years later, both of the authors made several trips to Denmark. Our visits to the *Folkeskole* there left us puzzled at first. The youngsters leaving the *Folkeskole* after nine or ten years of education, whether going into the university prep program or the vocational program, seemed very well prepared. But when we visited the lower grades of the *Folkeskole*, we found very little emphasis on academics. The teachers in those grades, when asked about what they were trying to accomplish, told us that they were mainly interested in what they described as "socialization," by which they appeared to mean helping youngsters to feel comfortable with themselves, to like the school, to get along with other children, and to develop character. They told us that their experience was that if these things were accomplished in the lower grades, they would provide a sound foundation for strong and steady progress in academics later on. There was an odd resonance of Japan here.

When the eighth-grade results of the Third International Mathematics and Science Study came out, the United States was disappointed at the relatively poor performance of our students relative to those of other countries. Later, when the fourth-grade results were released, we were very heartened, because our relative standing in these earlier grades was much higher. This is, however, just what we would have predicted. Other countries whose academic performance is much higher in the later grades appear to have chosen to differentiate the purposes of early education from later elementary and later elementary from secondary education more sharply than we have and to place less emphasis on academics in the early years than we and more emphasis on the social, personal, and moral development of the child than we do in those years.

The two cases we highlight here—Japan and Denmark—are not by any means identical. Japan consistently rises to the top of the distribution in international assessments of student achievement in the core subjects in the curriculum. The performance of Danish eighth graders on the TIMSS study, by contrast, was not very impressive, and another study of comparative performance on reading in the earlier grades in Europe also showed the Danes to be lagging. The Danes believe that it will all even out at the end of compulsory schooling, and so it will be very interesting to see how their students do when the results of the high school level TIMSS assessment are released in February 1998.

But the point is made. More than most other countries, parents and educators in the United States expect more in the way of cognitive development from very young children than their counterparts elsewhere, whereas others emphasize character and social development and love of school and learning instead.

One has to be careful in saying these things in the currently rather charged environment, for fear of being misunderstood. Many critics believe that one of the persistent problems of our elementary schools is their child-centered philosophy, which can become an excuse for expecting little of children and demanding less. No one is more focused on results than we are, and no one is more interested in promoting a rigorous academic curriculum. The point here is not the objective but the means of achieving it.

This line of argument leads to images of the early years of schooling that are nothing if not warm and inviting, classrooms in which all the students are made to feel at home, wanted, and valued. But it also leads to images of schools in which students learn to be responsible for their behavior toward others and to take responsibility for their own learning. These are years in which the child learns when competition is appropriate and when cooperation is in order. It is the period and the setting in which the society transmits to the next generation the fundamental values it holds dear.

The idea that character development is an important function of the early years of school is not new. But it fell out of fashion a generation or so ago when schools were accused of purveying majority values at the expense of the values of minority groups whose culture was therefore being expunged. Not sure of their ground, educators retreated from the field. It is ironic that it took an expert on business management, Stephen Covey, to remind us that the core values of all the world's great religions are much the same.[1] Covey's enormous success as an educator of businesspeople rests first and foremost on a moral foundation. Few Americans would disagree with the proposition that one of the most important outcomes of the early years of education should be internalizing such values as respect for others, honesty, fairness, compassion, civility, responsibility, tolerance, self-discipline, patience, and hard work.

The question, of course, is not whether such values should be taught but how. One way, of course, is through literature, and these themes should be at the heart of the study, analysis, and discussion of literary works. But the most powerful teaching in this arena has to do with the values that students see embodied in the way the school actually works every day, the way the adults in the school treat the students and one another. Great care needs to be taken to make sure that everything the adults in the school do reinforces and does not sabotage these values.

Taking these ideas seriously leads to interesting departures from American practice. In Japan, for example, students, not janitors, are expected to clean the school and to keep it neat, and it is students, not paid cafeteria workers, who serve the meals. Much of the work in Japanese classrooms is done in small groups, each one led by a student. Leadership of each group rotates among the students in it so that all students get to both lead and be led. The groups compete with one another, but the students within the group are collaborators. In this way, the way the school is organized and managed reflects the values it is trying to teach.

Having said all that, it is also true that by the end of fourth grade, these students must also have acquired the crucial tools of further cognitive development, and the most crucial tool of all is language.

What Schools Can Do: Make Sure Every Student Leaves Elementary School Fully Literate

There is an abundant and growing literature showing that students who leave the fourth grade unable to decode the written language, to comprehend simple text, and to write it are destined for a lifetime of difficulty and frustration. As such students go up the grades, they experience a vicious cycle. Because reading and writing are difficult for them, they read less and write less. Because they read less, their vocabulary does not grow at the same rate as it does for other children. Because further growth in both reading and writing depends in part on the acquisition of a larger vocabulary, they fall further behind the other children in reading and writing skills, which places them at a still greater disadvantage with respect to vocabulary. And so the downward spiral goes. Because English literacy is the key to learning every other subject in the curriculum, not excepting mathematics, these children fall further and further behind across the board.

The first obligation of the school when it comes to cognitive functioning is making sure that all children get on track and stay on track with respect to reading and writing. Nothing else in the formal curriculum matters as much as this does.

The fervor of the debate about how to make good on this obligation is very destructive. The advocates of whole language learning on the one hand and phonics on the other seem determined to fight it out to the finish so that the opponent is vanquished and forced to leave the field.

What is actually needed is balance. We subscribe to the views expressed by Marilyn Adams and Jeanne Chall, two of the nation's leading experts on reading, who see reading not as a single, undifferentiated skill but rather as a task the nature of which changes over time as one learns to read material of ever growing complexity and subtlety.[2] Early on in the process, what is most important is to decode the symbols that we use to write English sentences so that one can make the appropriate sounds in response to the symbols on the printed page. Later, when this skill is mastered, what is most important is to be able to make real meaning out of the sounds one has learned to speak, to interpret and critique the meaning intended by others, and to convey increasingly complex thoughts and ideas through one's own writing.

Phonics is the method of choice for helping young people to decode the language. We both sent our very young children to Montessori schools in part because we recognized the strengths of the Montessori method (which is heavily phonics-based) in helping young children learn how to decode the language. But later, just like Jacque Austin and the teachers in the Kennedy Elementary School, we turned to other methods (much more like those of the whole language movement) to help our children develop an appreciation for literature and the other uses of language.

But we do not mean to convey the view that English-language literacy is a simple progression from phonics-based instruction to literature-based instruction. The research shows that even when phonics should predominate, language is best learned in an environment in which what is being decoded relates to things about which the young child is genuinely curious. Similarly, later on, when decoding has been mastered and the child is reading real literature with interest and understanding, it is important to work at steadily improving the student's spelling and diction. Balance, then, is the watchword through the whole process.

We have met partisans of phonics who will give no quarter to those who want young people to read real, original, classic literature in elementary school and partisans of whole language who believe it is perfectly all right for students to spell in any way they wish and to invent their own diction or who believe that young people who enjoy writing will somehow come to practice good diction and spell correctly without ever receiving instruction on these topics. Worse, from our standpoint, are the teachers who, grade after grade, take no responsibility for the quality and accuracy of their students' literacy skills on the grounds that their students are not developmentally ready yet, thus blithely passing these students up the grades until they are in terrible trouble.

It is the touchstone of our approach to education that we believe that all but the most severely handicapped can reach internationally benchmarked standards in the core subjects in the curriculum, most especially reading and writing. It is crucial that no one fall behind and that at the first sign that someone is doing so, every effort is made to get that student back on track.

This commitment was fully in evidence at Kennedy Elementary School. You recall that Jacque and her staff took full advantage of the provisions of the Kentucky Education Reform Act that provided extra instructional time outside the regular school day for students who were falling behind. The same must be true during the school day, stealing time from other subjects, if necessary, to make sure that students are meeting the standards for reading as they progress through the grades.

The forced choice between making students repeat a grade and passing them on when they have not mastered the material is an artificial choice. Neither alternative is the answer. The best option is to monitor student progress constantly and, at the first sign that a youngster is falling behind, to put that student into afternoon, Saturday, and summer programs that will help the child stay even with the others. Every effort must be made to get and keep every youngster on grade level in the literacy program, whatever it takes.

Like every other craft, reading and writing improve with practice. For very young children, progress in reading is directly connected to the support these youngsters get from their parents, from curling up with a book and listening to a parent read, to having a parent listen to an account of what the child has read. Children from low-income families learn to read in the same ways that all other children do, but they often lack the books in the home, and their parents often lack the time to read to them that other children and their parents routinely get. Unless some provision is made in their school to compensate for the lack of these supports, these youngsters will fall behind. Maria Montessori, of course, developed her method precisely to meet the needs of such children, and this is why the Montessori method appealed so strongly to Jacque (though, as we pointed out, many of us who are not poor also choose this method for our children).

The record shows that much of this support can be provided not only by adult volunteers but also by older students or students of the same age who are a little more advanced. The advantage in the peer tutoring approaches is that the students who are doing the tutoring often benefit in greater measure than the students who are taught. Some years ago, a massive study of computer-aided instruction showed that peer tutoring (students tutoring students) was by far the most cost-effective method of improving the reading outcomes for students who are behind.[3] Some of the best-known elementary school improvement programs today rely exclusively or heavily on this technique. Many schools now pay dearly to have outside groups organize their tutoring programs when, with a modest effort, they could do the job themselves. Having older students tutor younger students can be made to work in the K–6 school. It works even better in districts that have K–8 schools. It is often hard to have older students tutor younger students when the latter are in another school building, but it can be arranged if they are on the same campus.

The evidence is also abundant that learning to read and learning to write are closely connected skills and that the latter facilitates the former. One of the most widely remarked features of our New Standards performance standards is the requirement that students read twenty-five books a year. We set this because of the evidence that nothing improves reading and writing skills like reading. The more you do, the more proficient you get. Here, too, one of the great sources of inequality in education is the differential access to books as between students from low-income and high-income families. Were it up to us, very high priority in the school budget would go to the purchase of a wide variety of challenging books for every grade and subject, enough to provide every classroom with an abundance of books and to make it possible to loan books to students to take home.

There are many local and national programs that have made it their business to provide books and volunteer tutors to help young people learn to read, from Reading Is Fundamental to President Clinton's reading volunteer program. We strongly encourage schools to take advantage of these programs and make them an integral part of their basic school plan.

So far, we have been discussing the teaching of reading and writing in English to the children of families whose native language is English. But the same standards need to be applied to second-language learners. This nation is experiencing a wave of immigration from non-English-speaking nations greater than any in our history. We do these youngsters a great disservice if we do not do everything in our power to enable them to become fluent English speakers. The overwhelming majority of these youngsters—and their parents—want to learn English as quickly as possible.

This ought not to mean throwing non-English-speaking youngsters into schools in which only English is spoken on a sink-or-swim basis. Non-English speakers should, wherever possible, be enrolled in classes in which their native language is the language of instruction until they have a decent command of English. But the effort to produce that command should be intense. These youngsters should get at least three times the number of English classes each week that fluent English speakers get. This way, early elementary students should be ready for English-only classes in a year or two; it will take longer for older students. But there is nothing to excuse our failure to educate the thousands upon thousands of students who participate in bilingual education programs year after year and still speak, read, and write poor English. The simple fact is that students who graduate without a good command of English will never have an equal opportunity to learn or to earn a decent living.

What Schools Can Do: Developing Literacy in Mathematics and Science

For many years, instruction in elementary mathematics heavily emphasized the rote learning of computational skills over the mastery of the basic concepts involved in the application of mathematics to everyday life. The result is students who were turned off to mathematics and often unable to use their computational skills to solve ordinary problems. Here again, the issue is balance. We would no more argue that computational skill is unnecessary than we would argue that it is unimportant to be able to decode the language, spell, or use good diction.

But it is very important for youngsters to see mathematics as a powerful tool for making sense of the world, both because that is the way they should use mathematics and because that is the best way to persuade them that the study of mathematics is rewarding.

Research on cognition over the past twenty years has made it clear that teaching that is harnessed to the way children actually gain knowledge about the world will be far more successful than teaching that is not so designed.[4] The old idea that children have to spend years mastering rote procedures out of any real-world context before they are ready to use them to solve practical problems is simply not true. They are much more likely to learn mathematics in the context of trying to figure out how long their shoelaces need to be for a shoe with a given number of eyelets, how many fish their fish tank can support if they are given data on how much room each fish needs, or how to divide a dozen cookies most fairly among seven people.

To do mathematics is to figure out the mathematical content of a real-world problem, formulate the problem in mathematical terms, and then solve it. Computation is one part, albeit a very important part, of that sequence. We are simply arguing that students should be taught how to do mathematics, not just computation, from the beginning, mastering the concepts as well as the skills involved and applying the skills and conceptual knowledge to actual problems at hand.

Much the same thing is true of science. The best way to learn science is to do it, in activities that lead to real understanding. Here, too, students must develop a strong conceptual grasp of the material as well as acquire the knowledge needed to do the science involved. And they must have a chance to use the concepts and knowledge to solve problems that arouse their curiosity and pique their interest.

What Schools Can Do: Strengthening Health and Physical Fitness

Studies by the military of the physical health of recruits over the past twenty years reveal an alarming slide in the physical condition of America's young people. From obesity to lack of physical stamina, from alarming rates of teenage pregnancy and rising incidence of tobacco smoking to the growing ravages of drug abuse, our young people are in trouble. However much we might wish that some other institution would assume responsibility for these problems, none seems ready to do so. The price for not dealing with these problems early is that they overwhelm us later. Youngsters in their late teens do not, in the main, do these things out of ignorance so much as emotional need. Once started, therefore, these behaviors are very hard to stop. But the record shows that information about the consequences of abuse and opportunities to build good habits, if provided in the early years, can make a big difference. Fortunately, there are many good physical fitness programs available.

What Schools Can Do: Setting the Same Expectations for Everyone

At the beginning of this book, we described the distinctly American practice of assigning children to ability groups when they first enter the formal school system as a particularly vicious form of tracking. It is vicious because the low expectations that these assignments create for many children follow them all the way through their formal education, effectively denying them the opportunity to obtain a good education.

In most of the northern European nations, it is illegal to group students by ability until they are at least fourteen years old. In Japan, it simply is not done. This does not hold the best of their students back (in fact, a higher proportion of their students perform at high levels), but it certainly does open up opportunities to those who are not in the top ranks that ours do not have.

We have already described how heterogeneous grouping as used in Japan can be used to manage classrooms and help students learn to be responsible for their own learning. It is, we think, very important for the lower grades in American schools to abandon the widespread use of ability grouping and to use methods of heterogeneous grouping to advance the learning of all youngsters. This is not intended as a blanket prohibition on the occasional use of ability grouping, where ability grouping is a legitimate strategy for bringing the skills of lower-performing students up to the standard. This may happen when students who are slipping are asked to stay after class or come in on Saturday or during the summer, for example, for tutoring and other special instruction. It is intended to prohibit the practice of assigning children thought to be "slow" to groups from which very little will ever be expected.

What Schools Can Do: Teaching Students How to Study

One of the interesting differences between the Japanese approach to elementary education and the American approach is the way each nation thinks about study skills. We Americans tend to think that students will somehow pick up the study skills that they need on their own. The Japanese do not believe that and devote time and effort in the early years to direct instruction on the subject of study skills.

Teachers in Japan routinely teach first graders how to organize their desks, use the bathroom, and other activities. Later the students are taught how to organize their pens and pencils and still later how to take notes that will enable them to summarize and reconstruct the logic line of a lecture or conversation, make an outline, organize a notebook, and so on. They will teach them, too, just what is expected of them in the classroom.

Colleges in the United States routinely report that incoming freshman lack the most basic study skills. Could it be that the simple step of directly teaching these skills could make a big difference in what and how much students learn in the elementary schools?

What Schools Can Do: Implementing the Class Teacher System

Other major changes will have to be made in the structure of the school to really connect with students. We are very taken by the effectiveness of the system of so-called class teachers used in various forms by a number of northern European and Asian countries, in which teachers follow student body cohorts through the grades. We could adapt the idea in this country by having teachers stay with a given group of youngsters for two or three years rather than the current nine or ten months. Elementary school teachers would be assigned a cohort of youngsters when they first enter kindergarten or the first grade and stay with that group until they finish grade 2. Another group of teachers would take over at grade 3 and stay with that group of students through grade 5, and so on through middle school and perhaps the first two years of high school or until they get their Certificate of Initial Mastery.

This is not some kind of management trick. The schools we have visited in northern Europe and Asia that use this practice are palpably different places. Having the teachers follow the students through the years creates an environment in which the teachers are much more likely to identify with and therefore care deeply about the fate of each individual student than they are in the prevailing system. Teachers in schools with this new structure who used to pass the student to the next teacher hoping for the best but fearing the worst will find that they are the next teacher. Third-grade teachers who know that they will have a particular student in the fourth and fifth grade as well will build long-term strategies to deal with problems that they might otherwise have felt they could do little or nothing about. They will feel strongly accountable for their students to both the parents and the other teachers in the school. Teachers in such schools get to know parents well and form deep partnerships with them over the years of the kind they might have had back when a teacher was expected to call home if the kids were out of line or needed something and the parent actually did something about it.

Most important, a deep, caring relationship will grow up among many more teachers, students, and families that will provide a secure foundation for the learning that then takes place. Imagine the immense pride that a teacher in such a system feels when students who have been under his or her care for years succeed later in life.

What Schools Can Do: Specialist Teachers in the Elementary Schools

For a long time, elementary school teachers have been expected to be jacks-of-all-trades. Perhaps this was wise when there was little emphasis on academic achievement in the elementary years and students were assigned to ability groups that lowered expectations to a bare minimum for a large proportion of students. But in an age when expectations are far higher, this method of organization is no longer appropriate.

A few years ago, a study revealed that although 76 percent of elementary teachers feel very well qualified to teach reading, only

26 percent feel qualified to teach life science.[5] But many elementary teachers do not do the job teaching basic reading skills that they should be able to do. And for many, mathematics is a challenge.

If the class teacher approach were adopted, it would make sense to have most class teachers be the English teachers, just as most class teachers in Europe are the teachers of the native language, and have other teachers specialize, too. English teachers could teach one or two other allied subjects. Other teachers might specialize in math and science. Schools might choose to pair up two teachers, one specializing in math and science and the other in English language arts and social studies and history and have them follow one or more classes through several grades together. No more teachers would be required than are required now. But most teachers would be better prepared, and many would be more at ease with the subjects they teach.

What Schools Can Do: Convert to K–8 Schools

Middle schools are the wasteland of our primary and secondary landscape. Most teachers would prefer to teach in elementary schools or high schools than to teach in middle schools. Caught between the warmth of a good elementary school and the academic seriousness of a good high school, middle school students often get the least of both and the best of neither.

The problems of our middle schools, we believe, are not unrelated to a distinctly American phenomenon. More than in most other countries, our parents have tended to "hand off" to the schools many responsibilities that in other counties remain with the parents. Some critics have explained this phenomenon by pointing to the high rate of women's (and therefore mothers') participation in the labor force. But the record shows that in other countries where the rate of female participation in the labor force is as high as or higher than in the United States, parents are prepared to

accept considerably more responsibility for their children's performance in school than is the case in this country and also to accept
full responsibility for aspects of student behavior, such as drugs and
sex, that in this country have become the responsibility of the
schools by default.

All these issues come to a head when the child leaves elementary school for middle school. That is typically when the student
physically leaves the neighborhood school and the protective shelter of the family for a more anonymous institution, when the class
group is broken up into separate classes by ability and subject, when
all the pressures of sexual maturation come into play, and when the
youngster first really tries to find his or her place in a confusing,
sometimes frightening, and often competitive world of peers below
the surface of the formal school world of classes and subjects.

We have noted a distinct advantage in districts that use a system of K–8 schools, followed by a four-year high school. Similar
advantages appear in other nations that use K–8 or K–9 systems.
Combined with the class teacher system, these advantages become
many times greater. The anonymity and rootlessness of middle
school is replaced by a feeling of community and social support typically found only in American elementary schools, and the increasing emphasis on academic content associated with the advance into
secondary education starts to flow down into the elementary grades.
In short, one often gets the best of the typical elementary and secondary education settings, rather than the worst. In some European
countries that use this system, the class teacher follows the students
all the way through, from first grade through eighth or ninth grade.
In others, the students have the same class teacher from the beginning through the sixth grade and then another class teacher to the
last grade in the school. Having schools organized in this way
greatly facilitates having older students tutoring younger ones,
which, as we noted earlier, benefits both. Not least, K–8 schools
would keep youngsters in their neighborhoods and close to home
and family at an age when they are very vulnerable.

What Schools Can Do: Getting Parents Involved

We just noted the distinctive American inclination to "leave it to the schools." On the whole, though, teachers often complain—legitimately in our view—that they are being held accountable for student behavior and performance for which parents in fact bear major responsibility. It is also true that many teachers are not eager to reach out to parents and draw them into their work for fear that the parents will interfere in some way with what they see as their professional domain.

Here again, we are struck by the differences between American practice on these points and prevailing practice in other countries, in both Europe and Asia. Before we introduce the specifics, though, it is important to point out that the idea of the class teacher is relevant here, because the fact that the class teacher follows the child through several grades makes the following practices both more useful and easier to implement.

1. Ask the parents of younger children to come with their children on the first day of school, and shake the hands of both parents and youngsters when they arrive. And greet them by name. This may seem a small thing, but in the nations where this is common practice, it establishes a reservoir of good feeling and goodwill among parents, teachers, and students that goes a long way. In many Asian and some European countries, the class teacher or another teacher will call on the parents in their home once or sometimes twice before the new school year begins.

2. At the start of the year, provide each student with a bound blank notebook to be shuttled back and forth daily between the class teacher and the parents of each student. This practice, common both in Europe and Asia, is very simple and very powerful. During the day, teachers will write messages to the parents or guardians in the book about the student—what they need to do at home, what they seem not to have done that they should have done, something that worries them about the student's health or

behavior. The student takes the book home and gives it to the parent, who may write a reply but must in any case sign the passage acknowledging that it has been read. But the parent may also originate a message to the teachers about, for instance, some problem at home or with the student in particular that the parent thinks the school should be aware of or a query about how the student is doing on a particular topic or a report on some success in the student's life outside of school that the parent would like the teachers to know about.

Where the technology is available, all of this can easily be done with e-mail systems to which both the parents and the teachers have access. But we wanted to share the low-tech version with you to make it clear that lack of an e-mail system is no barrier to the introduction of this effective practice. It works surprisingly well to build close bonds between home and school, turning parents and teachers into a strong team working on behalf of the student.

3. Offer programs that will bring parents into the school. This, you recall, is what Jacque did when she offered the preschool Montessori program free of charge if the parents of the children would come in to help out for two hours a week. It wasn't the help she wanted so much as the parents' presence because she knew that this would break the ice and start to build a strong bond between the families and the school staff.

What Schools Can Do: Family Resource Centers

Jacque, you recall, was so excited about being made a principal that she failed to understand that she was being assigned to a school no one else wanted, a school living in the shadow of housing projects that were home to students so poor and so lacking in hope that the teachers in that school had long ago stopped trying. Increasingly, a new phenomenon is emerging in the United States: neighborhoods and communities where there is no work. In these places, almost invariably in the inner city, it is not uncommon to find students who live lives of bleak despair uninformed by hope or any belief that they can succeed, students who sometimes have no home they can call their own, who are constantly sick and without a doctor, whose nutritional intake is on a par with youngsters in Third World nations and whose role models are people who live on (or beyond) the fringes of society. Violence and the constant threat of death are woven into the fabric of their daily lives.

Schools with such student bodies need help—sometimes a lot of help—in making sure that the manifold needs of these students for basic medical care, shelter, and food—to say nothing of love, affection, security, and a sense that they matter and someone cares about them—are being met.

You will also recall Jacque's comment that the state-funded Family Resource Center plays what has become a crucial role in the life of that school. The Commonwealth of Kentucky provides these centers for students who live in low-income communities. Like Jacque, we think that is good policy that has very high payoff in student achievement. These centers, at a minimum, need to be one-stop shops, located on or near the school grounds, where students and their parents can get easy access to the full range of health and social services they need.

But as Jacque's remarks imply, the staff of these centers can go far beyond the minimum to serve as an important resource for the school to track down youngsters who should be in school, keep youngsters in a given school even though their homes may be constantly moving, and so on.

In one center of this kind that we know of, the staff of the center and the school jointly register the student and his or her family at the beginning of the school year in one smooth process so that the family gets all the resources it is entitled to and both the school and the center staff get introduced to the family as a unit. In another center formed for the same purpose, the staff learned that many of the parents were too poor to have a family doctor and used only the emergency room of the local hospital for their medical needs, a very expensive process. Further analysis revealed that it would be cheaper for the local hospital to build a clinic on the campus of the school-family center and did just that, at its own expense.

Bringing together the wide range of agencies that intersect with the children and parents in low-income families is often not easy, and the work required to enable these typically hard-pressed agencies to go beyond collocating to genuine collaboration at the agency level is often very difficult. But the payoff can be enormous. Our own work in this area has been greatly facilitated by our partner, the Washington-based Center for the Study of Social Policy, which has developed very creative ways to redesign both the governance arrangements under which these agencies operate and the funding flows that typically determine the incentives for their staffs.

But whether one settles for collocated one-stop shops that bring the agencies together at or near school grounds or goes the distance to actually redesign the way the agencies work, the point here is that schools located in communities and neighborhoods of the kind we have been describing often cannot be expected to bring their students up to high standards unless they have access to the kind of resource represented in Kentucky by the Family Resource Centers.

What Schools Can Do: Planning to Improve Student Performance

Jacque told us that although her strategy for turning the school around relied heavily on adoption of the Montessori method, it would be wrong to consider that her strategy. Her unwavering strategy, she says, was to keep everyone focused on results and only results. In areas where the Montessori method did not produce the results they were after, they found something else that would.

This is what we think of as goal-seeking behavior. It does not come naturally. It is often derailed by all the myriad exigencies of life in schools. For most of us ordinary mortals, it is made much easier by having a method at hand, a set of steps to go through and questions to ask designed to help us focus on the goal and direct all our resources to the accomplishment of that goal. The rest of this chapter is a description of the steps we use to help schools to produce a school plan that will keep their faculties focused squarely on the objective. It offers a kind of planning discipline that is of benefit to all schools at all levels.

Don't be fooled by the chart in Figure 4.1 on the next page. It may look like a generic approach that could work as well for a soap manufacturing firm as for a school or district. But in fact we developed it in reaction to the generic schemes that others offered to us but did not work very well for educators. As you will see, its express purpose is to improve student performance with a system based on standards. It is results-oriented, emphasizing measurability, accountability, and constant monitoring. When we use it with school people, it is accompanied by a set of powerful tools for setting goals and diagnosing, monitoring, and analyzing performance that, taken together, enable school people to build a results-oriented culture that works. The basic steps of the planning system are as follows.

1. *Agree on purposes.* We begin by getting agreement on our vision and mission. By vision we mean a statement of our broad goals for the students, the kinds of people we hope we can help them be. By mission we mean a clear statement about what the role of the school will be in achieving the vision. And we also spend some time clarifying what we believe and elaborating a set of principles that will guide our work together. In our own organization, we call these principles our *core beliefs.* The first of the nine core beliefs we have agreed on is "All but the most severely disabled students must reach internationally benchmarked standards of achievement—no exceptions, no excuses." When we work with educators on evaluating their vision and mission statements and developing their core beliefs, we ask them to focus on whether those documents emphasize student performance and if not, why not.

You will remember that when Jacque Austin took the first steps in turning her school around, many long-time veterans at the school

Figure 4.1. Planning to Improve Student Performance: A Series of Questions.

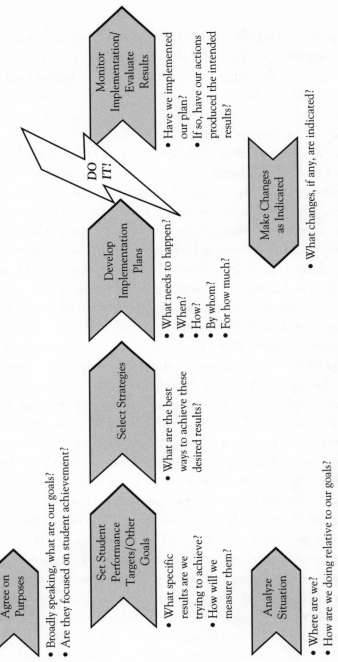

Agree on Purposes
- Broadly speaking, what are our goals?
- Are they focused on student achievement?

Set Student Performance Targets/Other Goals
- What specific results are we trying to achieve?
- How will we measure them?

Select Strategies
- What are the best ways to achieve these desired results?

Develop Implementation Plans
- What needs to happen?
- When?
- How?
- By whom?
- For how much?

DO IT!

Monitor Implementation/ Evaluate Results
- Have we implemented our plan?
- If so, have our actions produced the intended results?

Make Changes as Indicated
- What changes, if any, are indicated?

Analyze Situation
- Where are we?
- How are we doing relative to our goals?

Source: National Center on Education and the Economy, © 1997. Used with permission.

did not think that students there could achieve at high levels. They thought that the obstacles they faced in their home lives were so overwhelming there was little the school could do to overcome them. Jacque refused to accept the children's backgrounds as an excuse for poor performance. The school could not wait until "good" students showed up, she pointed out. "The parents are sending us the best children they have," she said. "It's not like they're keeping the good ones home."

2. *Analyze the situation.* This step begins by selecting a key set of measures or indicators of student performance, with the emphasis on achievement. What you are looking for is not an endless list of things to measure but a relatively small set of powerful indicators of progress toward your mission. It is crucial here to focus on ends, not means. You will want to know that kids are showing up at school and staying through the day. But that is only because you know that they are not likely to learn if they do not show up. Your objective is that they learn. The most crucial indicators are the indicators of learning. The indicators you select must be measurable. The cost of measuring has to bear some reasonable relationship to the value of the information you get. You want some indicators of current performance but also some that will predict future performance (so you can fix things that are going wrong before they get really bad). What do you most want to know about an individual student's performance? At what points in the student's career is it most important to know it? What do you most need to know about the performance of the student body as a whole (things like what proportion of students are getting to the fourth-grade benchmark when they should and what proportion of the students that enter high school stay in school and what proportion of those that do stay in school graduate to your standards)? What factors do you think most affect student ¡performance (things like health, attendance, school climate, and student satisfaction with the school), and how will you measure them? We have developed a list of over one hundred indicators that schools might want to choose from as they select the indicators that

are of the greatest value for them. The selection is crucial because in a results-based system, the results you select are the touchstone of the system.

In the case of Pasadena High School, the staff fixed on a very clear indicator of accomplishment in high school mathematics and selected a very clear indicator of the mathematics accomplishment of entering freshmen and used the data produced by the latter indicator as the basis for their program design.

3. *Set the student performance targets.* This is where the faculty says, "Here's where we want to be a year from now, and here is where we want to be in five years." You are putting down markers— significant, achievable performance targets that must be reached by a certain date. Here again, the aim is to have a relatively small set that you believe actually can be achieved and must be achieved to reach your goals—the proportion of your fourth-grade students meeting the fourth-grade reading standard a year from now and three years from now, the proportion of students meeting the eighth-grade math standards year by year for the next five years, the rate at which you will reduce high school dropouts year by year over the next three years, and so on. Select these targets carefully because you will be telling your community that you expect to be held accountable for achieving them, and you will actually be managing to them for years to come.

Pasadena High, you will remember, decided to set a target of 80 percent of students hitting their chosen measure of mastering math through geometry within five years. The staff would have liked to set the goal at 100 percent, but they did not believe it was achievable. What they did accomplish was impressive. And it left room to move the goalposts at the end of the five years.

4. *Select strategies.* A strategy is a best guess about what is most likely to get your students to the goals you have set for them. American education is a long and endless succession of fads masquerading as best guesses about what will work. We have a three-step approach that we believe is much more disciplined and much more likely to work than a random selection among fads of the week.

First, we lay out the broad canvas on which the plan will be drawn. It has five areas that will need to be filled in, each section with its own plan. The five areas or sections are captured in a kind of catechism that goes as follows:

You will not get the results you want until you define the results you want and settle on measures of student progress toward them. So the first area for planning (the one we just discussed) is **standards and assessments**. But getting the standards and measures right will not improve student performance unless something changes in the classroom, so you must create a **curriculum and instructional program** for the students. But for many students, especially those who live in impoverished circumstances, changing the school's curriculum will not matter much until **community services and supports** are provided that enable these students to come to school ready to learn. But doing all of these things will avail little until **high-performance management techniques** are used in the school and the district that will support instead of frustrate all the other changes made in the schools. And finally, all the needed changes in all four of these areas will never come about if the community does not understand them and does not support them, so **public engagement** is the fifth and final piece of the planning and action puzzle.

In our own work with schools and districts, we provide diagnostic instruments that help educators think about what they are doing in each one of these areas in a disciplined way. The idea is to do a careful assessment of the strengths and weaknesses of your current operations in each one of these areas in relation to the kind of performance you want for your students and your best guesses about what it will take to shape your work in each area to get the performance you want.

The diagnostic instruments are useful but do not by themselves provide a detailed guide to the best practices in each of the five areas just described. So having laid out the canvas, the second step in devising your plan must be to decide on the specific strategies you will use to get to your targets in each of these areas. For every target you have set, ask, Who does this best in the city, state, and nation? How do they do it? And how can we do it better? Who is best at helping dyslexic individuals overcome the limitations associated with that condition? Who has done the best job of teaching analytical geometry to youngsters from the barrio? What nations and schools know the most about teaching multiple languages to their students, and how do they do it? What is the most effective school organization in the world as measured by rate of improvement in student achievement for students like ours?

This is benchmarking, and it is not the same thing as doing a literature search. What you need is much more than a research finding. To do a good job of benchmarking, you need to talk to a lot of people at the site itself, satisfy yourself that something of real value to you actually happened there, come to understand the ways in which that site and situation are the same as and different from your own site and situation, make sure that you know how the people at the other site actually achieved what they reported, come to understand the kinds of compromises that they made that you might not have to make, get from them their own assessment of what they would do differently now that they have been through it, ask them to react to some of your own ideas about how to improve on their methods, and so on. This is very different from and much more than reading a research report. It is through a process like this that skeptics (they should always be among the benchmarking team) come to believe that it can actually be done and through the interactions that take place among the team members that a good plan is forged.

Most schools will not be able to afford many benchmarking trips, and most of the ones you do will have to be within a few hundred miles of your school. But you can do some of your benchmarking by phone, Internet, and e-mail. You can ask faculty members to do some benchmarking when they are going to Europe or Asia or even New York City or Seattle on vacation. (We have met many people from other countries and formed close, lasting relationships with them in just this way.)

This whole book was written using this technique. We have traveled all over the world looking for the most effective practices we could find and thinking hard about how best to adapt them to the circumstances American educators face. You can learn something from that—we hope—but you need to do it too. Not necessarily on the same scale or with the same reach, but certainly with the same purpose in mind.

What we are talking about here is the disciplined search for best practices, an antidote to the "Gee, I just got back from a terrific talk by Joe Schmo—we gotta do what he did!" approach to school improvement. The disciplined search for better ways to do the most important things the school does is the heart of the planning process.

Jacque, you recall, picked the Montessori program and the National Alliance, both serving as external partners, after a very careful analysis of her requirements. Pasadena High looked all over the United States for ideas, materials, and programs that fit its circumstances. When it found CMSP among the math and science programs funded by the National Science Foundation, it found a program that addressed almost every one of the elements of program design we just listed. But the Pasadena benchmarking team of teachers, parents, and students also found a house system they could use in posh Greenwich, Connecticut, and many other creative ideas that worked for them at Central Park East in New York's tough Harlem neighborhood.

The trick here is making sure that your strategies are actually matched to your goals. Remember that after the staff at Pasadena had agreed to their goal, Judy went to the math department, which proposed using a standard high school math text. Careful analysis of the situation in relation to the goal made it clear that a standard math text could not and would not get those students anywhere near the targeted goal. That is the kind of analysis that is needed to get to strategies that will work.

5. *Develop implementation plans*. This part is pretty straightforward. You will need to take the strategies you have selected and turn them into an action plan that specifies what is going to happen, who is going to do what, how they will do it, how much it will cost, and when it will be done. When each planning team has done its

part of the plan, the school's leadership team needs to meet and decide how best to allocate the available resources among the various planning teams and resolve any conflicts among them.

To say that developing an action plan is straightforward does not mean that it is easy, however. In the case of Kennedy Elementary, the principal had to hire teachers who were qualified in the Montessori approach to teach in those grades, and this meant she had to ask long-time Kennedy veterans to seek employment elsewhere in the district. This was difficult but, she was convinced, essential if the school was going to transform itself to achieve its goal of significantly improving student performance.

6. *Do it!* "What a dumb step," you just said. "Of course we would do it." Well, maybe. Schools and districts are funny places. Many of us have been in the habit of producing what are really compliance plans, plans produced to somebody else's order because that somebody else said we had to have a plan. So when it was done, we sent it in, it was checked off by the people downtown, and we threw it up on the shelf and never looked at it again. This time it is your plan, not their plan. So do it!

7. *Monitor implementation and evaluate results.* Are you actually doing what you said you would be doing? Did you actually do what you said you would do? What results did you get? Were they what you expected? If they were not, what does an analysis of the data suggest about what might have gone wrong and what you have to do to correct it? When these questions dominate the leadership and management team and general faculty meetings, you will be on the road to improvement. It requires almost an obsession with data and using data to figure out what is going right and what is going wrong and what you have to work on next.

8. *Make changes as needed.* Just like it says. This planning system is, as we said, about results. Making it work in most schools and districts requires not just new procedures but a new culture, a culture of results, a culture of continuous improvement, a relentless search for ways to do better next time.

We've ended this chapter on the K–8 school with several pages on planning. We did that because it is here in the K–8 school that all the foundations get laid, that youngsters learn to read well or badly, that they develop a facility for mathematics or come to look on it as a curse, that they acquire the subtle array of skills in relating to other people that make life a joy or withdraw into their own cocoon, that they develop the foundations of character that will serve them for a lifetime or become people who end up on the wrong side of the law.

All of these things are important. But none is more important than the first in the list—learning to read well. This is so because literacy is the key to all further learning and because—no point could be more important—children who do not learn to read well by the end of the second grade will *never* catch up to those who do.

Children who come to Kindergarten from low-income families typically are eighteen months behind in language development. By the end of grade 3, they fall as much as five years behind. The crucial grade is grade 1, where the effort to master the phonemic structure of language is paramount. Students who fail to become literate by the end of grade 2 may improve their reading ability over time with effort and good teaching, but they will never meet high standards of literacy, no matter what they do.

This is the conclusion of two colleagues in Australia, Peter Hill and Carmel Crevola, who have been reviewing a mountain of research done in many nations on reading and who have capitalized on that review to design a highly effective whole-school approach to early literacy development in Melbourne. That work focuses on bringing children from low-income families and with diverse language backgrounds up to high literacy standards. Both Hill and Crevola are associated with the Center for Applied Educational Research at the University of Melbourne. They are working on a book that describes their research and field work and includes a discussion of the results.

The intersection of Hill and Crevola's research on literacy and the research on class size leads us to a very interesting conclusion. We just told you what they have concluded with respect to literacy. The class-size research shows that, within a broad range starting at a class size of about fifteen and ending at an upper bound of about twenty-five, achievement outcomes are not much affected by class size, everything else being equal. These facts, we believe, have very important implications for planning and for school design. We would make every effort to keep class size in Kindergarten and grade 1 at or below twelve students, raising the size of the classes above that to whatever size is required by the total student enrollment and the number of teachers at the school. Hill and Crevola's approach depends heavily on close, daily monitoring of student progress on reading, on detailed matching of instruction to the student's progress, and on as much individual one-on-one support for the student as possible. All these requirements are greatly facilitated by small class size. All take very careful schoolwide planning and close collaboration among faculty, parents, and others who support the work of the faculty.

In some schools, this kind of thinking about class size will result in significantly increased class sizes in the upper grades in elementary school, assuming that there is no more money available overall. But we now know that the price to be paid if students do not really master the written word in Kindergarten and grade 1 is simply unacceptable. No trade is more worth making.

This proposal, however radical its implications, is a good example of what it will mean to plan for results when the stakes are high and the aim is clear. This is what it really means to care.

Interlude:
The Graphic Arts Academy

Judy B. Codding, Pasadena High School

After receiving their high school diploma, fewer than 15 percent of the students at PHS enter a four-year college or university. But we were doing little to encourage the remaining 85 percent to focus on their future after high school. After graduation, most of our students continued in the dead-end jobs they had while in high school, hung out on the street corner, or passed through the local community college, lasting little more than a semester. We needed to do something to ensure that our students had an opportunity to lead decent lives and to have a secure future after high school. The school needed to address the career transition issue, even if our country would not.

Our first step was to ask industry to come in and evaluate our vocational education programs. We invited Honda to evaluate our automotive shop and program, several local electricians to evaluate the electrical shop and curriculum, and other professionals to look at our wood, drafting, and printing shops and programs. The evaluation of our print shop echoed the reviews we got on all our vocational programs: the equipment was antiquated, the materials were outdated, the environment was poor, and the teachers were not knowledgeable about what was happening in industry. As one person said, "What's happening here is not only not educative, it's actually miseducative." So we offered the Printing Industry Association the challenge. Roll up your sleeves, join in an equal partnership, and help us make it better for our students and for your industry.

The Printing Industry Association (PIA) of Southern California has just under two thousand printing businesses as members. More than 80 percent of the companies that belong to PIA employ fewer than twenty people. In the mid-1980s, PIA conducted a self-evaluation to ascertain the industry's standing in relation to the future workforce. What the evaluation found was startling to them and made the PHS offer rather attractive: a potential shortage of thousands of workers by the turn of the century. PIA established an education committee. The association's members recognized that they had to attract new employees as well as retrain their present workforce. To run the complex machinery in a printing facility, workers needed strong reading, math, and problem-solving skills and eight to ten years of experience. PIA was extremely concerned with the low levels of knowledge and skills they saw in students graduating from southern California high schools. They felt they had something important to offer to us.

In February 1991, an advisory board was set up that included representatives from the Pasadena school district, Pasadena High School, a local printing company, PIA, Pasadena City College (PCC), and California State University at Los Angeles. During the six-month planning period, an intense effort was mounted to gather equipment, retrofit and redesign the old print shop, identify teachers with appropriate industry and academic backgrounds, develop standards, design an appropriate academic and applied learning curriculum, recruit students and their families, and otherwise lay the groundwork for a successful program. Without the extremely expensive equipment donated by the printing industry, the district would never have been able to operate the newly designed Graphic Arts Academy, our first attempt to establish a partnership academy and our first attempt to develop a school-to-work transition program.

The partnership academies at PHS are designed to engage all students in their learning and education: students who are heading for a four-year college or university, those who leave or complete high school and seek full-time work and then return to postsecondary education, those who enter the workforce and obtain employer-provided training, and those who work and continue their education simultaneously.

The Graphic Arts Academy has the following key features: a significant partnership with industry; partnership with Pasadena City College, California State University at Los Angeles, and the Regional Occupational Program of Los Angeles County; integration of academic and applied learning with our business and university partners participating as equal partners in curriculum and program development and in setting the standards for a specialized high school diploma, the Certificate of Mastery; and mentorships beginning in the junior year and paid apprenticeships for students in the summer of their junior year and the second semester of their senior year. Obtaining the Certificate of Mastery requires completing the requirements for a PHS diploma, a senior project, one hundred hours of community service, eight hundred hours of graphic arts instruction, and four hundred hours as an apprentice. Students who meet the standards for the Certificate of Mastery are guaranteed a job by the printing industry when they graduate and have the option of completing one year's work toward their two-year community college associate degree while still in high school. By the time the students in the Graphic Arts Academy receive their high school diploma and the Certificate of Mastery, they will also have taken the courses required for admission to the university system of California.

The Graphics Arts Academy admitted its first class in September 1991. The three-year course integrates academic study with technical training and includes both school-centered and work-place learning. In the sophomore and junior years, students take most of their courses in the Graphic Arts Academy building, situated on the main high school campus. Five instructors (as they refer to themselves) teach all students their academic and technical subjects with the exception of an early-morning foreign-language class. Classes are small, block-scheduled according to the daily needs of the program, and the instructors have common planning time. Coursework blends applied academic study in English, history, mathematics (the printing industry insists that all students complete math through algebra II), and science with technical training and hands-on experience on printing equipment. Field trips and guest speakers who describe career paths in the graphic arts industry are key components of the program.

The sophomore year in the academy is primarily for establishing strong academic and problem-solving skills. Students are exposed to a variety of jobs and career paths in the graphic arts industry (press operators, production support positions, design, plate setup and typesetting, scanner and camera operators, platemaking and proofing, cutter and folder operators, sales, printing management, shipping and warehouse positions, and administrative and clerical positions) through field trips and guest speakers. Students are required to do community service in graphic arts after school.

In the junior year, students continue in a rigorous academic program including taking chemistry and algebra II. At this time, they are introduced to a mentor and are placed in a paid summer internship experience with a nearby printing company. They are also responsible for running a printing business after school and have responsibilities in all production areas. Some of the students begin their college work during this year.

As seniors, students continue with their academic coursework and take advanced graphic arts courses at Pasadena City College, concurrently earning high school and community college credit. Overall, the daily schedule and environment of the seniors changes dramatically. An early-morning advisory period is followed by an economics class, and by 9:00 a.m. they have gone their separate ways—to their apprenticeship, classes at PCC, or advanced academic classes at PHS.

Nowhere have I seen more motivated students, more dedicated teachers, or a program that better meets the needs of its students than the Graphic Arts Academy. As Tashan [not the student's real name] told me, "This program has saved me. My mom thinks it's the best thing that has happened to me and our family. The teachers all want me to be a success. They talk to my mom all the time. They won't let me get a low grade. If I slip a little, I have to come in until I know the stuff. They make me want to work hard. They really do care about me—all of us. None of my teachers would have ever thought I could or would take algebra II and chemistry and go to PCC. It's cool. We are just like a family here.

I know I will be something for me and my mom and my little brothers and sisters."

I frequently went over to visit the academy, especially on a difficult day when I wanted to know that something was going right for the kids at PHS. On one particularly hot May day, Tashan greeted me and took me all around the academy. He was obviously proud. In the print shop, he explained that one of the big expensive machines, a Heidelberg computerized printing press, had stopped working and three of the students were trying to figure out what was wrong. I saw them huddled around a repair manual. They explained to me that they always tried to figure out what was wrong in hopes of fixing it before calling in a repair person. I looked over their shoulder at this very sophisticated repair manual that José, Roderick, and Jimee were reading, and I could easily understand why industry is so upset with schools today. The repair manual required a sophisticated level of reading comprehension and an ability to solve problems, troubleshoot, and use initiative, the likes of which I have never seen in the best high schools in this country.

After doing some reading and discussing (sometimes in heated Spanish), José got under the machine, Roderick got down near José, and Jimee started passing on directions, reading intently from the manual with Roderick's interpretations of what needed to be done. I stayed around to see whether they would be able to make the repair—it turned out to be a minor malfunction—and they explained to me what they did.

These kids, who not so long ago would almost certainly have dropped out of school, who had had real trouble reading, who were the kinds of kids that every teacher would rather have had in someone else's classroom—these kids were doing chemistry experiments sorting polar materials from nonpolar materials (because they understood that making a mistake about which is which could make a printing mess); they were making their own paper and then testing its weight, thickness, and gloss; they were writing their own poetry and then racing to set the type in which they could print it; they were learning to assess which kids had a special gift for writing or for drawing or for layout or for printing or for

*numerous other functions. These kids, who had known only gang alle-
giance and warfare outside of school, were realizing that they needed each
other in the Graphic Arts Academy.*

*But this makes it sound too easy! Programs like this require a new
way of thinking on the part of everyone—the high school (students, teachers, administrators, and parents), higher education (the community colleges and four-year institutions), and the industry partners. The Graphic
Arts Academy, right from the first meeting, presented an enormous
challenge to all. Implementation of the design was not easy for any of the
partners. I learned that changing a system as deeply embedded in law,
regulation, and custom as ours, is a tremendously long-term undertak-
ing. But I have also learned and feel passionately that schools can no
longer go it alone.*

Beyond the Comprehensive High School

We began this book by pointing out that our education system holds out the preparation of elites for the nation's selective colleges as the ideal, leaving most of the other students, the vast majority, to enter adult life with inadequate academic skills and very little in the way of the kind of technical knowledge and skills they will need for rewarding careers. In this chapter, we propose a system that would change that. It focuses on the structure of our high schools and on the boundary between our secondary schools and the postsecondary system of education. The system we propose owes a debt to the Danes.

The Danish Approach to Vocational Education

Young people in Denmark, as in most of northern Europe, start school a year later than we do. Following kindergarten, everyone goes to the *Folkeskole* for nine years. They can, if they wish, go for an additional tenth year. There is no stigma attached to this decision, and in fact, a growing number of students are taking advantage of this option in order to improve their scores on national school-leaving exams.

At the end of the final year, students may take the school-leaving exams. They are not required to do so, but most do because otherwise their options for good jobs and further education are severely limited. Students can decide in which subjects they want to be examined.

When a student finishes *Folkeskole*, there is no graduation ceremony; one is expected to go right on with one's education. But graduates are issued a certificate indicating the final examinations taken and the grades obtained on them. Educational institutions and employers all over Denmark will ask for this document from candidates for admission and employment. That is why almost all students choose to take exams and an increasing number stay on an extra year to do as well as possible on them.

Although compulsory education ends with the completion of *Folkeskole*, 93 percent of young Danes go on. What they go on to is simple but very interesting from an American standpoint.

A little more than one-third go on to the traditional northern European secondary school, the gymnasium. The gymnasium's three-year program looks to an American like what we would call a college-prep program. Its purpose is to prepare its students to take the exams to enter university. But the university program that they enter at the end of gymnasium is not at all like the first year of what we call college. The university programs are designed to prepare students for the professions—law school, medical school, engineering school, senior division work in the sciences in preparation for a career in physics, and so on. This is quite striking. Unlike the United States, with its open-admissions colleges, Danish universities admit only those capable of doing university-level work. Their gymnasium graduates, with twelve or thirteen years of schooling behind them, are vaulting straight into the third year of what we would think of as a selective college.

Most of the rest of those leaving the *Folkeskoler* for further education go to the technical and commercial colleges (college in Denmark provides what for most students are the tenth, eleventh, and twelfth years of schooling). There are two basic alternatives in these colleges. Students can go either into the technical or commercial gymnasium or into the "sandwich program."

The students who go into the technical or commercial gymnasium enter a program that, like the traditional gymnasium, lasts three years. They study to take exactly the same kind of exams at exactly the same levels, providing access to the same university programs as the students in the regular gymnasium. The difference is in the pedagogy. In the regular gymnasium, you will find the familiar textbook and class lecture approach that you would find in most serious American college-prep programs. But in the technical and commercial *gymnasier,* you will find classes that are largely based on projects—a learn-by-doing approach. Although the graduates of the technical *gymnasier* have gone to an avowedly vocational school, they are more sought after by employers than the graduates of the traditional *gymnasier* who major in math and science because, we were told, they have mastered the same substance but are more likely to show initiative, to be self-starters, to work well with others in groups, and to be more comfortable with real-world problems. More surprising, universities often prefer the graduates of the technical *gymnasier* because they think more analytically.

The sandwich program is the descendant of Denmark's old apprenticeship program. It is called a sandwich program because it consists of a period of so many weeks at school followed by a period of so many weeks at the worksite, alternating repeatedly until the young person passes the theoretical and practical exams. These programs are typically three and one-half to four years long. They begin with an initial period of about six months during which the young person can explore as many as a half a dozen different careers before settling on the one he or she wants to pursue. Once that choice is made, the student is expected to obtain an apprenticeship contract with an employer and enroll in the appropriate program at the technical or commercial college. If it proves impossible for the student to get a contract with an employer, the college must, by law, provide an experience for that youngster that simulates the experience of working at an employer's worksite. The apprenticeship contract can be terminated by either student or employer during the first three months. After that, they are stuck with each other.

When students enroll in the sandwich program, they are told which additional courses they need to take to prepare themselves for the university entrance exams. The result is that a student who enters any of these three programs—the traditional gymnasium, the technical and commercial *gymnasier*, or the sandwich program— can go on to higher education. There should not be any dead ends in this system. It is not a sorting system. It provides many different paths for students with different objectives, but no door is ever closed, no decision irrevocable.

What is truly astonishing is the level of accomplishment of the students when they reach their twelfth (or thirteenth) year. What would have happened to Jeff, the student introduced in the Prologue, if he had been going to high school in Aalborg? First of all, if he was in his ninth or tenth year (still in *Folkeskole*), he would not have had the option of "coasting through." He could not have avoided algebra by taking a course like "business math" or opted out of taking physics. When we asked Christine, a fifteen-year-old in her last year of *Folkeskole*, about the Danish curriculum, she explained, "In the Danish school, you can't choose all your lessons. . . . You have to take Danish, English, math, and . . . biology, geography, and history. When you get a little bit older, you get something called 'society' that's three lessons together [geography, history, and civics]. In the seventh grade, you can choose between German and French. In math [we study] algebra, trigonometry, geometry, fractions, statistics, a lot about that." In addition to biology, Christine said, all students were required to take chemistry and physics. They take two physical education classes a week, and they get to make some choices among cooking, sewing, and wood shop. But the choices are very few. It is virtually the same curriculum for everyone, and the expectations are the same for all.

At the end of ninth grade—or tenth if he chose to stay an extra year—Jeff would have had to sit for his exams, and when he had taken them, he would have gotten a leaving certificate from his *Folkeskole*. We asked Danish ninth graders to describe the certificate.

"It tells the grade that we ended on and the grades we got on the examinations [subject by subject]. And it tells the average, and then you can have a paper where the teacher writes what he thinks about you and your way of doing work."

"Do you ever show your certificate to anyone? Does the employer ask to see your certificate?"

"If you are going to be a metalworker or something, he wants to see your certificate to make sure that you can add two and two."

Another student was interested in becoming a flight mechanic. We asked him what one had to do to become a flight mechanic. He said that you have to go to a technical college but not to university. He would also have to get a contract with an employer. And to obtain a contract, he must present his certificate to document that he did well in school. "Could you be a flight mechanic," we asked, "and not know math, algebra, or trigonometry?"

"Not at all," he replied.

We asked the students whether the exams that one takes depend on whether one expects to be an air-conditioning mechanic, a flight engineer, or a cook.

"You most often choose all exams. Then you won't be standing there someday [unable] to get in somewhere. But you can say that you won't have German, for example, [if] you know that you don't need the topic or class."

Had Jeff grown up in Denmark, he would have known, as these students do, that getting a good job depends on taking a full set of exams when leaving the ninth grade and doing well on them. He would have had the option of taking no exams at the end of *Folkeskole*, but he would never have dreamed of exercising that option because he would know that every employer offering a decent job connected with engine maintenance and repair would expect him to have continued his education and would be very interested in how he did in school. Jeff could not see why he would ever need much math after school (because, as we saw, the employers in his town were prepared to teach him arithmetic if they thought he needed it and the community college had no math requirements), so he did not take it even though he was good at math and liked it. In Denmark, the math he skipped would have been required. The same is true of physics. So we can be sure that Jeff, who is unquestionably bright and able to do demanding academic work when he chooses to, would have emerged from the *Folkeskole* with a strong grounding in the core subjects in the curriculum.

What then? We know that Jeff, like many other American young people, would rather learn by doing whenever he has the choice. And he likes technical subjects. So he would have chosen to go to a technical college for the rest of his high school program.

The View from Aalborg

The city of Aalborg is the industrial hub of the Jutland peninsula, a rural vacationland in the north of Denmark. The Aalborg Technical College is its pride and joy, an institution occupying ten campuses scattered across the city. Its administration building and many of the classrooms and workshops are housed in an impressive complex on the crest of a hill overlooking the fjord, the city, and the stacks of a large cement company. It looks like no American high school we have ever seen but reminds us of the best vocationally oriented American community and technical colleges. The equipment, from the masonry workshops to the agricultural facilities and the metal and electrical labs and workshops, is state-of-the-art, and the classrooms are staffed by highly qualified teachers often responsible for both the initial training of their students and the advanced training of people who have been in their fields for many years.

Jeff's basic choice when coming to the college would have been whether to enter the technical gymnasium or the sandwich program of vocational training.

The technical gymnasium is located in a suburban area at the south end of town in a small cluster of well-kept low buildings that bustled with activity. We arrived late, just as school was getting out. The staff had to scramble to find a student who was willing to stay and talk to us. Anders is a handsome, articulate young man who speaks flawless, idiomatic English. He is in his last year at the technical gymnasium (equivalent to the senior year in an American high school). His mother is a bookkeeper. His father, he said, is a teacher who used to be a radio mechanic.

The curriculum at the technical college is project-based, as we indicated earlier. We asked him what sorts of projects he had worked on.

"I've made potato flour and marmalade and some safety equipment. Right now I'm making a weather station for my final project."

He told us that the general pattern for projects was that the student first produced a design, then built the project, and then tested it to see if it actually performed up to the standards on which the design was based.

"So my project has to measure the wind, how much humidity is in the air, the temperature inside and out, and what direction the wind is coming from. . . . I have to find out what I am going to use and order it from the school and make it myself, and write a report."

"Do you know the standards that are expected of you?"

"Well, the standards are pretty high. But my project is an electrical project, so they don't expect so much from the mechanical quality, but the electronics has to be perfect. It should work, and if it does not work, I have to find out why it doesn't work.

"We have projects in every subject. Now we are making a physics project with a refrigerator. We're trying to figure out how it works, how it can become more efficient, how much power it uses on an ordinary day, how we can make it better, and then write a report about it."

"What was your English project on?"

"I wrote about censorship of music in the United States."

"What did you find out?"

"I found out that a lot of people didn't want young people to hear what they wanted . . . so they put those parental guidance stickers on, 'explicit lyrics.' And then a lot of shops didn't want to sell the records because they had warning labels. That was quite an effective form of censorship, because if you can't buy the records, you can't listen to them. Logic."

"What about math?"

"We had to measure up some land and we used . . . a surveyor's instrument. We put some sticks in a field and measured the area between the sticks."

We wanted to know how demanding the math curriculum was in the technical gymnasium. Anders was taking A-level math, the more demanding level. Anders's technology course must be A-level, as well as his Danish course and at least one other academic course. Also, he must take and pass other A-level courses to get an overall pass.

"What is the content of A-level math?"

"It's pretty much everything. . . . We've got integration [calculus] and . . . vectors. Trigonometry is quite easy, but we have very advanced trigonometry."

"What about statistics?"

"We could choose it as an exam project, but I didn't. I chose [mathematical] models. We had one for how many fish there are in the North Sea. We could calculate from what they ate and how [many fish were] caught. And then we had something about vectors in space, sort of like 3-D vectors. It's very complicated."

"So the math you learn has to do with the projects that you want to take on?"

"Well, if we want to do, for example, the surveyor's project, then we have to learn a lot of trigonometry to do it. And it's been like that with all the things. All the subjects are linked together."

"Having the projects connected with what you are taught, it's much better than just being taught the stuff, because you can see what you can use it for and see that it's something real. . . . I think it makes much more sense to [link] the things, all the classes, because if you're in math class and you're just listening to the teacher and you're going, 'Oh, we're never going to use that in real life.' And the next day you're going to your electronics class and then you have to use the thing you learned in math the day before. It makes you want to learn more."

Echoes, we thought, of Jeff, for whom much of school was irrelevant because he could never imagine how he would use the knowledge he gained in school in "real life." But we wondered aloud whether this emphasis on project-based learning was coming at the expense of real mastery of the disciplines, so we asked the students at the technical gymnasium to compare their curriculum with the one that the students in the regular gymnasium were getting.

"Well, for starters, I've got a lot more physics than they have. I've got five physics classes a week, nine math classes, and ordinary [gymnasium] students have only got about three physics classes every week. And I think ours is at a more advanced level."

Who could have blamed us for assuming that Anders was headed for a career in science or technology? Actually, that had been the case.

"Well, originally I was going to study to be an engineer at the university, . . .[but now] when I finish, I'm going to the university and study English. I've really gotten interested in British and American society, and I want to study that."

"How is it that you are able to go from the technical gymnasium to a university and major in English?"

"This education [in the technical college has] got the same level as an ordinary gymnasium, so I can do anything that you can do with an ordinary exam. It is possible to go almost anywhere with this education."

What a far cry from Jeff's attainments and prospects! But suppose that Anders had not elected to go to the technical gymnasium but had chosen to go into the sandwich program instead. In that case, he might have followed the same path as Hans. Hans is in the last year of the four-year program for "fitters."

"I am nineteen years old. I live in a small town just outside Aalborg. I have one brother. He is a fitter, and my dad is a fitter, too. And I still live at home with my mom and dad."

"What is a fitter?"

"It means you work with metals . . . a lathe and milling machine and computer-controlled machines. And work something with your hands, make things fit together."

"When you were in *Folkeskole*, what did you think you had to know to come here?"

"Algebra, geometry and trigonometry, chemistry and physics."

"How about languages?"

"We had German and English."

"What did you do?"

"I just took English."

"So you came out of the *Folkeskole* knowing English and Danish?"

"Yes." (In fact, he speaks English very well.)

Hans has continued to study these subjects in the sandwich program at the technical college, along with the technical subjects in the workshops. His teacher, thinking that we might have concluded that the curriculum is entirely vocationally oriented, assures us that that is not the case, that part of the curriculum is devoted to making Hans a "whole person." We ask him what that means.

"I guess we look at it and say, 'He's supposed to be in the company for eight hours, but there will be twenty-four hours in a day, so there'll be a lot of spare time where he has to do a lot of other things for himself and for his family and for his friends." We are reminded by this remark of the art we have seen throughout the corridors of the technical college, of very high quality, selected by

Lars Mahler, the college's director (principal), and changed every month. Someone here really does care about a lot more than the professional skills of these young people.

Turning to Hans, we ask him how he spent the past four years. He explains that the first two school terms ran twenty weeks each, followed by shorter terms of ten, five, five, and ten weeks, respectively.

"And where have you spent the rest of your time?"

"I've been in the factory where I am an apprentice, to learn the things I have to know."

So about half of Hans's apprenticeship is spent in classes at the technical college and the other half at a machine shop in structured training.

We learn that at the fifteen-person machine shop, Hans is responsible for machining a variety of parts to very high tolerances and then measuring the results to make sure that the quality of the work meets the standards.

This is demanding work, but the program back at the technical college is designed to more than match the requirements of that work. When we began interviewing Hans, we found him working at a computer loaded with computer-aided design software.

We ask if the software design, programming, and CAD skills he is using have any application on the job at the machine shop, and he tells us no.

"Do you think that you will use them later?"

"Maybe, if I get to another firm."

Hans's teacher, Niels, explains: "We are not using the CAD only for designing but [also to help] the young people understand how things work together. When you can draw something at a station like this, using software like AutoCAD, you can, using some other programs, translate it directly to a machining program and put it into a milling machine or a turning machine. Today, there won't be many students who are allowed to use computer-aided design in the factory. But things are moving in that direction. Some factories are organizing themselves into small working groups where they are supposed to be able to use systems like this."

The next day, we would visit a factory not far from the school that makes heavy-duty pumps for use in rugged environments. Looking at their apprentices as we talked, the managers said, somewhat wistfully, that there would be many fewer jobs for these young people in the future, as the whole process becomes progressively more highly automated and the machines do almost everything in direct response to computer programs created in the process of designing the products. We recalled the vocational education teacher at Walt Whitman who despaired of ever having up-to-date equipment. Here, in Aalborg, the technical college was preparing its high school students to do the work that would be available when the current state-of-the-art machines become obsolete.

At the time of our talk, Hans was in his last school term before completing the program. Like all the other students in the class, he was sweating his exams, which would begin the following week. The exams would take an entire two weeks. We asked Hans what he expected.

"We will have to make something, but we do not know yet what it is because we do not choose it." The subject, of course, is chosen at the national level by the employer and union groups that set the standards for the sandwich programs nationwide.

"They choose a part. Then you have twenty-four hours to do the milled parts, twenty-four hours to do the turned parts on the lathe, and eight hours to put the things together so you have one completed unit." All students have to make the same item.

We asked Niels who does the judging.

"Two people come from industry—one from the union and one from the employer. And then there will be one of the teachers from my group, and those three people . . . have two days to measure all the [things made by the students] and fill out the forms and calculate the grade . . . according to the instructions, which are the same for all students."

"What happens when someone fails?"

"He'll have to do it again. [He'll go] back to the company to get some training. We'll call him in again and give him some special training for two or three weeks and then give him another test in August."

In addition to the three days for actually making the specified project, the students are allotted an additional four days for setting up the machines and doing all the calibration required. Then there is a two-hour exam directly related to the fitting work. Finally, the students must also pass exams in their academic subjects—Danish, English, the various subjects in mathematics and science, and so on.

We asked Hans what he has learned in the factory other than how to be a fitter.

"I have learned how to work with other people so you can make one thing, so it will be finished on time."

We ask about his work schedule.

"I meet at seven in the morning. Then I get out at three in the afternoon."

"How often do you show up late?"

Hans, thoroughly shocked by the question, replies, "Never!"

The employers in Jeff's community would have been shocked not by the question but by the answer.

Roland Østerlund runs the vocational education program of the Danish Ministry of Education. A big man, he considers his words carefully when he speaks. He brings to his subject a knowledge of vocational education as it is practiced around the world that is quite unusual. We ask him why Americans should not think of the Danish system as tracked.

"Selecting . . . is not tracking of the students because they would still have opportunities for continuing into higher education in whatever direction they like. But in the school form [they select], they would meet a culture that is flavored by the aim of the programs run by that particular kind of institution. That means you can have diversity in the system without tracking the students."

Roland points out that whereas enrollment in vocational education in many advanced industrialized countries continues to fall off at a rapid rate, it is well above 50 percent in Denmark and pretty stable. He attributes this in part to the knowledge on the part of parents and students that enrollment in vocational education programs in Denmark does not preclude later enrollment in higher education for anyone.

"Another very important feature of the system is that the programs preparing students for work would all be a combination of school-based education and training and work-based training.

"[Students] should be independent, able to work on their own. What you train them to do today might be outdated when they graduate from the program, so you have to prepare them to be able to continue their learning on their own."

One key to this kind of flexibility is what the Danes call "personal qualifications." "Right now," Roland tells us, "we are changing the [regulations] for a number of different courses to include specific targets relating to . . . personal qualifications: flexibility, sense of quality, creativity, communication, teamwork, and so on. The final craftsmen's test will include not only the traditional craftsmen's skills but also their creativity, their ability to work on their own, and their ability to find the information they need to solve a problem.

"There is a focus today on the learning organization. If you bear in mind that we already have a system where the major part of the education and training program is placed inside the company, this is not a strange idea in Denmark. If you learn things by doing them and meet the changes as they come when you work, you already have a focus on learning rather than teaching. In the school part of the system, we are in the middle of a process of moving the focus away from teaching and over toward learning—and in that sense giving the student the responsibility for learning and the accountability for the outcome."

What the Danes Taught Us

The system failed Jeff by consistently communicating a message that he did not need to know very much to succeed in life, by failing to provide any incentive to take tough courses or work hard in school, by expecting very little of him and providing less. This was not just a failure of his school and district but a failure equally of his parents and the employers in the community. The result is that Jeff has, by now, graduated high school with far less knowledge and skill than either Hans or Anders. His prospects for the rest of his life have been greatly—and needlessly—diminished.

We do not advocate adopting the Danish system of education and training. We focus on it here to make a simple point: in America, Jeff is not the exception; he is the norm. There are millions of students very much like Jeff who are leaving high school with a false sense of confidence in themselves and in their preparation for life. That is unforgivable. And it does not have to be that way.

The Danes taught us a number of things: that it is possible to construct a system in which the same proportion of youngsters go on to postsecondary education as currently in the United States, but most stay to get a degree because they are fully prepared to do college-level work; that it would be possible for our kids to complete the first two years of a real college program one or two years before they do now, thus saving an enormous amount of money and eliminating the waste of the last two years of high school, when so many of our kids simply coast; that we can create a hands-on form of college-prep program that will attract many kids like Jeff who are currently alienated by conventional college-prep programs; that we should not regard well-designed vocational education as a dumping ground for kids who either won't or can't make it in a college-prep program but rather as a first-class alternative for kids who are quite capable of demanding academic work but who want to work with their hands or do applied work when they leave high school; that American employers need not expect that they will have to teach arithmetic to their new employees; that those same employers could expect those employees to show up on time and put in a full day's work; that virtually all of the kids who do not go from our high schools to selective colleges could be emerging from our community colleges at the age of eighteen or nineteen with the same skills and prospects that only a handful of our best community college graduates now have.

What the States and Districts Can Do: Abolishing the Comprehensive High School and Creating a New Structure in Its Place

The current form of the American high school could not be more different from the Danish structure for the type of upper secondary education just described. Largely set in the 1950s, it was urged on the nation by James Bryant Conant, the former president of Harvard University and distinguished chemist, in his highly influential series of reports on the American schools.[1] But its roots go back further, to the interwar years, when American secondary education was transformed from the privileged preserve of the few to the mass institution we know today. In the 1920s and '30s, as noted in Chapter Two, American educators readily abandoned the classical ideal of a high school focused on the core curriculum and adopted what most saw as a more democratic alternative, a high school that would provide a much more diverse curriculum and many more paths than the classical high school. The core curriculum of the classical high school was deemed antidemocratic and therefore un-American. Something for everyone was definitely in.

Conant's contribution was to observe that the small high schools in America's small towns could not afford to engage specialist teachers and pay for the equipment that was needed to do a good job of teaching chemistry or modern languages, for instance. Only by bringing together many students, often from a large enrollment area, could the students and the dollars be assembled to provide such a curriculum. Of course, it wasn't for everyone, and so appropriate courses would have to be offered for those not going to college as well.

Some years ago, Arthur Powell, Eleanor Farrar, and David Cohen, in their landmark book *The Shopping Mall High School*, described the end result of these developments, a high school organized like a modern shopping mall in which everything one could wish for was available at every price and quality range to meet the needs of a very diverse clientele.[2] Something for everyone had achieved its apogee. On a single campus, one could get science in every form, from Advanced Placement physics to a general science course that contained little science at all. Courses in pop culture took their places alongside courses in Shakespeare. Drivers' ed and general shop had the same standing as precalculus and microeconomics.

We believe that the shopping mall—or comprehensive—high school is not an asset but a problem and ought to be abolished. We have argued throughout this book for schools that concentrate on a core curriculum set to very high academic standards and dedicated to the proposition that one must not only master the academics but also be able to apply what one has learned to complex real-world problems.

Doing that, we believe, is a full-time job, a job that no comprehensive high school in the nation is currently doing. First, all communities, even the Winnetkas and the Scarsdales, have youngsters who are not headed for Harvard, Yale, Columbia, and the University of Chicago, and they do not do very well by these youngsters. Second, these elite systems often do an excellent job of the academics but a much poorer job of helping these youngsters apply what they know to complex real-world problems. So the agenda we have in mind is an agenda that no one is doing well and that, if taken seriously, will present a challenge to even the most favored high schools.

Our proposition is simple: redefine high school.

High school should be about academics and applied academics. It should not be about pop culture, driver education, how to use a checkbook, or general shop.

Nor, especially, should it be about serious vocational education leading to a good career. Why? Because serious vocational education leading to a good career takes a kind and quality of faculty, equipment, relations with employers, and overall management that is very specialized and demanding. The idea that it can be the part-time occupation of the staff of a comprehensive high school is to condemn it to the inferior status that it has long had in the United States.

High schools should be asked to do one thing well, not many things in a mediocre way. And the one thing that they should be asked to do well is provide all of our students a first-class academic foundation for the rest of their lives.

In our scheme of things, this means that high schools would have two specific jobs. The first would be to bring all students up to the Certificate of Initial Mastery standard before they leave. This is, by itself, a very tough job, a job no open-admissions high school in America has ever attempted for a heterogeneous student body. The second would be to provide for CIM recipients who want it a post-CIM course of study in high school designed to prepare them for serious college entrance examinations.

In terms of the Danish model, the American high school would provide what the last year or two of the *Folkeskole* (grades nine and ten) provides and, as an additional option for students who want it, a program roughly similar to the regular gymnasium.

The pre-CIM high school would be much more focused than most high school programs. What it would be focused on is a program designed for one purpose: to get lower-division high school students to the CIM. Most courses would be required; there would be very few electives. Students who entered the high school behind grade level or who fell behind would be put in accelerated programs and given extra time during the school day, after school, on Saturdays, and during the summer to catch up. There would be no penalty, though, for the student who did not get the CIM by age sixteen or the tenth grade. The school would, however, feel a strong obligation to make sure that virtually all students received the new certificate by the time they finished high school. Whenever an individual student met the requirements for the CIM, that student would then be eligible to begin a post-CIM program of his or her choice.

In Europe, as we pointed out, the gymnasium actually incorporates the first year or two of what we call college, as well as the end of what we think of as high school. Our idea of the high school post-CIM academic program would work in a similar way because it would include both Advanced Placement courses and the opportunity to participate in the International Baccalaureate Program (designed for grades 11 and 12), both of which can lead to credit for as much as a full year of coursework in America's selective colleges. Thus the students in the high school we have in mind would enroll in that high school's post-CIM academic program in order to do their very best on the college entrance exams and to be able to skip as much as a whole year of college work, beginning college with the sophomore year in a way roughly comparable to the common European experience.

In sum, the redesigned high schools we have just described would be far more concerned with academics than most of our comprehensive high schools have been since the early years of this century. Their first task would be to get all their students to the Certificate of Initial Mastery standard. Their second job would be to offer a rigorous academic program for those students who have earned their CIM and want to prepare themselves for entrance to a demanding four-year college program. Needless to say, students who successfully complete such a program would have no need for remediation in college. They would be as ready for what we call college as any gymnasium graduate in Europe is ready for university (Figure 5.1).

Figure 5.1. The American High School—Redesigned.

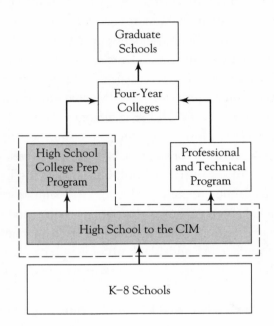

What the States and Districts Can Do: Providing Professional and Technical Education in Institutions Designed for That Purpose

But many students will want an alternative to the traditional four-year college, an alternative that will give them an opportunity to get involved in their careers sooner, that will provide a high-quality technical and professional foundation for that career, and that also provides a clear path to a four-year college and possibly graduate school later.

In Denmark, this opportunity, as we have seen, is provided by the technical and commercial colleges, which provide very solid programs leading to the university entrance exams and to national skill certificates, the standards for which are set by employers. It is a no-dead-end system, in that the students that choose the skill certificate program have clear pathways to the university exams.

The United States can and should have a system that does no less. Three key elements are required: the standards for these programs, institutions to offer them, and the cooperation of industry in providing the structured training that, for many careers, should accompany the classroom education the students can get.

The standards for university entrance examinations already exist. The occupational standards are being set by national industry groups as this book is being written, under the auspices of the National Skill Standards Board, created by President Clinton and the Congress for that purpose. These standards are intended to reflect the state of the art in their respective industries and to enable the students to acquire skills and knowledge broad enough and deep enough to enable them to cope with swiftly changing technology and even job descriptions in their chosen fields, very much as the Technology College in Aalborg was equipping its students to deal with metalworking technology that was still over the horizon.

Among the institutions that now offer some form of vocational education are regional technical and vocational high schools, community colleges, technical colleges, and proprietary schools. Some of these institutions have very solid programs now. Some others have become dumping grounds for students whom no one else wants. Many others lie somewhere in the middle, with programs that might have served in the past but have a long way to go to reach the level of quality that we have seen in Aalborg and in some community colleges in the United States.

And there lies the challenge to the states—to rebuild our postsecondary vocational education system to make it the most modern, highest-quality vocational education system in the world. It is a measure of this country's single-minded preoccupation with college that we have starved our vocational education system of support and allowed its standards to slip well below those of our competitors elsewhere in the world. All the Jeffs in our high schools deserve a high-quality choice other than the Universities of Michigan or Iowa States or Macalesters. It should be possible for them to enroll in a program like those in which Anders and Hans were enrolled.

The military's role there, once large, is now diminished. Civilian programs of the kind we have in mind exist in the United States, but employer participation is spotty and weak, and there is not yet a set of clear national occupational standards to guide the work of both the educational institutions and the students, there is no clear standard for admission to such programs, and the path from such programs to further higher education and higher degrees is often blurred at best.

The National Skill Standards Board and the industry partnerships it is creating will produce the standards. The rest is up to the states. Funding streams are needed that will enable students who have received the Certificate of Initial Mastery to attend postsecondary vocational institutions that provide programs leading to the new national occupational certificates. Governance arrangements for the vocational institutions should be changed to require much more industry participation in every aspect of the work of the vocational institutions. Funds are needed to enable the institutions to acquire up-to-date technology and instructors. And the states need to develop incentives that will reward institutions that succeed in getting their students to the new national occupational standards and provide consequences for those that take the students' money and give them little in return.

Not least important, the states need to establish clearly what academic credit will be given by state higher education institutions to students who have acquired particular national skill certificates.

In many cases, we believe, these skill certificates will be sufficiently demanding in academic terms to warrant the concurrent award of a community college associate degree, thereby entitling the holder to transfer into a four-year college at the junior-year level. The technical and professional preparation programs should be seen not as an alternative to college but as another way to go to college. The national skill certificates should be seen not as the last stop in the educational process but as another step in a continuing education process.

The idea of students leaving high school as early as the age of sixteen to go on to some form of postsecondary education may seem radical to many people. But the state of Minnesota has had a law on its books for many years now that makes it possible for any Minnesota youngster who has reached the age of sixteen to go to any postsecondary institution that will admit him or her and take along to that institution the state funding that would otherwise have gone to the school district. No disasters have occurred in Minnesota as a result of this law; it has worked very well.

The high school diploma, once highly valued by employers, is no longer valued. Our proposal does raise the question of what to do about the high school diploma and high school graduation. There are at least three options for handling both issues. First, the CIM could become the diploma. Second, districts or states could make the award of the diploma contingent on having received the CIM. Or third, they could award diplomas in the future, as at present, on the basis of seat time, to those few students whose disabilities are so severe as to make it impossible to reach the standards and the handful who could do it but simply will not, and award both the diploma and the certificate to the vast majority who do reach that standard. Each of these options has its merits and drawbacks, many of which we have discussed elsewhere. Different jurisdictions will make different choices among them. The main point is that there is a wide range of credible ways to adopt the certificate system while continuing to honor in some form the rather formidable American commitment to the high school diploma.

What the Schools Can Do: Building the New High School

If the primary task of every high school is to get every student to the Certificate of Initial Mastery standard, the high school must be redesigned for that purpose. The first step in that redesign will be to develop a highly focused curriculum for students who do not yet have their CIM. Just as there are very few electives in the Danish *Folkeskole*, there should be very few electives in the lower division of high school. Courses of study should be defined for a small core of courses in English language arts, mathematics, physics, chemistry, biology, earth sciences, geography, history, economics, foreign languages, the fine and applied arts, and physical fitness. This is our list of subjects. You will have your own. But note that the list is short.

These courses of study, taken together, are the curriculum for everyone until they have their certificate. Each of these courses should have an accompanying end-of-course examination that assesses student mastery of the material in the course to the standard set for the Certificate of Initial Mastery. Focusing on a few demanding courses, combined with making sure that the remaining courses are aimed at thoroughly learning the most important topics, should make large gains possible.

The planning system we described in the closing pages of Chapter Four, or something very much like it, will be required to track student progress toward the CIM standard and to adjust the program of the school to make sure that everyone is on track to get their certificate. Each student coming into the high school will have to be assessed to see where they are against the standards, and that information will have to be made available immediately to the teachers so that they can put together a program matched to the students' needs. With common, required courses and defined courses of study, it will be possible to develop grading systems for student work that are not idiosyncratic to each teacher, but which use common rubrics. So a system for continuous assessment using grades can be developed in which an "A" is an "A" is an "A" no matter which teacher a student has. This will make it easier for a student pursuing the CIM and will make it easier for the teachers to jointly assess the progress of their students.

Adolescence is a very vulnerable time for young people. Just as their bonds to their own family weaken, their bonds to the adults at school weaken as they enter what for many turns out to be the vast, anonymous institution called high school. Some turn to gangs, others shrink into themselves, and many just enter the youth culture in a way that can often be destructive.

We think that high schools must do several things to counteract these influences: first, assign every member of the professional staff as an advisor to a group of students and make sure that this person stays in touch with each student's parents and with the student; second, change the master schedule so a group of teachers shares responsibility for a set of students, and those teachers have specific times during the week to meet together and talk about how the students are doing and correct course where necessary; and third, create "houses" within large high schools in which this group of teachers and their shared student body can physically reside and in which they can build some sense of community.

This idea of a shared community of students and teachers within the larger institution can have many ramifications. It could include an extension, for example, of the class teacher idea, in this case meaning that some or all of a student's teachers follow that student through the required curriculum leading to the Certificate of Initial Mastery. It could mean that all the teachers meet to see how the students are doing on the writing standards, and that the teachers of history, for example, end up sharing responsibility with the English teachers for making sure that students who are not doing well on the requirement to produce a persuasive essay improve those skills. It will surely mean that the teachers in the group will collaborate on decisions about how to use the available time within and beyond the regular school day to get their students to the CIM standard as quickly as possible. Abolishing Carnegie units and focusing on the design and redesign of courses needed to get their students to the CIM will inevitably lead to unique ways to carve up the school day, ways that reflect the specific needs of the students in the group.

Sharing the same group of students should make it possible for teachers to reduce the number of students with whom they come in contact.

Even if the economics of the local situation result in large class sizes, the reduced number of students each teacher comes in contact with will mean that the teachers will know their students better, and that should greatly improve the outcome for both student and teacher. Not the least of the ramifications of building these communities of students and teachers within the high school is the enhanced potential for the moral development of the students. Everything the faculty does—even more than what it says—sends a moral message. From the fairness of the grading system to the fairness of the discipline that is meted out, these highly impressionable young people learn what adults really value. When the group is small, the way the group works is highly visible, and it is much more likely that the adults involved will take real responsibility for the moral and ethical messages they send.

Our emphasis here on doing what must be done to make sure that virtually all students receive the Certificate of Initial Mastery should not in any way convey a diminished image of high school. For those students who want to stay on after receiving their CIM, there should be a wide array of demanding courses in many subjects and some that may just be fun. Many, by design, will be college-level courses carrying college credit. We have emphasized the pre-CIM changes that must be made because of our overriding concern that every student leave high school with the strongest possible foundation for the future.

What the Districts and States Can Do: Organizing to Support the New System

The new academic certificates will motivate students to take tough courses and work hard in school only if two things happen: first, if businesses and postsecondary institutions make it clear that students are more likely to get good jobs and get into college if they have the certificate, and second, if students are permitted to get on with their lives when they get the certificate, rather than having to serve time in high school until they reach the age of eighteen in order to get their diploma or similar certificate.

Making good on those promises would require a district or state to work hard to get business leaders and postsecondary institutions in the area or the state to sign on to the idea of the certificate. It is not necessary to get all the businesses or postsecondary institutions to do this, just enough to make students pay attention. In our experience, chambers of commerce, the state business roundtable, the state affiliate of the National Association of Manufacturers, and similar business organizations are eager to participate in such endeavors because their members are often desperate to find some legitimate role they can play in improving the knowledge and skills of young people available for front-line jobs. The idea that students could work for a piece of paper that certifies to prospective employers that they possess a stated set of knowledge and skills and can perform at a specified level is very attractive to businesspeople. Many states in addition to Minnesota already have laws on their books permitting high school students who meet certain minimum requirements to enroll in community college before they get their diploma.

It is very important that when you announce that you are going to implement your own version of the academic certificate in your state or district, you are able to announce at the same time just what options will be available to students when they get their certificate and that those options include some way to begin their postsecondary studies if they want to. And it is perhaps most important to have your business community and your postsecondary community saying clearly that youngsters who obtain the new academic certificates will get preference in hiring and in college admissions in the state's public and private institutions. As we saw in the case of the Graphic Arts Academy, this alone will motivate students, parents, and teachers to do their very best to make sure that students actually reach the new standards on which the certificates are based.

What States and Communities Can Do: New Professional and Technical Programs

The programs we have in mind would last from two to three years, with about half of that time spent at the worksite. The classroom work would not be geared to the needs of a particular job or employer but rather to a broad array of entry-level jobs in a large family of industries, all leading to better and more demanding jobs over time, thus qualifying the students who enrolled in these programs for many good jobs and opening thereby a wide range of opportunities when the program is completed.

In the interlude that preceded this chapter, you found a description of the Graphic Arts Academy at Pasadena High School, which John Porter, then director of high schools, Judy, and her colleagues designed as a precursor of the kind of program we have in mind. Establishing that program was a fight every step of the way, mainly because there was no infrastructure there to build on. As time goes by, it will be easier, partly because the National Skill Standards Board is developing the national standards that are needed to drive such programs and partly because the states are starting to build governance and financing mechanisms to facilitate the local development of such programs. And organizations like Jobs for the Future, our National Alliance and Workforce Development programs, and the National Alliance of Business are offering technical assistance to states and districts to give them the hands-on help they need to design and run effective programs.

But most of the work is still ahead. Though businesses are eager to get better-qualified help, there is no tradition in this country, as there is in Denmark and many other nations, of business providing structured training to young people as part of their formal education. And the states will need to pass legislative packages affecting the structure of their higher education systems, the laws relating to the structure of high schools and the granting of high school diplomas, and the flow of money through the higher and lower education systems to implement the ideas we have sketched out here.

We have no choice, though. There is a great irony here. Even though, as we said in Chapter One, this country has opted for a smorgasbord curriculum in the high school, we have at the same time produced a sound curriculum for and concentrated our attention and resources on only the youngsters who we believed were bound from an early age for four-year colleges. Like Jeff, the student we described in the Prologue, the rest have spent their high school years either as dropouts meeting their destiny in dead-end jobs if they could get them or biding their time in high school waiting for their diploma, often no more qualified for employment or life than the youngsters who dropped out earlier.

The program we described here, combining classwork in high school and community college with structured training at the work-site and working toward an employer-designed qualification, has been used for decades by many European nations to provide the majority of young people with a much better shot at success than we have given them for half a century. It is time to build that bridge for them. If we do not, none of the rest of the ideas in this book will bear fruit for most young people; they will not see the point of investing their own effort in their education, and if they do not make an effort, they will not learn much.

What High Schools and Districts Can Do While Waiting for Changes in State Policy to Be Made

We have proposed major changes in the institutional structure for education and training, many of which will require substantial changes in state policy. Is there anything that schools and districts can do while waiting for those changes to be made?

Of course there is. In the interlude that precedes this chapter, we described what Judy and her colleagues did at Pasadena High in the early 1990s. They used "meeting the standard for geometry" as a stand-in for the CIM. The printing trade association agreed to set occupational standards for the students who enrolled in the Graphic Arts Academy. The employers in the printing trades agreed to equip the academy, provide worksite training slots for the students and develop curriculum for the academy students. And the local community college and four-year college agreed to join the high school in providing a range of related courses that enable the students to get college credit for many of the courses in the graphic arts curriculum sequence, college credit that these students had when they got their high school diploma. Is this everything we have in mind? No. Is it a rough approximation of all the key features of what we have in mind? Absolutely. The academic and occupational standards are there. The curriculum combining head and hand is there. The combination of classwork and structured worksite training is there. And the motivation provided by clear routes to further college education and good jobs when the standards are met is there, too.

Much has happened since Pasadena High sewed the Graphic Arts Academy together out of the best parts available at the time. The New Standards performance standards and performance assessments are available. Courses of study that will make it possible to use those standards and assessments as the basis for awarding a Certificate of Initial Mastery will be available in 1998. Not long thereafter, the first occupational skill standards should be published by the National Skill Standards Board. And many states are putting into place workforce development systems designed to support programs of the kind that we have described. But even where that is not the case, the example of Pasadena High makes it clear that one can always start from just one school to build the systems we need to make sure that all the Jeffs everywhere will have a better shot at good careers and a decent life than the Jeff we described at the beginning of this book.

What Schools Can Do: Helping All Youngsters Prepare for Work and Careers

Preparation for work is only one of the purposes of education. But virtually everyone who enters school eventually leaves to do work of some kind. Some people might work in the home, others in a local mall right after high school, and still others as doctors after college and professional school. But we all go to work.

We have just argued for development of a new program of technical and professional studies that should be available as an option to young people who get their Certificate of Initial Mastery. Many, of course, will choose to take a strong college-prep program.

But all of these young people need more and better preparation for what awaits them when they go to work than they typically get now. The United States does less to prepare its young people for work than any other industrialized nation, and what it does, it does less well than any other nation.

Every school district needs to make sure that all youngsters get good counseling assistance beginning in the middle school years to help them think about what they might want to do when they get their Certificate of Initial Mastery, what kinds of work adults do, and how students can get a feel for the kinds of work that they might find interesting and rewarding. All countries in northern Europe do this. Many make it possible for youngsters from elementary school on to visit workplaces and shadow adults in their work roles to find out what they do and talk to them about it. Some countries require that schools do this for no less than a week a year. One or two actually require that the students have an opportunity to shadow their working parents in this way at their place of employment.

Japan and other countries we have visited strongly encourage firms of all types and sizes to make videos about themselves and the work that is done by the people who work for them and deposit those videos in school libraries. Many of these firms also send representatives to the schools to give talks about what they do and the skills that they are looking for in entry-level employees.

Some Americans see something sinister about such initiatives, as if permitting—to say nothing of encouraging—employers to do   ·
such things is tantamount to turning the school into a supplier of labor for rapacious employers who care nothing for the welfare or

future of our young people. We strongly disagree. There is nothing sadder than the hundreds of thousands of young people who hit the streets of America every year wholly unaware of what employers are really looking for, unprepared for any job that has a future, and with therefore little to look forward to before they have even turned twenty. Or the hundreds of thousands who make it into college only to drift through the experience for a while, drop out (true of two-thirds of those who enroll), and land equally unprepared on the streets. One does not have to be a captain of private industry to be concerned about the degree to which we have left our young people unprepared for work.

For most of us, it seems very natural to give a young person a hand up. We acquiesce when a friend calls to ask us to interview a son or daughter for a job or to give some job-hunting advice or to set up an interview with an influential contact. Some of the jobs our sons and daughters get in this way are just minimum-wage summer jobs. Sometimes they are the first job out of college, the one that starts them on their career path. We take this web of connections so much for granted that we never think about what it would be like for a young person who has no access to such a network.

But that is just what it is like for millions of inner-city youth who grow up among adults who do not themselves have decent jobs or perhaps any jobs at all. It is hardly surprising that these young people often lack good work habits and real work skills. Nor is it surprising that many of these same youngsters see no point in working hard in school, because they can see no payoff for themselves.

Wegmans Food Markets in Rochester, New York, addressed this problem by offering part-time employment to youngsters identified by the Rochester City School District as likely to drop out of school, provided that the youngsters stayed in school. If they graduated from high school, they would be entitled to a college scholarship from Wegmans. The company provided mentors at work to help the students succeed on the job. Wegmans asked its employees to volunteer to tutor the participants in their academic subjects to keep them from failing at school. And for every thirty program participants, the company provided a full-time youth counselor, available seven days a week, twenty-four hours a day. The dropout rate was cut by more than half, and of those who stayed in the program, more than half went on to college. The program has now spread to other employers in Rochester, with steadily rising numbers of students involved. This is not a matter of technical and professional education; it is a matter of strategic employer involvement in the life of the schools and their students. Wegmans has since gone on to participate in the Syracuse youth apprenticeship experiment, which fits nicely into the general proposal for technical and professional education we have described in this chapter. The point is simple: it is very important for employers to play a much more active role in the education of our young people than they have in the past; for the young people who currently have the weakest connections to work, employer participation may be nothing less than essential. The schools cannot do the job by themselves.

We opened this chapter by reminding the reader that this country has held up the ideal of the selective college and treated all those who do not reach that ideal as various losers. Scarsdale High School, where Judy spent fifteen years, is a good example of those rare schools that concentrate in a single-minded way on that ideal—on getting its students into selective colleges. Few believe they can afford to do that, which is why most have long since become shopping mall schools.

Because Scarsdale is focused exclusively on one single task and function, using a demanding academic curriculum to get virtually all of its students into selective colleges, it can become very, very good at that task. Our proposition here is very simple: let's give every high school in America that task, let every high school focus on getting every student to the CIM standard, and, after that, on the same demanding curriculum that you will find in Scarsdale for those who want it. If it is good enough for Scarsdale, it should be good enough for the rest of us. There is no substitute for providing the Jeffs of our world with first-class academic preparation. Much of the book is devoted to showing how that might be done in a practical way.

But the premise of this chapter is that that is not enough. For many people, the school-to-work movement has turned into an alternative education movement, another way to get all students to meet high academic standards in high school. For us, meeting that goal is necessary but not sufficient. Beyond the CIM, a great many of our students want and need a way to acquire the professional and technical skills and knowledge that will enable them to pursue rewarding careers. The elites, who are just as vocationally minded as anyone else, get this skill and knowledge in the graduate professional schools. We owe an alternative to the many people who do not want and perhaps cannot afford to pursue a baccalaureate degree and graduate school right out of high school.

Our aim in this chapter was to show how this country can restructure its education system to provide both a first-class academic foundation for everyone and a fine professional and technical education after that for those who want it. The key word here is restructure. Make no mistake—this is a new purpose for American education, and a new structure will be required to achieve it.

Interlude:
Accountability, Chicago-Style

Patricia Harvey, Chicago Public Schools

Even today, I wince when anyone reminds me of the famous comment by William Bennett, made when he was secretary of education, to the effect that Chicago was the worst school district in the nation. It may have been that comment that galvanized the framers of the 1988 Chicago reforms. To them, the central office—bloated, unresponsive, corrupt, as they saw it—was the enemy. And the savior was to be the parents and the community. The state law they pushed through the legislature emasculated the power of the central office, gave control of most of the district's funds to schools, and created what amounted to elected school boards for each school, controlled by the parents of the children attending that school. Each of these boards had the power to hire and fire the principals, select the teachers, determine the curriculum, and decide how the money was to be spent.

The schools were going to be the scene of the action. I'd grown up on the South Side, joined the Chicago Public Schools when I was twenty, and never looked back. In 1988, I was working in the central office. But with these reforms in place, I wanted nothing more than to be out in schools somewhere. That is how I came to be principal at Hefferan Elementary School on the West Side for four years.

When I took over, Hefferan was among the hundred worst-performing schools in the city. When I left four years later, it was square in the middle of the pack, an enormous move up the achievement ladder. It had been named by the U.S. Department of Education as one of the twelve "National Centers of Excellence in the United States." The school had visitors from every corner of the globe. Senator Paul Simon, Mayor Richard Daley, and a host of others would regularly drop by to show off the school to their friends and guests. Companies were doing everything they could think of to help the school—one firm gave every child a pair of mittens, a hat, and a scarf every winter. A group of 150 African American professionals organized a chapter of Proud to Read Aloud and trooped in regularly to tutor the kids who needed it. A dentist organized a dental clinic, and a doctor organized a voluntary medical clinic. The Japanese embassy volunteered to teach Japanese to every Hefferan student. I had even made converts of the local drug dealers, who once caught a local thief in the school's parking lot and nearly beat him to death, saying as they did so, "Don't mess with our school!"

I did not get these results by being a wallflower. I was known downtown for "creative insubordination." I was tolerated because I got results.

That was more than the district itself was getting. Overall, the result of the 1988 reforms was that, though some schools were getting better results, many were getting steadily worse. The idea that community control would be the solution to the problem was at best naive. The reformers had assumed that if parents were in control, they would see to it that their children got a good education. Accountability would be immediate and real because the customers would run the show. But what happened was quite different. Many of our parent communities are made up of desperately poor people who saw the schools as a heaven-sent source of employment for people who badly needed jobs. Teacher aides and hall monitors proliferated. And the new boards became an easy mark for snake oil salesmen and true believers selling solutions to the schools' problems. Schools newly flush with as much as $2 million in discretionary funds went out and purchased one of everything, and the school budgets became Christmas trees.

Five years after the reform legislation was passed, Ted Kimbrough, who had been superintendent during the reform years, announced that he would not accept another contract, said that his job had almost killed him, and declared that the reform was not working. The people behind the 1988 reform immediately started organizing to make sure that Kimbrough was succeeded by someone who shared their views. In the meantime, an insider was made acting superintendent.

Eventually, Argie Johnson, from New York City, was selected to be superintendent. Argie has a very strong commitment to the students that just shines through. And she has a deep interest in curriculum issues that also made her a strong candidate for the job.

Some people in the community were urging Argie to make me her deputy, but she was busy with other things and I was not interested. I loved my school and could only shake my head at the situation Argie faced in the central office. A fifteen-member school board, driven by factional fighting and headed by a woman who would eventually go to jail, was making the superintendent's life miserable, and perhaps most damaging, she was unable to assemble a team on which she could depend.

When Argie was interviewing for the superintendency, she had, more or less on the spur of the moment, come up with an idea for dividing the schools in the district into three tiers of performance levels and devoting special attention and resources to the schools in the bottom tier of performance. Later, as she was forced by circumstances to deal with one crisis after another, she was unable to develop this idea and in fact came under attack for proposing the "labeling" of schools whose students were performing poorly.

But I thought there was considerable potential in this idea and was eventually persuaded to join Argie's administration with the assignment to take the idea and turn it into a real program. We reached out to Tony Bryke at the University of Chicago, Pete Martinez at MacArthur, and others, and together we started to plan a new future for the Chicago schools. We asked ourselves what we wanted Chicago schools to look like, how we would define and measure performance, how we would identify underperforming schools, and what kind of help we would have to provide for them. Not least, we asked ourselves about accountability—to whom should the schools be accountable, for what, and what should the consequences be when they fail to perform? We redefined the three-tiered *system Argie had advocated; it now stood for accountability, intervention, and support.*

Even as this design work on the accountability program got under way, the school district was crumbling before our eyes. Student performance at the secondary level continued to decline. Parents were going on hunger strikes. And then a giant projected budget deficit was announced—on the order of $300 to $400 million. Argie did not have control of the budget; her chief financial officer reported directly to the board. Rumors were rife about an imminent state takeover and the possible breakup of the Chicago Public Schools.

The state held all the cards because only the state had the money to bail the district out of the deficit. I was asked to head a small team of district staff people to go to Springfield to meet with the committee the legislature had appointed to recommend the key points of the new reform legislation that would bail out the Chicago schools. I pointed out to the committee that they could not hold the superintendent and central office accountable for the poor performance of the students because the 1988 legislation had stripped the central office of any control over programming, budget, and staffing and removed every tool that central might have used to get the schools to pay attention to student performance. That legislation had given central no function at all.

We asked for new legislation that would enable central to hold the schools accountable for student performance and to deliver the kind of assistance to failing schools that would give them a chance at success. We urged the legislative committee to create a model of governance and organization for the district modeled on the governance and organization of modern corporations. The recommendations we were making were buttressed by the recommendations of a powerful group of Chicago leaders who were advising the state and city on the resolution of the budget crisis and saw the need for a complete overhaul of the 1988 reforms. Almost every one of our recommendations wound up in the legislation that was passed.

Perhaps the trickiest issue the legislature had to deal with was governance. It was clear that the fifteen-member elected board was wholly dysfunctional. The Republican governor decided to abolish the elected board and give control of the district to the Democratic mayor. The hall gossip had it that he was doing so because he was sure the mayor would fail and was reportedly astonished when the mayor stepped up to the plate and accepted the responsibility.

All that remained when the new reform legislation was passed was to put the new team in place. The mayor created a small appointed board composed of people he could trust and tapped his budget chief, Paul Vallas, a longtime associate, to take on the job of CEO, the successor to the superintendency in the new system. And he appointed his chief of staff, Gery Chico, to the key position of board chairman.

Paul asked me to take on the newly created position of chief of accountability, which meant creating the means for turning the system's performance around. So we had two crowds at the top, the politicos and the educators. We sniffed around each other like dogs. We wanted to think; they wanted to act. We were used to an environment in which people at least pretended to be nice to one another; they fought all the time and cussed one another out. We thought we were above politics; politics seemed to be all they ever thought about.

Gradually, though, we came to realize that we needed each other, and later we came to greatly respect each other. In time, Paul Vallas became a Chicago icon. He is brilliant, an astonishingly quick study, decisive, and shrewd, and we needed all of that more than we knew. He has a seemingly limitless memory and a capacity to be going as strong at the end of a fourteen-hour day as at the beginning. He is very impatient—wants it done and wants it done now. Over and over, he stresses the need to communicate with each other and with the people of Chicago, something he never stops doing himself.

In some magic way, Paul, Gery, and Mayor Daley understood what the people of Chicago wanted from their schools and gave it to them, and what they thought the public wanted was what we thought the kids needed. I see now that the idea that the schools should be above politics is absurd. Politics is about deciding what is to be done with public money, about who gets what, about which values will win out. Politics is about *mobilizing support for what you believe in. Paul and Gery understood that the public wanted to know that its money would not be wasted, that the achievement of the students would go up and someone would be held accountable when the students did not learn.*

Those are not bad things. They are good things. And they are what the mayor gave the people of Chicago. And while he was doing it, he gave us educators—those he trusted—wide latitude to get the job done. But the price of autonomy was bringing home the bacon, getting the job done. The city hall crowd never did what we educators had always done— celebrate the problem. They were interested only in solutions.

Our accountability plan was not complicated. We put our lowest-performing schools—not enough of them, but enough to make a good start—on probation. Every school on probation gets a probation manager. We recruited probation managers from the ranks of people in and beyond the Chicago area who had a reputation as first-rate educators. Some were retired, and others had full-time jobs. We got Catholic school principals, college professors, retired urban and suburban superintendents, principals at successful Chicago schools—anyone who had really done the job before and was willing to take on the assignment. No one did it for the money, because we did not pay much. They all did it for the kids and to give hope to some beaten-down professionals.

We gave the probation managers real authority. Schools not under probation, as I mentioned before, had the power to decide how the funds available to the school would be spent and what the school program would be, but schools on probation would have to get their plans and budgets approved by the probation manager. Furthermore, the probation manager had the authority to recommend the removal of any staff member of a school, including the principal. If these measures were not enough, the probation manager had the further authority to recommend that a school that was not responding be reconstituted from scratch if necessary.

This is authority with teeth. But you can find other accountability plans with teeth. The feature of our plan that makes me proudest is our emphasis on the help we provide to the schools in trouble, the help they need to succeed. It begins with the probation managers themselves, the highly regarded experts and practitioners who are the shock troops of this campaign. But we also required every school on probation to pick a recognized assistance organization—the National Alliance or any one of a number of organizations based at local colleges or universities—and take advantage of the perspective and direct assistance that such an organization can provide. The first year that a school is on probation, the district foots the entire bill for this external assistance. Thereafter, the schools on probation are expected to pick up an increasing share of the bill until they are paying the whole cost.

When we started this accountability program, we put 109 schools on the probation list. Fewer than 15 percent of the students in these schools were performing at or above the national average on our standardized tests. Now, only two years later, almost all of these schools, most of which had been in an unrelenting decline in achievement for seven years running, have shown gains, some of them quite large. We are not where we want to be yet, but we have turned a big corner.

6

Rebuilding "Central" for Accountability

I n the interlude preceding this chapter, the central office was perceived as the villain by the first set of reformers and as the hero
by the second. Charismatic and competent as the current leadership of the Chicago Public Schools is, it would be a mistake to see
the issue in terms of personalities and governance structures, as if the
solution to the central office problem is simply to make sure that the
right people are in charge and reporting to the mayor.

As we see it, the real issue here has to do with the structure and
function of the central office, how its role and the role of the people in it are defined, the incentives that operate on them, and how
their roles and functions relate to the roles and functions of the professionals in the schools. These are new questions. Until recently,
the answers were clear and simple: central office leadership meant
exercising power and demonstrating expertise by telling the people
in the next layer below in the organizational hierarchy what to do
and how to do it.

There is a long and honorable history behind that conception
of the job. At the beginning of the reform era between the world
wars, city school systems almost everywhere were politicized and
corrupt, fonts of patronage and votes for municipal politicians.
Angry reformers, pinning their hopes on the new methods of scientific and professional management then enjoying great favor in
American business, swept aside the old forms of organization and

installed professional managements and school boards whose design was based not on political forms of organization but on the board of directors of the admired firms.

Following the industrial model, the new superintendents slowly built bureaus and departments and staffed them with professionals whose job it was to oversee the principals and the teachers, informing them of directives and making sure that these directives were carried out, purchasing the resources the district needed—from erasers and toilet tissue to teachers—and deploying those resources to the places that in their judgment needed them most. They were the first professional managers our burgeoning school districts had ever had, and they were very much needed.

The growth in the size of district central offices accelerated greatly in the years following passage of the Elementary and Secondary Education Act of 1965. Most of this growth has been the result of people added to administer and provide direct services connected with categorical state and federal programs. As a result, central offices added people with much more expertise in curriculum, instruction, assessment, and other specialized areas than ever before. Though many have since lost their jobs in cutbacks, those that remain have also greatly multiplied the number of people who can say no to the people in the schools.

A former mentor aptly described the situation: "Everyone now has the brakes," he said, "and no one has any of the motors." This is not a picture of power rampant; it is a picture of weakness personified. Years ago, one of us was interviewing school board members, superintendents, other senior central office staff, and principals. We were trying to find out who had the power to change things. More exactly, we were trying to find out who thought they had the power to change things.

The school board members felt that they had only one voice among many and that experienced superintendents were quite skilled at keeping them from matters having to do with the substance of education. Superintendents thought it unlikely that they would last to the end of their first contract, were grimly aware that their subordinates were there before them and likely to be there long after their departure, and figured that they would be very lucky to make any progress on more than one or two priorities before their enemies on the board won a majority and either fired them or bought out their contracts. Second- and third-level officials in the central office felt overwhelmed when asked to make major changes, say, in math curriculum with only one math person on staff for fifty schools. These mid-level officials saw themselves as caught between schools that felt no need to pay attention to what the central office thought and a superintendent who expected major changes in the schools tomorrow. Principals, of course, perceived themselves at the bottom of a pyramid of people, all of whom could say no, none of whom would deliver, and some of whom would surely hold them—the principals—accountable for something they could not themselves deliver. The teachers, of course, had no illusions of power at all.

Some years ago, researchers did a survey of principals and central office personnel in districts. All were asked to identify the most successful principals. There was no overlap in the two sets of responses. The central office people, it turned out, defined a successful principal as someone who did whatever was asked by the central office and did so in a timely way (that is, such principals demonstrated good "compliance" behavior). The principals defined a good principal as someone who succeeded in getting from the central office what was needed to run a good school.

There are good schools even in cities that are enduring rough times. But they are typically run by principals regarded in the central office as renegades, people who are marching to their own drummer, have their own following, and are the least likely to follow the rules central office sets. Sooner or later, these shooting stars flame out, exhausted from the never-ending fight with central office personnel, who, understandably, insist that this principal play by the same rules that apply to everyone else.

In Chapter Three, we noted that many districts have addressed these problems by instituting what they misleadingly call "site-based management." But, as we said, this often takes the form of school councils that have stipulated roles in deciding what the school will do about a wide range of matters. District rules define who gets to sit at the table and how these people are chosen.

But a council solves none of the problems we just described. It simply makes them worse by adding yet another layer to the already thick sandwich of people who feel powerless and frustrated. The council is composed of people who are not held accountable for outcomes. Bad principals throw their hands in the air, saying, "The council made a bad decision, but I'm obligated to carry out their will." The good ones co-opt the council as best they can. Meanwhile, central continues to say no, not yes. The truth is that if nothing changes in the organization and management of the central office, the changes made in the schools will not last.

There is a way out of this box. But before we describe it, we need to describe . . .

How "Central" Really Works

Mike Strembitsky, now our colleague at the National Center on Education and the Economy, became superintendent of schools in Edmonton, Alberta, in 1973 and remained superintendent until 1994. In his two decades on the job, Mike slowly and deliberately transformed the Edmonton school district into an organization that answers to the criteria developed by the world's leading organizational analysts.

Seventy-six thousand students attend two hundred public schools in Edmonton, the economic hub of northern Alberta province. An oil boomtown in the 1960s, it is now a major working-class city with a fairly diversified economy, serving as the commercial and financial hub of northern Alberta and the capital of the province.

Mike first came to Edmonton's central office on temporary assignment in 1968, as an elementary supervisor. He went on a kind of a lark, he says, because he could not believe that mentally competent people would behave the way the people in "central" behaved. He wanted to understand how people came to think the way they thought.

Though hired as a supervisor of social studies for grades 4 through 6, Mike had budget authority for maps and globes for the whole grade range, K–12, for the district. He came up with a reasonable formula for getting this money to the schools and letting them make the decision as to what maps and globes they needed most. When one school received its map and globe budget, Mike got a call from an assistant principal, who asked whose money it was. "I already have maps and globes coming out of my ears. Can I spend the funds on anything I need?" Mike thought this a reasonable question and went off to check with higher authorities. The answer, of course, was no. The funds were available only for maps and globes. It was up to the science director in the central office to provide money for the biology models this school needed, if he wanted to. The assistant principal shot back, "So I can spend $575 on maps and globes that I don't need but will get nothing for the biology models that I do need? You've been in central for only four months, Mike. I remember when you were one of us!"

Mike had a conviction, which has gotten stronger over the years, that in any given case, the decisions ought to be made by the person who will be held responsible for the results. He had always been puzzled by the idea that central made all the decisions about how to allocate the district's resources when it was obvious that the school staffs, not the central administrators, were responsible for the results achieved with students.

So later in 1968, when he was appointed to the position of assistant to the superintendent, Mike decided to start with something simple, the money for supplies. Why not allocate the money that central spent on school supplies to the schools? No! exclaimed the finance chief; the money could be spent only where it was budgeted by central. Period. Full stop.

So Mike and a colleague in the curriculum area came in over a weekend, figured out a rough allocation formula, wrote a memo to the principals distributing the money and stipulating the conditions under which it could be spent, and distributed the memo so that it would be in the schools first thing on Monday. An emergency meeting of the senior staff ensued. In the end, the finance office recognized that the train was out of the station and adopted a more enlightened philosophy: "If you're going to do it, it should be done right." And so they built a better allocation system.

A few years later, Mike was appointed acting superintendent when the previous superintendent left. Being very young, Mike thought himself ineligible for the permanent position. But he acted as if he were the superintendent anyway, and the board liked what he did and gave him the job.

The new superintendent continued to try to give real control over the budget to the principals. But at the initial rate of progress, it would take fifty years to make a substantial dent in the problem. So during his honeymoon period with the board, he asked for and got authority to hire a former district employee, Alan Parry, who had left for a job in Ottawa, to fill a position that Mike created for him, "system planner."

Alan, a brilliant maverick who had no use for the usual protocol, worked according to his own clock. But he and Mike marched to the same drummer, and together they took the system head-on. Mike put Alan in charge of creating a pilot system within the larger system, a renegade system that would operate according to a new set of rules. Mike selected the principals of seven schools as the initial participants. They reported to Alan and Alan reported to him. Very simple.

But the barons in central were still there, in the form of department heads and division chiefs. Finance was the biggest problem. Its officials argued strenuously against giving any more spending authority to the schools, on the grounds that the integrity of the whole financial system depended on Finance retaining control. The schools, they said, had always behaved in a way that threatened to "break the bank." Left to their own devices, they would see to it that the bank was quickly broken.

The finance chief was not only a good political bureaucrat but also a good technician. He made it plain to the board that he could not be held accountable for the financial integrity of the district unless he controlled the finances directly. Mess with that, he said, and you risk the financial integrity of the district.

Later, Mike discovered that what the finance officer had said was literally true. As the end of each year approached, budgets were balanced by moving money among the various major line-item accounts, trimming some here and adding a little there to make it come out right. If most of this money was allocated to the schools at the beginning of the year, this juggling would no longer be possible. Finance would have to put a lot more work into making accurate estimates of revenue and expenditures at the beginning of the year. Good planning would be essential.

But the finance office was hardly the only obstacle to change. Almost every other senior officer at central was adamant that school staffs simply did not know enough to budget and spend money responsibly. It was obvious, they said, that central should worry about policy and money, the schools about educating kids. When pressed to tell Alan and Mike what it actually cost on a per-school basis to provide the service or equipment or supplies for which they were responsible to the schools, they filibustered or provided outrageously low estimates. Mike was undeterred; accountability and authority had to go hand in hand, and he was going to make it happen, at least in the pilot schools.

In the beginning, Mike and Alan thought that there were rules of thumb that central used to create unit budgets and that they only had to find out what those rules of thumb were to figure out what portion of the district budget should reasonably be given to the seven pilot schools. But they soon learned that although there were such rules, the rules had little to do with the access each school had to central's resources. Access to resources depended in many cases on how the principals played the game with the people at central. The principals who were greediest and who were the most responsive to central's every wish were likely to wind up with the lion's share of resources, regardless of the formulas. "You scratch my back and I'll scratch yours" was the real allocation formula.

That is how central really works, not just in Edmonton or in Canada but almost everywhere in the United States. Most people are not heroes—they "go along to get along." If we want a different result, we will have to redesign central so that for everyone involved, it pays to produce results for students.

Redesigning Central for Results: The Edmonton Model

Mike began by attacking the "all brakes and no motors" problem. He made a simple rule: everyone was to have only one boss. Only the boss could say no. For the teachers, that was the principal. For the principal, it was the regional superintendent. For the regional superintendent, it was Mike. That was the line, and the line included only a tiny proportion of people in central. If you were not in the line, you were staff or support. Very few administrators were defined to be staff; most were in support.

You may say that your school district, too, has a very short line, like the one we have just described. But the real issue here is authority. If the line is short and there are few people in it but many more have the authority to say no, the problem has not been addressed. The key lies in what Mike did about the authority of the people on the support side of the organization.

All support positions, accounting for the vast majority of employees in central, were stripped of budgets. Now they had to recover the costs of their departments through spending decisions made by the schools. Because the money—more than 90 percent of all the resources coming into the school district—was given to the schools, it was up to them to decide how much to spend on staff and how much to spend on maps and globes. They got a 25 percent discount if they spent their funds on services supplied by central, but if they wanted to spend more to get what they thought were better goods or services elsewhere, they could do so. Mike says that in retrospect, he would recommend putting a scheduled phase-out of this discount in place at the beginning. For the first time in their professional lives, the staff of the central service functions had real competition—other services, better services, customized services, and cheaper services. So they hustled.

The results were remarkable. The story of the maintenance department is a good example. The rules had been clear and unchanging for years. Each school interior got repainted every seventeen years, whether it needed it or not. When it did get painted, it got three coats of paint everywhere. When the painting was over, the staff had to put everything that had been taken off the walls back where it had been, if they could remember where that was. When the new regime went into effect, many of the schools thought that it made sense for them to repaint those parts of their school that got especially heavy wear, giving the rest of the school one coat, if necessary. They wanted the work done when the students were not in the building. And they were not interested in waiting their turn for the seventeen-year cycle to come around to them. Maintenance balked; the rules are the rules.

Fine, said the schools, and they started going outside the system to get their painting work done. About that time, the head of maintenance retired. The new chief had a different idea. He offered a new service. He would hire a special crew to come in at night. The crew would bring a Polaroid camera and shoot pictures of everything on the walls. Only walls and trim that the school wanted painted would be painted, and they would get the number of coats of paint that the schools had ordered. No work would be done during the regular school day, and everything that had been on the walls would be returned to the walls in its original position.

The system we just described did not, of course, apply to all services at central. Transportation, payroll, accounts payable, and hiring, for example, were exempt. But almost all others, including printing, legal services, contracted services, custodial services, maintenance, textbooks, furniture, and equipment were included. Some services, like the curriculum department, were given a greatly reduced budget and then told that they had to make up the difference with funds that the schools decided to spend on them.

With these two moves—shortening the line and sending the budget for support services to the schools—Mike made good on what we have already described as one of his cardinal principles: that control over resources should go to those who will be held responsible for results. If the schools are going to be held accountable for student results, then they should control the resources that are needed to produce those results. But who, exactly, is the school—the principal or the school council, if there is one? Mike's response is simple and consistent: If you are going to hold the council accountable for the results (that is, each of its members will get the rewards when students succeed and feel the consequences if they fail), it should be the council that gets to decide how the resources will be used, and it should report to the regional superintendent. If it is the principal who will be held accountable, the principal should get the resources and make the decisions about how they will be used. By this reasoning, to which we wholly subscribe, it is unacceptable to put decision-making power in the hands of a school council whose members are accountable not for student performance but to their own individual constituencies for whatever their constituencies choose to hold them accountable for. If it is the principal who is held accountable for the results and who therefore exercises the power, does that mean that the principal should be free to act as an autocrat, irrespective of the views and feelings of all the other participants? Mike's answer is that they should be free to act like an autocrat, but they will assuredly fail if they do.

That is because Mike defined results in terms of student achievement and customer satisfaction. Just as in the best current industry practice, Mike defined the customer as whoever has to use the product of your work, whether you are the superintendent or the person who welcomes visitors to the principal's office. He implemented a simple but very effective system of satisfaction surveys. Some populations were surveyed every year, others in alternate years. These extensive questionnaires were administered anonymously to teachers, students, parents, other community members, principals, central office support staff, and others. They became a very powerful tool to weed out weak staff members, not because Mike summarily fired people who got low ratings, but because people who got low ratings for two or three years running chose to resign rather than face the continued embarrassment.

Mike found that in a results-oriented environment with strong accountability, principals had a strong incentive to involve the staff and parents, but it was counterproductive to tell them whom to involve and how to involve them. The system produced strong leaders, people who were willing to take chances to get results, and these strong leaders were people who knew how to get everyone involved while keeping them on an agenda focused on results.

Like everything else, the power of the Edmonton system lay as much in the details of its execution as in its grand design. Mike knew that for the plan to work, control of the money would have to reside at the school level in fact, not just in theory, and the way money was allocated in the first place would have to be perceived as fair, the very opposite of the "you scratch my back and I'll scratch yours" system that had been in place for so long.

So Mike set the system up so that the principals would be able to move money from function to function (from staff salaries to textbooks, for example), not just within a function. He completely changed the district planning cycle so that funds were allocated in the spring based on projected enrollments (so that the schools could actually plan for the school year before that school year had begun), with adjustments made in the fall on the basis of actual enrollments.

A fair system of allocation of funds meant the use of objective criteria for funding that were public and adhered to. The system

Edmonton used was to decide on a basic amount to be allocated for each pupil (the same amount across the whole system) and then an additional amount for every student who cost more to educate for a particular reason. Thus students from a low-income background would come with an additional allocation, a student who was severely handicapped would come with a higher allocation than that, a student who was both severely handicapped and came from a low-income family would get a still higher allocation, and so on. The superintendent and board involved the whole staff and the public in deciding on these allocations, so they ended up having very broad support.

The funds for the categorical programs were distributed by these formulas in accordance with national and state law but as an integral part of the allocation system just described. The principals no longer reported to special categorical funding program officers at central for these programs but rather to the regular line, which ended the special status of these programs in central hierarchy. For the first time, the principals could plan one integrated program for the whole school.

The practice of many urban districts of hiring a large fraction of the teaching staff in a hiring frenzy during the last days of summer and the first weeks of the fall term is a personnel disaster, often leading to poor-quality staff and faulty staffing structures. Making it possible for the schools to do realistic planning for the fall enabled them to decide what kind of faculty they wanted and make offers in the spring to the most capable people available. Important changes were made by agreement with the teachers union in the seniority system to increase the ability of the school faculty to choose compatible colleagues while still protecting the rights of individual teachers. The schools could select whomever they wished, without regard to seniority, as long as they selected teachers who were on the district staff list (all members of the union). When reductions in force took place, however, seniority played a role in determining who was laid off.

But the flow of the dollars and radical thinning of the line in central did not by themselves guarantee that authority to make decisions would be aligned with accountability for the results of those decisions. All too often in the past, someone in central had told principals that they could not do what they wanted to do because it was illegal or against the regulations. Finding out which law or regulation was being violated was virtually impossible. So Mike had the district publish an annual guide containing all the relevant laws, rules, and regulations, gave it to the schools, and made them responsible for abiding by it. So the schools were accountable for results (defined as we have described) and for staying within the law, and they had all the flexibility, funding, and information they needed to do both.

What can we say about the incentives that operate on the people in this system? The incentives for students have not changed much. The incentives for the people on the support side in the central office have changed radically; if they are not genuinely responsive to the school faculties, they will be out of a job. The incentives operating on the school staff and many others in the central office are more subtle. All of us want to be effective in our work. Earlier in this chapter, we described the pervasive feeling among virtually all the actors on the public education scene that they could not be effective because someone else, they thought, had all the control. The system we have just described has the opposite effect; it creates a widespread feeling of having greater control leading to greater effectiveness.

But are these intrinsic incentives enough? Mike himself is not so sure. Had he stayed longer in Edmonton, he would, he says, have worked on the problem of student incentives and on creating stronger incentives for the faculty of each school to improve student performance against better measures of that performance. We have already described how the Certificate of Initial Mastery can be used as a powerful incentive to motivate student effort. And we have described New Standards as an example of a linked system of standards and assessments that incorporates both a worthy set of goals for students and a powerful means of assessing progress toward those goals. To get an idea of what stronger incentives for the faculty might look like, we need to turn to Kentucky.

Incentives for the Faculty: The Kentucky Model

The Kentucky model originated in a 1985 lawsuit brought by sixty-five school districts asking the courts to declare the Kentucky school finance system unconstitutional. In 1989, the Kentucky Supreme Court did much more—it declared the entire state education system unconstitutional and required the legislature to design a new one. The state Senate took the lead in creating the new system, advised by David Hornbeck, a lawyer who later went on to become the director of the National Alliance and then superintendent of schools in Philadelphia.

The result was the Kentucky Education Reform Act (KERA). The act abolished the state department of education and the jobs of the people in it. It mandated the creation of statewide goals for student performance and a statewide assessment matched to the goals. It created a new state department of education. Whereas the old department's mission was to regulate the inputs to the schools, the new department's mission was just the opposite: to regulate the system based on its results (described in terms of student achievement) and to administer a whole new system of incentives designed to maximize the effort that school people would put into improving student achievement.

The Council of School Performance Standards was established to develop the standards. The new state department of education was charged with developing the new performance assessments required to gauge student progress toward the standards. KERA mandated the creation of a school council for each school that had the statutory responsibility for deciding how its budget (allocated by formula) would be spent and what the school program would be.

The school council was to consist of the principal, three teachers, and two parents. Local school boards were stripped of their authority to decide school budgets.

The new law abolished in one stroke all the existing laws and regulations that determined the inputs into the schooling process, from teacher-pupil ratios to the length of the standard period in the school day. And it specifically gave to the schools—not the districts—the authority to determine the curriculum, student assignments, the daily schedule, instructional practices, and use of school space. So the school councils' authority to determine the budget and program were sweeping. The state provided a curriculum framework to guide their work, but they were not required to use it. This sweeping authority was matched by an equally powerful set of incentives that were designed to make student performance the overwhelmingly important determinant in their decision-making process.

These incentives consisted of rewards when the schools' performance as measured by student achievement improved and consequences when it did not. KERA created a statewide fund. The money was to go to schools that met a performance target that required the school's students to do better on the performance assessment than they had the year before. The faculty of each school would decide whether these cash awards would be used as salary bonuses by the staff or to augment the school budget or both, but the bonuses could not be used as a new base salary for the following year. Schools failing to reach their performance targets were required to submit a school development plan to the state and could get assistance from the state development funds. But if they showed declines in two cycles in a row or if performance declined by more than 5 percent in one cycle, they were declared to be "in crisis." The state was required to appoint a Kentucky Distinguished Educator (typically an outstanding teacher trained for this task by the state) to come to the school and advise it; the school in crisis was required to take that advice. Those faculty members who chose not to do so could be fired. The Kentucky Distinguished Educator was also required to evaluate the staff of schools in crisis every six months and recommend to the department of education that each faculty member be retained, transferred, or dismissed. A department team was empowered to shut down such schools altogether, if necessary. The legislation included a comparable set of rewards and consequences for school districts.

Comparing the Three Models

Let's compare the Edmonton model with the Kentucky and Chicago models.

In all three cases, control of the program and budget of the schools moved from central to the school. In Edmonton, "school" meant the principal. In Kentucky, it meant the school council, on which the principal sits as chair. In Chicago, the first reform vested control fully in the council and the second shifted some of that power back toward the principal. But in varying degrees in all of these cases, Mike's rule was generally observed: control over the resources was vested in the person or body that would get the rewards if there were good results and would suffer the consequences if things went badly. In all of these cases, many or all of the rules and regulations that had been in place to determine the inputs into the educational process were swept away. In their place were a set of incentives related to the schools' success or failure in producing results. In the case of Edmonton, the results were a compound of customer satisfaction and student performance, with an emphasis on the former. In Kentucky and Chicago, all the emphasis was on student performance. Edmonton relied mainly on intrinsic rewards; Kentucky used them, too, but relied mainly on monetary rewards. Though Chicago initially relied on intrinsic rewards and a system of very stiff consequences for poor performance, it is moving toward the addition of extrinsic rewards for continuous progress. Kentucky and Chicago both formally identify their worst-performing schools and provide them with special consequences as well as targeted assistance. Chicago's assistance plan is probably the more aggressive. None of these jurisdictions started out with incentives to motivate student performance, though both Chicago and Kentucky appear to be moving in that direction.

What Jurisdictions Can Do: Being Clear About What Roles Belong to "Central" Versus What Roles Belong to the Schools

What is truly interesting in our comparison is that we are comparing what a state did with what two large districts did. In one case, "central" is the state; in the other two, it is the district.

Taking the three examples together, we can synthesize a model of the relationship between central and the school in which it does not matter whether central is the state or the district:

What Central Does

1. Sets the student performance standards, including and especially the requirements for a school-leaving certificate set to an internationally benchmarked standard for sixteen-year-old students

2. Decides on the measures of student performance that will be used to assess progress toward the standards

3. Decides on other common measures of results, including customer satisfaction measures

4. Decides on who the responsible individual or group will be at the school level and the way in which that individual or individuals will be chosen and relieved of their positions

5. Decides on what results at the school level will be rewarded and on the rewards that will go to the responsible individual or group at the school level

6. Defines poor results at the school level and decides on the consequences that will attend those results for the responsible individual or group at the school level

7. Decides on the formula to be used to allocate resources to the schools and makes those allocations in a timely way

8. Negotiates contracts with all certified unions

9. Sets standards for teachers, hires teachers who meet them, provides strong orientation and training programs for new teachers, and maintains a list of teachers and other staff available for employment by the schools

10. Publishes a compendium of the laws and regulations by which the schools must abide and distributes it to the schools

11. Monitors the compliance of the schools with those laws and regulations, including audits of the schools' financial, personnel, and performance reporting systems

12. Collects data on results at all levels of the system and publishes those data

13. Administers the system of rewards and consequences, including the system by which central takes control of low-performing schools, if necessary

14. Provides information about effective programs, arranges for an aggressive program of assistance to the worst-performing schools to enable them to succeed, and monitors outside providers of educational services to schools

15. Decides on a method of assigning students to schools that maximizes competition among public schools while at the same time safeguarding the rights of protected classes (meaning that schools are not permitted to select their students based on race, gender, ethnic background, parents' income, handicapping condition, or religion)

16. Arranges, if necessary, for the provision of the support services required by the schools, including, for example, textbooks, maintenance, food services, and transportation

What the Schools Do

1. Decide on a leadership and management team for the school that will collaborate and involve the entire school community in developing and implementing the school's goals and plan

2. Decide on a code of behavior for the student body to which the students, parents, and faculty agree and which establishes order and discipline in the school, based on the consensual code

3. Add their own standards and goals to those of central

4. Decide on the measures, in addition to those required by the district and state, they will use to assess progress toward their goals and methods they will use to track progress continuously

5. Search for the best practices being used anywhere to get students similar to its students to targets like their own

6. Use the results of that search to decide on curricula and instructional programs designed to get their students to the target standards, including print materials and technology to be used

7. Decide on the best staffing structure to implement the instructional program

8. Decide how to organize the school, how to assign students to classes, what the master schedule will be, and whether there will be after-school, Saturday, and summer school programs

9. Decide on the best way to use the nonpersonnel resources available to the school to get their students to the standards

10. Decide what skills and knowledge the staff will need to execute the plan and what professional development program is best suited to provide those skills and that knowledge

11. Decide how the school wants to involve parents, social service and public health agencies, employers, and others in the life of the school and build a plan to make that involvement successful

12. Build an operational plan and operating budget that will make the best use of the available resources

13. Implement the plan and continuously revise it on the basis of the data on student performance gathered by the school and by central

14. Decide, on the basis of the school's own goals, whether the school should actively recruit a body of students and parents interested in those goals, construct a recruiting plan and implement it

15. Provide all information required by central for its monitoring and auditing functions

You may have noticed that we have argued in support of all but four of these thirty-one items of responsibility—the last two on each list. They have to do with parent and student choice among schools, our conception of what it means to be a public school, the way in which support services get provided to schools, and the idea of central auditing the schools. This set of issues arises in the context of our choice of the word *central* to describe both the Edmonton and Chicago central administrations and the role of the Kentucky Department of Education.

We have used the term *central* here to make a point. The principles we have described could be applied to the case in which *central* refers to a school district board of education and its central office, but it could just as easily refer to a state board of education and its central office, the state department of education.

Across the United States, enthusiasm is growing for charter schools—schools that are typically freed from the bureaucratic constraints of the local school district administration and from many of the constraints of state education policy as well. So one can imagine the principles for defining the role of central here being applied to a school district organization or to a state department of education with respect to its responsibility for managing its charter schools.

But whatever form of central emerges from the charter school debate, we are most emphatically of the view that public money should not go to private schools that are substantially free of all regulation. They must, as we see it, be public schools in that they would be funded not on the basis of the wealth of the parents who chose to enroll their students in that school but on the basis of a statewide formula like that of Edmonton, which assures that schools with comparable student bodies get comparable resources; they should be required to enroll students without discriminating against any protected class of student; and they should have to live within the collective bargaining laws that apply to the public schools. Crucially important from the standpoint of the main themes of this book is that they should have to accept the statewide standards for students, agree to administer and report scores from the state-adopted assessment set to the state standards, and be directly subject to a statewide incentive system of the kind we have described in Kentucky and Chicago. In such a scheme, all of the legitimate objectives of the charter school advocates could be accomplished while enhancing equity and greatly improving student performance.

What Jurisdictions Can Do: Building a Strong Accountability System

You could interpret this chapter as an adaptation of the lessons learned from business management to the world of public education, seen through the eyes of people who have actually done it.

What we want to do now is take you from general management to the solution of a particular problem: How do I build an effective accountability system for my district or state? Rather than answer that question in the abstract, we will instead ask you to imagine a school district of, say, 25,000 students or more and imagine that the following steps are taken in that district. Many variations on this scheme are both possible and advisable, depending on the opportunities and constraints in any particular location.

1. *Choose the student performance standards you will use.* We use the New Standards performance standards, but your state may have its own standards. In any case, we would urge you, if possible, to use internationally benchmarked performance standards in what you regard as the core subjects in the curriculum. The standards should make it very clear what kinds of student work will meet the standards, should not require that more be taught in the available time than can be taught, should represent both expert judgment and the commonsense judgment of various publics, should provide clear guidance to teachers as to what they should teach and clear guidance to students as to what they need to know and be able to do, and should be oriented to what performances students should be able to demonstrate that would convince ordinary Americans that they will be well prepared for life as a parent, citizen, and worker. The standards you use will drive every other element of the accountability system. So you must be sure that they have wide support among the relevant constituencies.

2. *Choose the indicators that will be used to drive the incentive system and the measures of progress you will use.* We would choose

- Measures of student performance against the standards

- Dropout rates

- Retention rates

- Customer satisfaction (as measured by periodic surveys of the satisfaction of parents, students, teachers, other faculty, the general community, employers, higher education admissions officers, and other interested parties)

Keep your list short, preferably as short as this list.

3. *Develop incentive systems (systems of rewards and consequences) that will motivate students to reach the student performance standards.*

Develop a system for awarding a certificate to every student who meets the standard you've established for student performance in the core subjects in the curriculum. Organize key employers and colleges in your area behind this idea, and help them communicate to your students that preference in hiring and admissions will be given to graduates who have earned this certificate.

4. *Develop incentive systems (systems of rewards and consequences) for school faculty and other district employees that will reward those who contribute to improved student performance and provide consequences for those who fail to do so.* Establish a point below which the measured academic performance of a school is unacceptable and a system for placing such schools on academic probation. The key elements in such a system are these:

- Engaging a highly qualified academic probation manager for each school.

- Requiring that the staffing plans, hiring, budget, and program plan of a school on academic probation be approved by the probation manager.

- Authorizing the probation manager to recommend the expedited dismissal of any member of the staff of a school on probation, subject to the laws and regulations.

- Requiring every school on academic probation to select an approved external technical assistance provider or school reform network to affiliate with and to use the assistance that organization or network provides.

- Authorizing the probation managers to recommend the reconstitution of any school on academic probation. Any staff member of a school on probation that has been recommended and approved for reconstitution would lose his or her job unless that staff member is offered another job in the district by another school.

Create a reward system for the schools that are contributing to substantial year-to-year improvements in the performance of the whole student body. Several such systems have been designed. The key common features of such plans that we would recommend include the following:

- The rewards go not to individual faculty members but to the whole faculty and are based on the performance of the whole student body (with safeguards so that a faculty cannot get the rewards by concentrating its attention on a small segment of the student body at the expense of the other students).

- The rewards are based on the progress that the school makes against its earlier performance, rather than on reaching a fixed target that is the same for all schools (if the rewards depended on reaching a fixed target, only the schools with the most advantaged student bodies would receive the rewards).

- The rewards can be added to the school budget or distributed as a cash bonus to the faculty and staff of the school, a decision to be made by the faculty and staff.

- The formula setting the targets for the release of reward funds is calibrated so that a smaller gain in each successive year will trigger the rewards and so that the cumulative gains over a fixed and common period of years will bring all schools up to the desired standard (for example, 95 percent of the student body meeting the standard) by a certain date.

- The formula setting the targets is designed so that schools are not able to improve their chances of reaching the targets by forcing poor-performing students to leave the school or by not counting them in the student performance data (which is why dropout and persistence data must be included in the key indicators).

- The formula setting the targets, though heavily weighted toward student performance indicator data, also includes some weighting for the school's customer satisfaction data (parents and, at the secondary level, students).

Create a reward system for district support staff that is designed to reward responsiveness to school needs as the schools see those needs. What we have in mind is calculating what proportion of the total district budget is accounted for by services that go from the district level to the schools and putting that money in the school's discretionary budget, to be spent either on the central services or services purchased from others, at the discretion of the schools. This system will provide a powerful incentive for district-level support units to provide competitive services at a competitive cost or go out of business.

Create a feature in the compensation system for all district staff that will reward performance. From the superintendent on down, annual increments in salary, or bonuses, or both, should be related to the gains in student performance and to measures of customer satisfaction, at the appropriate levels—meaning that a principal's salary, for example, should be related to the performance of the students in his or her school and to the satisfaction expressed by parents, students (at the secondary level), the teachers, and other staff in the school. Here again, gains in student performance should be weighted most heavily in the formula.

5. Create a resource allocation system that will align control over resources with accountability for results. Because this plan assumes that direct accountability for improving student achievement rests with the principal and the staff of the school, it follows that control over the resources needed to do that job should also rest with the staff of the school. Thus not less than 85 percent of the total resources available to the district should be distributed to the schools for expenditure at their discretion, along with substantial discretion over such matters as the staffing structure for the school, who is hired to join the school's staff, and what outside services are contracted for and with whom.

The primary principle to be used to distribute the funds to the schools should be that the funds should reflect the makeup of the student body. That is, the district should assign, as a matter of policy, weights to students with different characteristics (students who are severely handicapped would get a different weight in the distribution formula than students who have limited English-speaking ability, and both would get a different weight than a student who had neither of these characteristics) and, using this differential weighting, award a budget total to the school based on numbers of students of each weight assigned to the school. Such a formula should be designed to take into account the differential cost associated with educating students of each set of characteristics.

Support services offices in the central office would receive their funds from two sources. To the extent that such offices supplied services to other central office units, funds for those services would be included in the annual budget. To the extent that the services provided were intended for the schools, the funds to pay for those services would be recovered from the schools, as the schools decided to purchase those services from the central office service units.

6. Create an organizational structure for accountability in which everyone knows what he or she is responsible for and responsibilities are distributed in a way that corresponds to accountabilities. Make sure that each person in the organization reports to one and only one person. Define the "line" as running from the principal to the superintendent. This will make the line very short and the number of people in it very small. Make it clear that only people in the line are authorized to say "no" to people below them in the line.

Make it clear what units in central have line functions, staff functions, and support functions. Reduce the number of people in the superintendent's cabinet to no more than six, and make sure that the majority of them are line supervisors of schools. Group all the officers responsible for staff and support functions under the remaining cabinet members.

Bring all special resources (teachers of students with special needs, Title I teachers, and so on) under the control of the principal to the maximum extent permitted by law, and allow the principals to use the dollars represented by those resources as flexibly as the law allows while holding the principals accountable for the outcomes mandated by the laws under which these funds are provided to the schools.

At bottom, what we have described in this chapter is a revolution in the organization and management of public education, a revolution that utterly changes not only the way schools are regulated but also the incentives that operate on everyone involved, from students to professionals, managers, and service providers. Almost every piece of this system is in place somewhere in the United States or elsewhere in the world. But nowhere, yet, have all the pieces been put together. Most important, there is not yet anyplace where strong incentives for the students to achieve have been combined with strong incentives operating on the professional staff to help them achieve. When these elements are combined, they will without doubt produce unprecedented gains in student performance.

Epilogue
What We Owe Jeff

This book started with a story of a young man just about to leave high school and begin his career, a young man of whom little was expected and who achieved far less in school than he was capable of achieving. The staff of his high school was very caring. The community was very supportive. But the staff and the community had let Jeff down badly. He was becoming an adult in a world that would demand far more knowledge and skill as the price of admission to a rewarding career and competent citizenship than Jeff had attained. Jeff, we believe, is not the exception but the norm all over the United States. And there are many students, especially those who live in our great cities and impoverished rural areas, who leave high school with less skill and knowledge than he.

We had the feeling as we interviewed the people of Plainsville that they were sleepwalking through time, and we wanted to shake them gently, to make them wake up. Didn't they know that jobs for people with Jeff's knowledge and skill were drying up everywhere? Why couldn't they hear the voice of the community college counselor telling them that their sons and daughters were not learning enough in school to take the programs at the community college that lead to good careers? Why were the employers of Plainsville willing to settle for less than employers in many third world countries? Many of the educators we met in that high school knew that the school's programs were failing the students, not the other way

around; why were they doing so little about it? Jeff's dad acknowl-
edged that his son had done just the minimum to slide through
school, but when asked about his biggest problem with the schools,
he cited the poor record of the sports teams. They were all sleepwalking through time.

How could this have happened? How could all of us be willing
to settle for so little when we could have so much more? The answer
is that each group of actors in this drama sees itself as trapped,
unable to move. The employers would like more capable applicants,
but they see themselves as having to select from among the students
who are available. The teachers want more for themselves and the
students, but they see themselves as powerless to change the institution in which they work. The parents see the school as responsible for educating their children, and they do not see themselves in
a position to change what the school does. For most of these people, changing the schools is someone else's job, not theirs. So we
drift. And the students coast.

Our aim in this book is to show that this need not be, that it is
possible to build a system from the materials at hand that will enable
virtually all American youngsters to leave high school with a fine
education. Much of this book has been devoted to detailing the
panoply of initiatives it will take to do the job: high standards that
focus on the kind and level of student work that meets the standards;
new assessments that capture not only whether the student has mastered the knowledge and skills that are needed but also can apply
that knowledge and skill to the complex real world problems that he
or she will face as an adult; new curricula that focus on mastery of
the concepts that underlie the disciplines, thus enabling students to
learn new things quickly all their lives; new teaching methods that
focus on teaching for understanding and leave no one out; new uses
of available time that will give every student the time needed to
reach grade level in a high standards system and to stay at grade
level; a new form of high school diploma that demands that all
students can meet high standards, not just a few; new organizational

structures designed to leave no one behind and to refocus the American high school on academics, while at the same time providing new routes to high quality professional and technical education for those who want a hands-on approach to post-secondary education; new forms of high quality professional development that enable teachers to develop the skill and knowledge they think they need to improve their schools; new accountability systems that reward students for reaching the standards and their teachers for getting them there and that provide real consequences for both educators and students when those goals are not reached; new resource allocation systems that put the authority to determine how the money will be spent in the hands of the principals and teachers who will be held accountable for student progress; new planning systems that focus everyone's attention on results; new school organizations that will forge much closer bonds between students, teachers, and families; a reallocation of responsibility for educating children between the school and the community that will get the community much more involved in the education of its children than ever before; a redesign of the central office that will empower school faculties to take charge of their own destiny and make the bureaucracy downtown much more responsive to the needs of the schools, while at the same time tightening accountability for student performance all along the line; and much else. Every one of these changes is being pioneered somewhere in the United States right now. The payoff when they are brought together in one place will be enormous.

But, important as it is, this long and challenging agenda is only half the story. These are the technical elements of the agenda, the things that policy and practice can do. But they are not the crux of the matter. More than anything else, it will take a renewed moral commitment to our children and a willingness to set aside established ways of doing things in favor of a single-minded focus on results. None of our proposals will carry the day absent the conviction that virtually every student can achieve high standards and the iron determination to see that they do so.

The distance between what our children do achieve in school and what they could achieve is explained more than anything else by the fact that we expect so little. This is the single most important message sent to us by Plainsville, where there was nearly universal acceptance of mediocre performance. If that continues almost everywhere, then little will be done. The will to change begins with rejection of the status quo. A few leaders cannot do it alone.

And that is intimately connected to the fact that everyone must take responsibility for doing their part. Much of this book has been about personal responsibility—especially on the part of students, faculty, and parents. There is no substitute for the student accepting personal responsibility for taking tougher courses and working harder, for the teacher doing whatever it takes to get his or her students to the standards, for the parent to make sure that Jeff and Tiffany are doing their homework, for the employer to provide opportunities for structured training on the job, for the community center to offer after-school programs that build basic skills. We pointed out that the incentives operating on all of these actors now are not likely to produce these responses, and we made proposals for changing the incentives so that they will be much more likely to foster individuals' taking responsibility more often. If those incentives are going to work, they have to be put in place. And that will take political will at every level of the system, from the school to the statehouse. Jacque, Judy, Pat, Paul, Mike, and the Kentucky and Illinois state legislatures took a great deal of flak when they changed the rules in their schools, districts, and states. The results for the students are there for all the world to see.

But it is all too easy to go through the motions, to embrace the agenda of standards-based reform without doing what is really required. All over the United States, we see new standards, but standards that are very weak; we see standards with no assessments (which are useless) or assessments that are not matched to the standards (which are worse than useless); we see accountability systems with no teeth; we see accountability systems with plenty of teeth but no effective help to drowning schools (as if changed incentives by themselves would do the trick); and we see much talk about results without real plans for producing them.

The trick here is to develop an education system in which ordinary people can routinely produce what are now regarded as extraordinary results. That it is possible to do this has been proven many times over. Unfortunately, many adults have a big investment in the system that exists, and that makes it very hard to make the tough choices needed to implement the standards-based system that the students, who have no voice, so badly need. Making those choices will require first rate leadership at every level in our society.

We have focused in this book on the institutions that make up our education system. It is easy when you do that to forget the students—the infinite variety and compelling reality of their individual aspirations, hopes, and fears. Books like this rarely talk about the flesh and blood of these young human beings. Sure, students attend class, take notes, study, write examinations, get remediated, graduate, or drop out; but only rarely in books like this do they breathe. No one gets sick, moves across town, worries about having friends, falls in love, gets pregnant, comes to school hungry, or sees his parents get divorced. Any teacher knows that when children come to the schoolhouse door in the morning, they do not enter just as students of the quadratic equation and irregular verbs. They come as boys and girls, young men and women, with all the energy and hope and joy that youth is heir to. Who speaks for them? Others will speak for the work force, the economy, the needs of society. Someone must speak for the children.

This is not sentimental patter. It goes to the heart of our responsibilities as parents, members of the community, and educators. If children are to grow as we want them to grow, if they are to become thinking people with imagination, sensitivity, creativity, empathy, and the capacity to love, then they must be treated with respect and love. Respect and love start not with expecting less, but expecting more. But even as we pursue higher standards of achievement, we must never stop helping children to develop emotionally, socially, and physically as well as intellectually. There are no contradictions here. William Butler Yeats had it right when he defined the acme of human experience as "blood and intellect and imagination" coursing vigorously together. What matters most in God's design has something to do with nurturing the young. It is the job of all of us.

We have called on Jeff and Anders and Hans and Tiffany and other young people to remind us all that, in the last analysis, this book is not about incentives and curriculum and the master schedule; it is about giving all of these young people a shot at a better life than they will otherwise have.

Resource A
The National Center on Education and the Economy

This book is the work of an extended family called the National Center on Education and the Economy, a not-for-profit organization based in Washington, D.C., with offices all over the United States. Founded in 1988, the National Center has been deeply engaged in developing the agenda described in this book and in collaborating with individuals and institutions everywhere to make that agenda come to life in districts and states for students, teachers, parents, and administrators.

During most of our early years, we concentrated on developing policies that states and the federal government could use to make it easier for people at the local level to do the things we advocate in this book. We are continuing to work on the policy framework, benefiting from what has been learned along the way both in this country and abroad, and providing technical assistance on policies to support standards-based reform to government at the state and national levels.

The National Center on Education and the Economy is now developing the tools, technical assistance, and professional development resources that educators everywhere will need to implement the agenda we described here.

Among those tools are the student performance standards developed by New Standards, a partnership of the National Center with the Learning Research and Development Center at the University of Pittsburgh, seventeen states, and six school districts. These performance standards, excerpts from which can be found in Resource B, represent a whole new approach to academic standard setting, for all the reasons described in Chapter One. New Standards has also produced a matching set of performance examinations in mathematics and English language arts, available from Harcourt Brace Educational Measurement.

The same team that developed the performance standards and assessments is now busy creating National Center curriculum materials matched to the standards, along the lines described in Chapter Two. These highly innovative materials are based in part on what we have learned about curriculum in those countries where student performance is highest. The curriculum materials are in turn matched with a set of ideas about instruction also drawn from the best practices in the world.

Our National Alliance program offers technical assistance to states and school districts that are interested in implementing some or all of the ideas we have described in this book. This includes everything from assisting with the redesign of schools to get students to high standards to assistance with the design of standards-based state and district accountability programs, from assistance with the development of a Certificate of Initial Mastery that has strong community support to help with setting up standards-referenced planning systems.

Our Workforce Development program provides assistance in the development of strong state and local standards-based school-to-work transition systems with real employer involvement; it also helps to link these programs to statewide workforce development systems.

Many parts of the organization join together to provide a wide range of professional development programs designed to support the technical assistance work. Here, too, our approach is rather unconventional, drawing together all our tools into a fully integrated professional development system that reaches out to everyone from chief state school officers to teachers. The professional development can stand alone, but it works best as the glue that ties a comprehensive implementation program together. The professional development program uses technology at every turn, but ultimately it depends on face-to-face participation and the active involvement of participants.

All of this work is going on in some of the nation's largest school districts and some of its most rural schools, from Hawaii to New England.

You may contact us by telephone at (202) 783–3668 or by mail at the National Center on Education and the Economy, 700 11th Street, NW, Suite 750, Washington, DC 20001. Or visit our Web site (http://www.ncee.org).

We look forward to hearing from you!

Resource B
New Standards Performance Standards

The New Standards performance standards are derived from the national content standards developed by professional organizations. They cover four subjects—English language arts, mathematics, science, and applied learning at the elementary, middle, and high school levels. They consist of three parts: performance descriptions, samples of student work, and commentaries on the work samples. They are packaged in separate volumes for elementary, middle, and high schools.

We have selected one example of a performance description and several examples of student work samples and commentaries to provide an overview of the New Standards performance standards. The examples are found on the following pages.

The standards are organized as follows:

English Language Arts

1. Reading

2. Writing

3. Speaking, Listening, and Viewing

4. Conventions, Grammar, and Usage of the English Language

5. Literature

6. Public Documents (high school level only)

7. Functional Documents (high school level only)

Mathematics

1. Number and Operation Concepts

2. Geometry and Measurement Concepts

3. Function and Algebra Concepts

4. Statistics and Probability Concepts

5. Problem Solving and Mathematical Reasoning

6. Mathematical Skills and Tools

7. Mathematical Communication

8. Putting Mathematics to Work

Science

1. Physical Sciences Concepts

2. Life Sciences Concepts

3. Earth and Space Sciences Concepts

4. Scientific Connections and Applications

5. Scientific Thinking

6. Scientific Tools and Technologies

7. Scientific Communication

8. Scientific Investigation

Applied Learning

1. Problem Solving

2. Communication Tools and Techniques

3. Information Tools and Techniques

4. Learning and Self-Management Tools and Techniques

5. Tools and Techniques for Working With Others

The New Standards performance standards consist of three parts:

- Performance descriptions—descriptions of what students are expected to know and be able to do that is most essential to learn in each discipline

- Samples of student work—examples of actual student work matched to the performance descriptions

- Commentaries on the student work—comments that draw attention to the features of the student work that meet the standard

Exhibit B.1 contains the performance descriptions for the English language arts standard: reading at the elementary level (grade 4).

Exhibit B.1. Performance Descriptions: English Language Arts

Reading

Reading is a process which includes demonstrating comprehension and showing evidence of a warranted and responsible interpretation of the text. "Comprehension" means getting the gist of a text. It is most frequently illustrated by demonstrating an understanding of the text as a whole; identifying complexities presented in the structure of the text; and extracting salient information from the text. In providing evidence of a responsible interpretation, students may make connections between parts of a text, among several texts, and between texts and other experiences; make extensions and applications of a text; and examine texts critically and evaluatively.

A The student reads at least twenty-five books or book equivalents each year. The quality and complexity of the materials to be read are illustrated in the sample reading list. The materials should include traditional and contemporary literature (both fiction and non-fiction) as well as magazines, newspapers, textbooks, and on-line materials. Such reading should represent a diverse collection of material from at least three different literary forms and from at least five different writers.

B The student reads and comprehends at least four books (or book equivalents) about one issue or subject, or four books by a single writer, or four books in one genre, and produces evidence of reading that:

- makes and supports warranted and responsible assertions about the texts;
- supports assertions with elaborated and convincing evidence;
- draws the texts together to compare and contrast themes, characters, and ideas;
- makes perceptive and well developed connections;
- evaluates writing strategies and elements of the author's craft.

C The student reads and comprehends informational materials to develop understanding and expertise and produces written or oral work that:

- restates or summarizes information;
- relates new information to prior knowledge and experience;
- extends ideas;
- makes connections to related topics or information.

D The student reads aloud, accurately (in the range of 85-90%), familiar material of the quality and complexity illustrated in the sample reading list, and in a way that makes meaning clear to listeners by:

- self correcting when subsequent reading indicates an earlier miscue;
- using a range of cueing systems, e.g., phonics and context clues, to determine pronunciation and meanings;
- reading with a rhythm, flow, and meter that sounds like everyday speech.

This is a sample reading list from which the students and teachers could select. This list is not exclusive. Acceptable titles also appear on lists produced by organizations such as the National Council of Teachers of English and the American Library Association. Substitutions might also be made from lists approved locally.

Fiction

Brink, *Caddie Woodlawn*;
Cleary, *Ramona and Her Father*;
Coerr, *The Josefina Story Quilt*;
Cohen, *Fat Jack*;
De Saint-Exupery, *The Little Prince*;
Hamilton, *Zeely*;
Hansen, *The Gift-Giver*;
Lord, *In the Year of the Boar and Jackie Robinson*;
Mendez and Byard, *The Black Snowman*;
Naidoo, *Journey to Jo'Burg*;
O'Dell, *Zia*;
Ringgold, *Tar Beach*;
Speare, *The Sign of the Beaver*;
Yep, *Child of the Owl*.

Non-Fiction

Aliki, *Corn Is Maize: The Gift of the Indians*;
Baylor, *The Way to Start a Day*;
Cherry, *The Great Kapok Tree*;
Epstein, *History of Women in Science for Young People*;
Greenfield, *Childtimes: A Three-Generation Memoir*;
Godkin, *Wolf Island*;
Hamilton, *Anthony Burns: The Defeat and Triumph of a Fugitive Slave*;
McKissack, *Frederick Douglass: The Black Lion*;
Politi, *Song of the Swallows*;
Sattler, *Dinosaurs of North America*;
Fritz, *And Then What Happened, Paul Revere?*;
McGovern, *The Secret Soldier: The Story of Deborah Sampson*.

Poetry

Ahlberg, *Heard It in the Playground*;
Blishen and Wildsmith, *Oxford Book of Poetry for Children*;

De Regniers, Moore, White, and Carr, eds., *Sing a Song of Popcorn*;
Giovanni, *Ego-Tripping and Other Poems for Young People*;
Greenfield, *Honey, I Love and Other Love Poems*;
Heard, *For the Good of the Earth and Sun*;
Janeczko, *Strings: A Gathering of Family Poems*;
Koch and Farrell, eds., *Talking to the Sun*;
Lobel, ed., *The Random House Book of Mother Goose*;
Manguel, ed., *Seasons*;
Mathis, *Red Dog, Blue Fly: Football Poems*;
Silverstein, *Where the Sidewalk Ends*.

Folklore

Griego y Maestas, *Cuentos: Tales from the Hispanic Southwest*;
French, *Snow White in New York*;
Huck and Lobel, *Princess Furball*;
Louie and Young, *Yeh-Shen: A Cinderella Story from China*;
Luenn, *The Dragon Kite*;
Goble, *Buffalo Woman*;
Steptoe, *Mufaro's Beautiful Daughters*;
Steptoe, *The Story of Jumping Mouse*;
Kipling, *The Elephant's Child*;
Lee, *Legend of the Milky Way*.

Modern Fantasy and Science Fiction

Andersen, *The Ugly Duckling*;
Bond, *A Bear Called Paddington*;
Dahl, *James and the Giant Peach*;
Grahame, *The Wind in the Willows*;
Lewis, *The Lion, the Witch and the Wardrobe*;
Norton, *The Borrowers*;
Van Allsburg, *Jumanji*;
White, *Charlotte's Web*.

Children's Magazines

Weekly Reader;
Creative Classroom;
Social Studies for the Young Learner;
World (National Geographic);
News (Scholastic);
Action (Scholastic).

Other

Newspapers, manuals appropriate for elementary school children, e.g., video game instructions, computer manuals.

Exhibit B.2 is a student work sample of a standard-setting performance with commentaries from an English language arts task (Drift Aways) at the elementary level. Students were asked to write a poem with strong imagery. Prior to writing their own poem, the students spent a week reading from various collections of poems and studying imagery, rhythm, poetic language, and form. The work samples show the progression through three drafts to a final product. The capital letters pointing to sections of the student work are keyed to the commentary that follows the student work.

Exhibit B.2. Student Work Sample and Commentary: Drift Aways

Draft 1

Jan. 12, 1995

<u>'Feelings, Drift Aways</u>

When you know you can't forget someone
Because of how you miss them so much,
And no matter how much you try
You can't.

When you know you can't forget someone
Even though because they died,
They're making your life miserable
You can't.

When you know you can't forget someone
Even if you know they can't come back,
But you wish with all your heart they could,
They can't.

To Uncle Jerry, who I
wish would come back
with all my heart,
please, come back.

Exhibit B.2. Continued

Draft 2

Mar. 9, 1995

Drift Aways

Wicked women! <----- Ⓐ

Small cat.

Poor (defenceless) creature.

When you know you can't forget someone

Even if they all of a sudden just drift,

Drift away.

When you know you can't forget someone

Even if (there) just a cat.

Tiny cat,

Giant jump,

Three story jump,

Down,

　　Down,

　　　Down,

Into the hole.

Like my Uncle Jerry,

That cat, Bunnie,

(Whitch) still have hope for,

Just drifted away.

↑   Drift Aways.

Ⓐ

Exhibit B.2. Continued

Draft 3

Mar. 9, 1995

² Drift Aways

Wicked women!
Small cat.
Poor defenseless creature.
When you know you can't forget someone
Even if they all of a sudden just drift
Drift away.

When you know you can't forget someone
Even if they're just a cat,
Tiny cat,
Giant jump,
Three story jump,
Down,
   Down,
      Down,
I nto the hole.
   Like my Uncle Jerry, ⟵ - - - - - - - - - -Ⓑ
That cat, Bunnie,
Which I still have hope for,
Just drifted away.

   Drift aways.

Exhibit B.2. Continued

2Drift Aways

Wicked woman!
Small cat.
Poor defenseless creature
When you know you can't forget someone
Even if they all of a sudden just drift
Drift away.

When you know you can't forget someone
Even if they're just a cat,
Tiny cat,
Giant jump,
Three story jump,
Down,
    Down,
        Down,
Into the hole.
Like my uncle Jerry,
That cat, Bunnie,
Which I still have hope for,
Just drifted away.

Drift aways.

Performance Descriptions Assessed by This Task

- Conventions: Demonstrate a basic understanding of the rules of the English language.
- Conventions: Analyze and subsequently revise written work.
- Literature: Produce work in at least one literary genre that follows the conventions of the genre.

Commentary: What the Work Shows

Ⓐ The student identified three misspelled words in the second version (see circled words) and corrected them for the final version.

The student demonstrated, through virtually error free writing, the ability to manage the conventions of the English language.

The student made effective changes in the form of the poem. The early three stanza draft has long sentences that imitate prose in form and rhythm. The final four stanza format makes use of imagery, line breaks, and white space to create mood and rhythm.

Ⓑ The student made appropriate and substantive changes from draft to draft, e.g., adding the parallel between the loss of the cat and the death of her uncle.

The student draws an analogy between an occurrence she once witnessed and the larger question concerning the finality of death.

Ⓒ Ⓓ The poetic devices used in the poem, such as alliteration, repetition, and the gentle image of drifting away as a metaphor for death, suggest an understanding of poetic language and how to make proper use of it.

Ⓔ The use of line breaks and white space to produce a strong poetic form, e.g., "Down, Down, Down," demonstrates an understanding of poetic form.

Exhibit B.3 is a student work sample of a standard-setting performance with commentaries from a mathematics task (Cubes) at the middle school level (grade 8). Students were given a three-part question about volumes and surface areas of cubes. Students were given fifteen minutes to answer the questions.

Exhibit B.4 is a student work sample of a standard-setting performance with commentaries from a mathematics task (Points and

Segments) at the middle school level (grade 8) also. Students were given a task: points and segments. Students worked on this individually in class and as homework.

Exhibit B.3 focuses on geometry and measurement concepts, and Exhibit B.4 focuses on function and algebra concepts.

Exhibit B.3. Student Work Sample and Commentary: Cubes

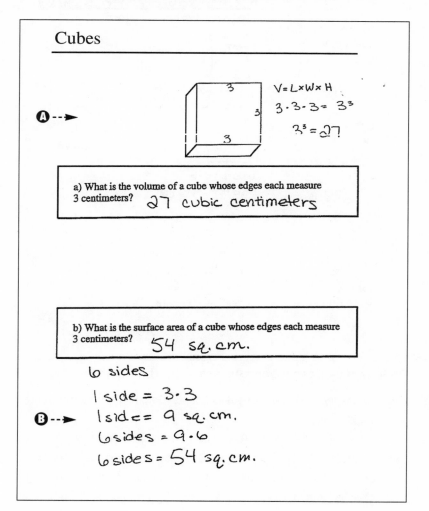

Cubes

Ⓐ --▶

$V = L \times W \times H$

$3 \cdot 3 \cdot 3 = 3^3$

$3^3 = 27$

> a) What is the volume of a cube whose edges each measure 3 centimeters?   27 cubic centimeters

> b) What is the surface area of a cube whose edges each measure 3 centimeters?   54 sq. cm.

Ⓑ --▶

6 sides

1 side = 3·3

1 side = 9 sq. cm.

6 sides = 9·6

6 sides = 54 sq. cm.

Exhibit B.3. Continued

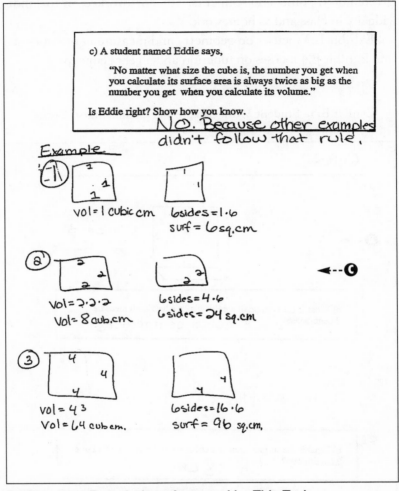

c) A student named Eddie says,

"No matter what size the cube is, the number you get when you calculate its surface area is always twice as big as the number you get when you calculate its volume."

Is Eddie right? Show how you know.

NO. Because other examples didn't follow that rule.

Example.

(1) vol= 1 cubic cm   6sides=1·6
              surf = 6sq.cm

(2) Vol= 2·2·2   6sides= 4·6
     Vol= 8 cub.cm   6sides= 24 sq.cm   ◄--C

(3) vol = 4³   6sides=16·6
     Vol= 64 cub cm.   surf= 96 sq.cm.

Performance Descriptions Assessed by This Task

- Geometry and Measurement Concepts: Determine and understand length, area, and volume.
- Mathematical Skills and Tools: Use formulas appropriately.
- Mathematical Communication: Organize work, explain a solution orally and in writing, and use other techniques to make meaning clear to the audience.

Commentary: What the Work Shows

Ⓐ Work on the first question illustrates understanding of volume.

Ⓑ Work on the second question illustrates understanding of surface area. Equals signs (=) are used a little carelessly, though. Colons (:) or arrows (→) would be more appropriate links; or equals signs could have been retained while clarifying just what is equal or the same. For example, "Area of 1 side = 9 sq. cm."

Ⓐ The explanation of the answer "27 cubic centimeters" is very clear and concise. A minor observation is that the student labeled three edges of the cube "3," but she did so in only two of its three dimensions.

Ⓒ Several examples are given to counter Eddie's claim, not just one example. Not only is Eddie's claim not true for all cubes, it is false for most cubes.

Exhibit B.4. Student Work Sample & Commentary: Points and Segments

The Task

Students were given the following task:

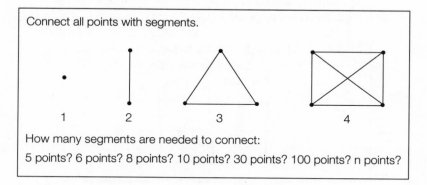

Connect all points with segments.

| 1 | 2 | 3 | 4 |

How many segments are needed to connect:
5 points? 6 points? 8 points? 10 points? 30 points? 100 points? n points?

Students were then cued on how they might proceed:

Make drawings for some of the above. Hints: Make a table. Look for patterns.

The task called for students to explore a relationship (between numbers of points and connecting segments) and to recognize a pattern and generalize it. More specifically, in asking how many segments are needed to

Exhibit B.4. Continued

connect 100 points, then n points, the task invites a closed-form generalization, such as $n(n-1)/2$, instead of an open-ended form, such as $1 + 2 + 3 + 4 + \ldots + (n - 1)$. The open-ended form is not well-suited for finding solutions with large values of n.

Other manifestations of this problem are the popular "handshake problem" often posed to elementary school children (see *New Standards Performance Standards*, Volume 1) as well as the common formula for high school students new to the method of proof-by-induction, $1 + 2 + 3 + 4 + \ldots + (n - 1) = n(n-1)/2$ [or $(n^2-n)/2$].

Exhibit B.4. Continued

already connected to B and E. I
made two more lines that connected it
C and D. Then B is connected to
A and C. so 2 lines connect it to
D and E. Then C is now connected to
all but E. so you draw one line
and no all are connected together. 3+2+2
+1 = 10. I used this same method to
connect the 6 point figure. I came
up with 6+3+3+2+1 = 15 segments.
I did it for 8 points and got 8+5+
5+4+3+2+1 = 28 segments. for 10 points
it was 10+7+7+6+5+4+3+2+1 =
45 segments. I saw a pattern, it was
always (n points ×1) + (n-3)×2) + (n-4)+(n-5)+
n-6) and so on until you had
n- the number right before n. So
for 30 it would be 30+27+27+26+25
and so on down to +1=435. I knew there
had to be an easier formula so I
made a chart that looked like this

n points	2	3	4	5	6	7	8	9	10	30
lines	1	3	6	10	15	21	28	36	45	435

100	n

Exhibit B.4. Continued

D --> I tried many different things to find
the relationship between the top
number and the one below it but with
no success. Then I tried dividing the
bottom number by the top number, and it
made a pattern. $1 \div 2 = .5$ $3 \div 3 =$
1 $6 \div 4 = 1.5$ $10 \div 5 = 2$ $15 \div 6 = 2.5$
$21 \div 7 = 3$ $28 \div 8 = 3.5$ $36 \div 9 = 4$

E --> Each time it went up by $\frac{1}{2}$. Then I said
what can I do to the top number to get
the number to multiply it by. Then I
found this $((n \div 2) - .5) \times n$ as the
formula and it worked. So for 100
points it would be $100 \div 2 = 50$
$50 - .5 = 49.5$ $49.5 \times 100 = 4,950$
points Shortened it would be like this

B --> $((100 \div 2) - .5) \times 100 =$ the bottom number
of lines

$n \times (n \div 2) - 5) =$ line segments

Exhibit B.4. Continued

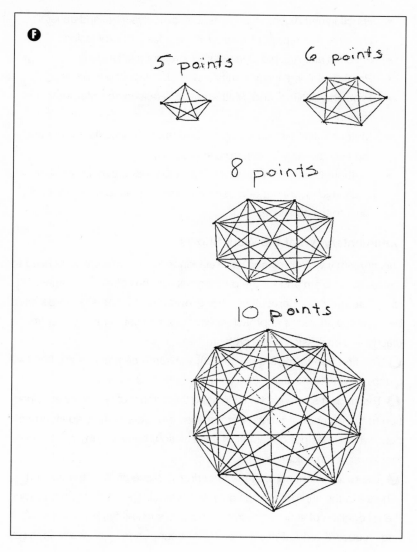

Performance Descriptions Assessed by This Task

- Function and Algebra Concepts: Discover, describe, and generalize patterns, and represent them with variables and expressions.
- Function and Algebra Concepts: Represent relationships.
- Problem Solving and Mathematical Reasoning: Implementation.
- Problem Solving and Mathematical Reasoning: Mathematical reasoning.
- Mathematical Communication: Use mathematical language and representations with appropriate accuracy.
- Mathematical Communication: Organize work, explain a solution orally and in writing, and use other techniques to make meaning clear to the audience.

Commentary: What the Work Shows

This student's work provides clear evidence for the strategies he used to tackle the problem and for the development of the solution in stages. This response provides particularly strong evidence for the standards cited because the student's approach seems too unusual to have come from a teacher-led discussion of the problem.

A The first two terms are $n + (n - 3)$, the same quantity as the first two terms of the more "classic" $(n - 1) + (n - 2) + \ldots + 3 + 2 + 1$.

B The student succeeded in expressing the number of segments as a function of the number of points. Parentheses are repeatedly used incorrectly here, which does not detract from this solution, but is worthy of correction for clearer communication.

E The recognition, here, of the recurring increase of $1/2$ in the fraction s/n (where s is the number of segments) is powerful. The student went beyond the recognition of simple quadratic functions such as $f(n) = n^2$ or $f(n) = cn^2$ and "reduced" a quadratic pattern to a linear pattern. The work does not communicate well the reasoning used to conclude that $s = ((n \div 2) - .5) \times n$. The student's phrase, "Then I found this," leaves the reader to wonder, "How?"

G Giving the points alphabetical names is central to the clarity of the student's explanation.

Exhibit B.5 is a student work sample of a standard-setting performance with commentaries from a science task (Compost) at the
high school level.

Exhibit B.5. Student Work Sample and Commentary: Compost

Students were asked to design and conduct an experimental project that
would improve the environment at their high school. The assignment, given to
students in an environmental science class, followed a unit on the chemistry
and biology of ground and water pollution.

Students worked on this task in a group in class with peer feedback and
the opportunity for revision.

Our Compost Pile Project:

(A)

Plan: We want to find out what kinds of insects help compost turn from just waste to useable mulch
and soil helper. We also would like to know what conditions help to speed up the breaking down of
the compost. Our final goal is to recommend the best placement of the school compost pile we are
recommending to Mr. W   . This will depend on light and water needed and if the pile needs
insects that he might see as not desirable near a school. roaches, flies etc.)

Procedure:

(E)

1. The materials we used for the Compost Column were : 8, 2 liter bottles and the cutting thing
(with razor blade) and glue guns. We used the instructions for making the bottles from the Bottle
Biology book.

2. Construct two bottles (see our drawing)

3. We filled the compost part of the bottles with grass clippings, fruit waste, and leaves. we put the
same stuff in both bottles. We mixed the compost up in a pail and placed half in one and half in the
other. We also measured the mass of the bottle with the compost in it to make certain. We
adjusted the amount to account for a 12 gram difference in the bottles because of extra glue on
one.

4. We put one bottle in a direct sunlight part of the room and the other in a location that only has
sunlight in the morning. We selected right in the middle window in the back of the room facing
south with full sun from 7AM until 6PM and on the east side of Mr. G.   's room where there is
sun only from 7AM until about noon. We found that the south window also gets about 10 degrees
hotter. This may effect our results. (these two locations are similar to the sun times of our two
proposed sites for the school compost pile).

5. We watered both bottles and recorded the amount of water added each day. This needed to be
the same in both bottles because we did not want to get more than one variable in our light
experiment.

(O)

5. We took out a small sample of the compost (YUCK) and examined it with a hand lens and the
microscope. WASH your hands and only do this again when you really have to! We recorded our
observations in the data. (later we voted to use gloves).

6. We did this for 2 weeks until we could identify some of the animals that came in with the
compost and are helping to decompose the stuff (we think). We used a book on biology to help with
identification. This was the most difficult part

(J)

7. We were asked to throw the bottles away (it was very wasteful) after five weeks because they
seemed to be the home of a big bunch of fruit flies. We decided to keep one compost column going
and cover the top with a fine mesh cloth to keep the fruit flies in and continue our experiment.
Also we wanted to use it when we present our idea of a compost pile to Mr. W

Exhibit B.5. Continued

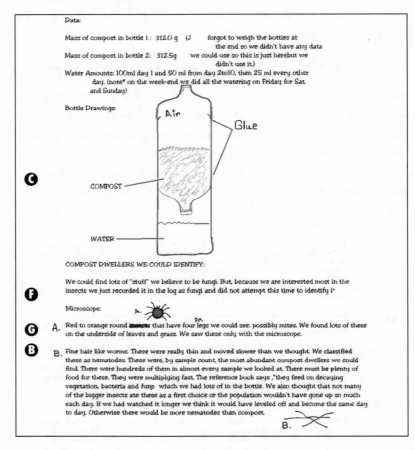

Data:

Mass of compost in bottle 1 : 312.0 g   (J   forgot to weigh the bottles at
                                              the end so we didn't have any data
Mass of compost in bottle 2: 312.5g   we could use so this is just herebut we
                                              didn't use it.)
Water Amounts: 100ml day 1 and 50 ml from day 2to10, then 25 ml every other
      day. (note* on the week-end we did all the watering on Friday for Sat.
      and Sunday)

Bottle Drawings:

Air

Glue

C

COMPOST

WATER

COMPOST DWELLERS WE COULD IDENTIFY:

We could find lots of "stuff" we believe to be fungi. But, because we are interested most in the
insects we just recorded it in the log as fungi and did not attempt this time to identify i⁺

F

Microscope: A.

G   A. Red to orange round insects that have four legs we could see: possibly mites. We found lots of these
            on the underside of leaves and grass. We saw these only with the microscope.

B   B. Fine hair like worms. These were really thin and moved slower than we thought. We classified
            these as nematodes. These were, by sample count, the most abundant compost dwellers we could
            find. There were hundreds of them in almost every sample we looked at. There must be plenty of
            food for these. They were multiplying fast. The reference book says ,"they feed on decaying
            vegetation, bacteria and fung which we had lots of in the bottle. We also thought that not many
            of the bigger insects ate these as a first choice or the population wouldn't have gone up so much
            each day. If we had watched it longer we think it would have leveled off and become the same day
            to day. Otherwise there would be more nematodes than compost.

                              B.

Exhibit B.5. Continued

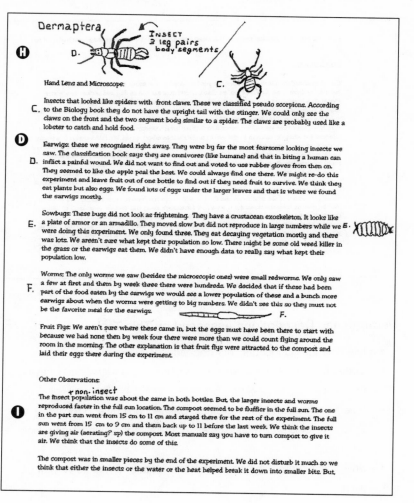

Dermaptera

INSECT
3 leg pairs
body segments

D.

C.

Hand Lens and Microscope:

C. Insects that looked like spiders with front claws. These we classified pseudo scorpions. According to the Biology book they do not have the upright tail with the stinger. We could only see the claws on the front and the two segment body similar to a spider. The claws are probably used like a lobster to catch and hold food.

D. Earwigs: these we recognised right away. They were by far the most fearsome looking insects we saw. The classification book says they are omnivores (like humans) and that in biting a human can inflict a painful wound. We did not want to find out and voted to use rubber gloves from then on. They seemed to like the apple peal the best. We could always find one there. We might re-do this experiment and leave fruit out of one bottle to find out if they need fruit to survive. We think they eat plants but also eggs. We found lots of eggs under the larger leaves and that is where we found the earwigs mostly.

E. Sowbugs: These bugs did not look as frightening. They have a crustacean exoskeleton. It looks like a plate of armor or an armadillo. They moved slow but did not reproduce in large numbers while we were doing this experiment. We only found three. They eat decaying vegetation mostly and there was lots. We aren't sure what kept their population so low. There might be some old weed killer in the grass or the earwigs eat them. We didn't have enough data to really say what kept their population low.

F. Worms: The only worms we saw (besides the microscopic ones) were small redworms. We only saw a few at first and then by week three there were hundreds. We decided that if these had been part of the food eaten by the earwigs we would see a lower population of these and a bunch more earwigs about when the worms were getting to big numbers. We didn't see this so they must not be the favorite meal for the earwigs.   F.

Fruit Flys: We aren't sure where these came in, but the eggs must have been there to start with because we had none then by week four there were more than we could count flying around the room in the morning. The other explanation is that fruit flys were attracted to the compost and laid their eggs there during the experiment.

Other Observations:

The insect population (+ non-insect) was about the same in both bottles. But, the larger insects and worms reproduced faster in the full sun location. The compost seemed to be fluffier in the full sun. The one in the part sun went from 15 cm to 11 cm and stayed there for the rest of the experiment. The full sun went from 15 cm to 9 cm and them back up to 11 before the last week. We think the insects are giving air (aerating? sp) the compost. Most manuals say you have to turn compost to give it air. We think that the insects do some of this.

The compost was in smaller pieces by the end of the experiment. We did not disturb it much so we think that either the insects or the water or the heat helped break it down into smaller bits. But,

Exhibit B.5. Continued

since the bits went smaller faster in the sunny bottle, the sun/temperature may have had a lot to do with it.

CONCLUSIONS:

(K) Our recommendation is that the compost pile be placed on the south side of the building just behind the driver's ed. simulator trailer. This location gets full sun all day and is close to a water faucet. The insects we saw with our experiment were not harmful. We saw no roaches or house flies or maggots. We do think that you should only use yard waste and maybe fruit waste from the cafeteria (salad stuff is OK too). We did not use any meat food waste and that might draw more flies. If we have time we will experiment to find out which insects do the most good in a compost pile and see what we can add to the pile to make their numbers go up. We think that it is a waste to throw all that yard waste from all the grass away when we could make compost that other's could use for gardens or soil building. Since our experiments showed that the full sunlight bottle broke into smaller pieces faster and seemed to decompose faster, the full sun location would be better. This is because we would like the compost to break down quicker so that it can be used. The smell of the compost goes down after the first week. But, if you are constantly adding material to the pile it may stay a little smelly. The only disadvantage of this location is that the wind usually blows out of the southwest and the pile will be upwind from the new building. We thought that by placing it by the simulator it would be far enough away (112 feet we measured) to dilute the smell and not cause a problem. The smell is the only bad effect of this location. The location was the best sun and the closest to water. We think we could find a way to cut down the smell if it became a problem. We are willing to contact local lumberyards to see if they will donate the chickenwire and the 2 x 4s to construct a compost pile that we can start using in May. Thank you for your time and reading our lab report.

Performance Descriptions Assessed by This Task

- Life Sciences Concepts: Interdependence of organisms.
- Scientific Connections and Applications: Big ideas and unifying concepts.
- Scientific Tools and Technologies: Use technology and tools.
- Scientific Tools and Technologies: Acquire information from multiple sources.
- Scientific Communication: Represent data and results in multiple ways.
- Scientific Investigation: Controlled experiment.

Commentary: What the Work Shows

(A) (B) The work shows understanding of the interdependence of organisms, including populations, ecosystems, and food webs.

(C) The compost bottle was a small scale model in which the variables could be controlled, then scaled up to the compost pile recommended in the conclusions.

D The discussion of the earwigs' niche shows an understanding of the interdependence of growth, population stress, and predator/prey relationships, all evidence of an understanding of change and constancy, and of cause and effect.

E The students created the tools to make this investigation possible, overcoming the obstacle and impracticality of two full-size compost piles.

F **G** The precision of the language, "we believe to be fungi" and "possibly mites," is excellent.

G **H** Drawings are used effectively.

The work shows consideration of appropriate resources by scaling down the compost pile to conduct the investigation accurately and practically in a pop bottle.

I **J** The work also shows attention to safety and consideration for others.

This work shows thorough and appropriate documentation, both in the procedures and in the descriptions of the organisms that provide enough detailed information for others to replicate the investigation.

The writing contains some spelling and grammatical errors, but these do not detract from the quality of the report.

I The conclusion is drawn from evidence.

K The conclusion of the report is an appropriate recommendation to the school principal, "Mr. W.," as to where the school should keep a compost pile.

Evidence of peer review is not included in this report.

Exhibit B.6 is a student work sample of a standard-setting performance with commentaries from an applied learning task (Electro-
Hawk 1) at the high school level.

Exhibit B.6. Student Work Sample and Commentary: ElectroHawk 1

Students were required to complete an application project that would develop
their skills in gathering and using information, communication, and problem
solving, and help them to become self-directed learners. The students defined
the project and acquired a mentor from outside the school to assist them. The
students were supervised by a teacher throughout the process of developing
a proposal and planning a presentation of the project. This student designed
an electric car for a local competition.

The student worked as a member of a team to get most of the work
done. This student was also the actual driver of the car in competition. The
team worked with an adult mentor and a teacher advisor. The students were
required to maintain a journal to record the time they spent on the project.
The work culminated in a presentation to interested adults and peers.

The student wrote a three and one-half page proposal describing the project. He created a time line and maintained a journal. He also performed an
analysis of the record of performance. Excerpts from each of these pieces
follow and provide a glimpse of the proposal, time line, journal, and analysis.
Following the student work is a section describing what the work shows in
relation to the standards.

Exhibit B.6. Continued, *Proposal Excerpt*

Application Project
Proposal Paper

Have you ever wanted to go for a ride into the future? Or maybe drive an almost non-polluting vehicle? For my application project, I propose to build a full size, fully drivable, fully operational solar/electric car. I am currently, and will continue to build, and improve an electric vehicle. I, along with the aid of 4 other students, and the watchful eye of Mr._____, and Mr._____, am currently building this vehicle in the_____Technology Department. The vehicle, along with the many tests and upgrades, should be completed by the end of July.

I have chosen to build an electric car for my application project almost by coincidence. _____High School received an electric motor, a speed control, and two batteries from P.U.D in early November. In return, we must build an electric or, solar-electric vehicle. Immediately I jumped at the rare opportunity to build the ElectroHawk 1. Unfortunately it took us until after December to get a team together to build this vehicle. This is the main reason that I have started my application project in the middle of building this vehicle.

There are many skills that have helped me along the way, as well as many new skills I have acquired while building this vehicle. Some of the most important skills I have are those pertaining to my familiarity of the various tools (saws, drills, grinders, sanders, etc.) used to fabricate the vehicle. I have been around these different tools all of my life since my father owns a custom woodworking company. I have also taken many classes in the Technology Department, teaching me the safety skills necessary to operate all the tools. I also feel that I get along well with others which helps to build a stronger team, and more important, a higher quality electric vehicle. Without a high quality electric vehicle, somebody will get hurt.

The variety of skills I plan to attain from this project are those related to metal works. I have already learned how to "tack" or make small welds, as well as what is necessary to cut metals. I will also have a better

Exhibit B.6. Continued, *Proposal Excerpt*

Next we have to locate a chain as well as a sprocket that matches the required gear ratio of the rear wheel sprocket. Mr._____has been putting his time in to locate these items since he seems to have the best understanding of exactly what we need.

After deciding what needs to be done on the rear suspension, and gearing, we need to begin work on the front axle and suspension. This task includes many variables such as: how the vehicle will be steered, how the suspension will attach to the vehicle, as well as wheel size. Mr._____has told us that he knows someone who builds front suspension kits, and that it might be possible to order one. Mr._____has told us about a unique front suspension he has designed based on three-wheel bikes he saw while visiting the Oregon coast.

Once we have the entire chassis finished we can begin mounting and wiring all of the electrical components such as speed control, throttle, and batteries. Our vehicle is very compact, and finding adequate space will be difficult. We also need to wire up the vehicle, and from the schematics, it does not look easy.

After everything is wired up, and in place we will begin going over all of the rules and regulations to make sure that we are legal and able to race. There will be a practice day when all of the competing vehicles will turn out at_____Speed Way to take practice runs, as well as have a judge look over our vehicle for anything we may be missing.

Finally, after everything is completed we will begin doing tests and trials. Our main goal of running the various tests will be to find any flaws in the structure that may be present and get the vehicle running at it's most efficient levels. We will also begin lightening the vehicle at this point to see what the least amount of material is needed to make the vehicle hold together.

When presentation time comes I will have many ways of showing what I have learned. I hope to have a journal, several pictures, and several graphs and charts showing the vehicles rating of efficiency increasing as

Exhibit B.6. Continued, *Time Line Excerpt*

Application Project
Time Line

March 30, 1995:   Completed

By this date the mock-up will be completed
and work on the metal chassis will
commence.

April 14, 1995:   Completed

By this date the chassis will be completed
and work on the rear suspension will commence.

April 21, 1995:   Completed

By this date the rear suspension will be completed
and work on the front suspension will commence.

May 9, 1995:

By this date work on the front suspension will be
completed and work on wiring the car will
commence.

May 6, 1995:

Work on wiring the car will be completed and
safety checks will be performed. As well as checks
to make sure our vehicle can satisfy the rules.

May 9, 1995:

By this date all safety parameters will be met,
and performance testing of the vehicles systems
will begin.

May 13, 1995:

The vehicle will be taken to_____speedway
to get looked over by a judge that will check to make
sure that we meet all the necessary guidelines.

Exhibit B.6. Continued, *Journal Excerpt*

the brackets that hold the tire to far forward. To correct this we thought it would mean rebuilding the entire rear suspension. Fortunately I got the wheels upstairs turning and found an alternative. The piece in the front of the axle that was blocking the tire could just be cut off and moved forward. A roll bar was also put on the vehicle. Mr. also welded up the car instead of having us do it mainly for safety reasons. We also have a partially completed battery box to hold and keep the batteries from leaking and possible putting the driver in danger. A front axial also got started today as well, but it still needs allot of work.

4/18-(4 hrs)

Today I managed to get work off so I would have more time on the car. We got the rear axial completed and now all we have to do is attach it. This will take very precise work making it happen so that we can get the axial on straight. We also began major work on the front axial and suspension. This is proving to be more difficult then we were hoping trying to build the suspension around the axial itself using the unique system that we decided to use.

4/19-(5 hrs)

Today the magic happened. The rear axle and suspension was placed in the car. Before we did this though we had to cut some very precise holes into the frame to give the axle something to connect to. This means that we have 4 total holes that need to line up perfectly. And we are relying solely on our measurements. And when the moment of truth happened, the axial went in nice and snug, and the suspension had very little play. We also worked more on the battery compartment. It is nearly completed. We also began making decisions as to where we want to place electrical components onto the vehicle. We are going to be calling it very close. It will be a late night Thursday for sure.

4/20-(8 hrs)

Today we worked almost solely on the front suspension. I worked most of the day machining the front axial making it the correct size for the wheel to fit on. I am wondering if this axial is strong enough to support itself since it is barely 1/4" thick. I also got pizzas for dinner tonight donated by. I also completed a battery box

Exhibit B.6. Continued, *Journal Excerpt*

to protect the driver from acid spills in the event of a role-over. We also connected the support for the axle and completed the front axial.

4/21-(10 hrs)

Tonight was the longest night I have ever worked on this car yet. We worked until midnight. We kind of had to since the practice run is tomorrow. Tonight we worked on many things. Our first priority was to check if our front axial steering system was going to work. Apparently the angle the steering system was at wouldn't work. it didn't have a sharp enough turn. So to adjust it we had to increase the angle of slope. After doing this our turning radius was dramatically increased. We also attempted to wire the vehicle and place all of the insides of the vehicle. This proved easier said then done. The schematics made almost no sense at first but we managed to get most of it done. Mr._____spent most of his evening looking for things we needed such as correct sized nuts, sprockets, chains, mirrors, and other equipment. We all eventually got a little cranky by the time 12:00 rolled around so we decided to call it quits and return early in the morning to finish all of the little unimportant items.

4/22-(6 hrs)

Today was safety inspection and practice day. before we headed off for the race track we still had a few things that needed to be done. Some minor adjustments as well as electrical wiring. We worked hard and fast to get everything done that needed to be done. We still didn't get it all done. it came time to head off to the track so we packed up and decided to finish our work there. Once we arrived at the race track we immediately began work on the electrical system and gearing. And just as quickly as we got started working on the car peoples curiosity grew as other teams came over to get a glimpse of our unique steering system. After about two hours of hard work, and safety inspection we finally rolled the car onto the track. And then the moment of truth came with Mr. as our test pilot. He pushed the throttle forward, there was no response, he pushed the throttle again and still there was no response. I began going over all the wires in the system. Turns out to be a wire disconnected from the motor. Very quickly we got the wire connected back on only to realize that our chain wasn't tight so again we responded quickly moving the tire back. And then it was time to test our creation. Mr.

Exhibit B.6. Continued, *Analysis Excerpt*

	A	B	C	D	E	F	G
1	Lap #	Time (sec)	M.P.H.	RPM of Wheel	RPM 42/9	RPM 42/11	RPM 42/13
2	1	79	15.95	279.54	1305.47	1067.86	902.93
3	2	54	23.33	408.96	1909.86	1562.24	1320.95
4	3	55	22.91	401.53	1875.13	1533.83	1296.93
5	4	56	22.50	394.36	1841.65	1506.44	1273.77
6	5	53	23.77	416.68	1945.89	1591.71	1345.87
7	6	50	25.20	441.68	2062.64	1687.22	1426.63
8	7	46	27.39	480.09	2242.00	1833.93	1550.68
9	8	46	27.39	480.09	2242.00	1833.93	1550.68
10	9	48	26.25	460.08	2148.59	1757.52	1486.07
11	10	51	24.71	433.02	2022.20	1654.13	1398.65
12	11	46	27.39	480.09	2242.00	1833.93	1550.68
13	12	45	28.00	490.76	2291.83	1874.68	1585.14
14	13	45	28.00	490.76	2291.83	1874.68	1585.14
15	14	49	25.71	450.69	2104.74	1721.65	1455.74
16	15	51	24.71	433.02	2022.20	1654.13	1398.65
17	16	48	26.25	460.08	2148.59	1757.52	1486.07
18	17	48	26.25	460.08	2148.59	1757.52	1486.07
19	18	45	28.00	490.76	2291.83	1874.68	1585.14
20	19	50	25.20	441.68	2062.64	1687.22	1426.63
21	20	44	28.64	501.91	2343.91	1917.29	1621.17
22	21	43	29.30	513.58	2398.42	1961.88	1658.87
23	22	42	30.00	525.81	2455.53	2008.59	1698.36
24	23	42	30.00	525.81	2455.53	2008.59	1698.36
25	24	44	28.64	501.91	2343.91	1917.29	1621.17
26	25	43	29.30	513.58	2398.42	1961.88	1658.87
27	26	44	28.64	501.91	2343.91	1917.29	1621.17
28	27	42	30.00	525.81	2455.53	2008.59	1698.36
29	28	42	30.00	525.81	2455.53	2008.59	1698.36
30	29	45	28.00	490.76	2291.83	1874.68	1585.14
31	30	42	30.00	525.81	2455.53	2008.59	1698.36
32	31	42	30.00	525.81	2455.53	2008.59	1698.36
33	32	44	28.64	501.91	2343.91	1917.29	1621.17
34	33	42	30.00	525.81	2455.53	2008.59	1698.36
35	34	44	28.64	501.91	2343.91	1917.29	1621.17
36	35	42	30.00	525.81	2455.53	2008.59	1698.36
37	36	42	30.00	525.81	2455.53	2008.59	1698.36
38	37	43	29.30	513.58	2398.42	1961.88	1658.87
39	38	44	28.64	501.91	2343.91	1917.29	1621.17
40	39	46	27.39	480.09	2242.00	1833.93	1550.68
41	40	41	30.73	538.63	2515.42	2057.58	1739.79
42	41	47	26.81	469.87	2194.30	1794.91	1517.69
43	42	44	28.64	501.91	2343.91	1917.29	1621.17
44	43	44	28.64	501.91	2343.91	1917.29	1621.17
45	44	46	27.39	480.09	2242.00	1833.93	1550.68
46	45	45	28.00	490.76	2291.83	1874.68	1585.14
47	46	45	28.00	490.76	2291.83	1874.68	1585.14
48	47	46	27.39	480.09	2242.00	1833.93	1550.68
49	48	45	28.00	490.76	2291.83	1874.68	1585.14
50	49	48	26.25	460.08	2148.59	1757.52	1486.07

Exhibit B.6. Continued, *Analysis Excerpt*

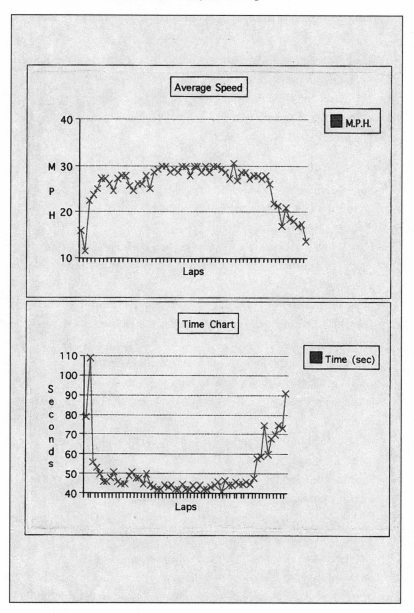

Performance Descriptions Assessed by This Task

- Problem Solving: Design a product, service, or system.
- Learning and Self-Management: Learn from models.
- Learning and Self-Management: Review own progress and adjust priorities as needed.
- Learning and Self-Management: Evaluate own performance.
- Working With Others: Participate in the establishment and operation of self-directed work teams.

What the Work Shows

Problem Solving: The student designs and creates a product, service, or system to meet an identified need; that is, the student:

- develops a design proposal that:
  - shows how the ideas for the design were developed;
  - reflects awareness of similar work done by others and of relevant design standards and regulations;
  - justifies the choices made in finalizing the design with reference, for example, to functional, aesthetic, social, economic, and environmental considerations;
  - establishes criteria for evaluating the product, service, or system;
  - uses appropriate conventions to represent the design;
- plans and implements the steps needed to create the product, service, or system;
- makes adjustments as needed to conform with specified standards or regulations regarding quality or safety;
- evaluates the product, service, or system in terms of the criteria established in the design proposal, and with reference to:
  - information gathered from sources such as impact studies, product testing, or market research;
  - comparisons with similar work done by others.

The proposal explains the genesis of the project: the P.U.D. (Public Utilities Department) provided the school with an electric motor, a speed control, and two batteries as the basis for designing and building an electric or solar-electric vehicle for entry in a competition with other schools in the local area.

The process of design of the vehicle emerges through the "Proposal Paper," "Time Line," and journal. The proposal records the plan the student envisaged early in the process. This plan is reflected in the timeline. The journal provides insight into the reality of the design process, especially the ways in which the students responded to problems they encountered as the design took shape.

Learning and Self-Management Tools and Techniques: The student learns from models; that is, the student:

- consults with and observes other students and adults at work and analyzes their roles to determine the critical demands, such as demands for knowledge and skills, judgment and decision making;
- identifies models for the result of project work, such as professionally produced publications, and analyzes their qualities;
- uses what he or she learns from models in planning and conducting project activities.

Learning and Self-Management Tools and Techniques: The student reviews his or her own progress in completing work activities and adjusts priorities as needed to meet deadlines; that is, the student:

- develops and maintains work schedules that reflect consideration of priorities;
- manages time;
- monitors progress toward meeting deadlines and adjusts priorities as necessary.

Learning and Self-Management Tools and Techniques: The student evaluates his or her performance; that is, the student:

- establishes expectations for his or her own achievement;
- critiques his or her work in light of the established expectations;
- seeks and responds to advice and criticism from others.

The proposal and journal reflect the student's expectations for his own achievement. The journal also records the student's analysis of his work in light of those expectations. The entries focus on the efforts he and his fellow team members made to reach a satisfactory result, rather than a detailed analysis of the student's own performance. There is also evidence of seeking and responding to advice, especially from the teachers who provided assistance to the team.

The student's recognition of his accomplishment is evident throughout the written work, as is his pride which comes through in a humble voice.

Tools and Techniques for Working With Others: The student participates in the establishment and operation of self-directed work teams; that is, the student:

- defines roles and shares responsibilities among team members;
- sets objectives and time frames for the work to be completed;
- establishes processes for group decision making;
- reviews progress and makes adjustments as required.

It is clear from the journal entries that the work was a team effort, though there are few references to the definition of roles and responsibilities or of the processes the team established for decision making. The journal also makes it clear that the students took responsibility for the project despite the close involvement and assistance of their advisors.

The proposal and timeline establish the objectives and time frame and the journal provides evidence that the team reviewed their progress and made adjustments as required.

Resource C
New Standards Reference Examinations

In addition to developing student performance standards, New Standards developed *Reference Examinations* in English Language Arts and Mathematics. These examinations are part of a complete assessment system of performance examinations and portfolios referenced to the *New Standards Performance Standards*.

Designed to help achieve high performance, these standards-based performance assessments:

Emphasize performance tasks developed with the help of thousands of classroom teachers

Offer three levels—elementary, middle, and high school

Have been field tested across the nation

Are professionally scored by Harcourt Brace Educational Measurement

Provide timely reports of student, classroom, school, and district performance in relation to the standards

Respond to Title I requirements for testing in mathematics and reading or language arts and for developing challenging content and performance standards for all children

Take into account international standards

The *New Standards English Language Arts Reference Examination* ties to the *New Standards Performance Standards* for reading, writing, and conventions. The student-constructed responses are scored holistically and provide a snapshot of the kinds of work students can do in an on-demand situation. The *Reference Examination* is designed to work in conjunction with a portfolio system to provide additional information about student performance.

Three levels are available (in English only)—elementary, middle, and high school—with items developed to be administered at the end of fourth, eighth, and tenth grades, respectively. It is expected that some students might achieve these levels earlier and others later than these grades.

The exam is organized into three sections, administered over three class periods:

An Independent Writing Task, a report of information, that asks students to use details

An Integrated Reading and Writing Task that asks students to answer short, open-ended questions and then produce a piece of text-based writing to demonstrate comprehension of an informational passage

A few well-crafted multiple-choice questions that ask students to respond to questions that deal with either reading comprehension, inference and analysis, or editing rules and guidelines

The assessments emphasize skills that are fundamental to many types of readings and writing: the careful selection of details and the ability to relate specific details to an overall theme or idea. Thus, the assessments reinforce the idea that reading and writing are highly integrated activities.

Exhibit C.1. Independent Writing Task Sample

This task asks students to write about a given topic, while encouraging them to organize their ideas, express them clearly, choose words carefully, and use correct spelling, grammar, and punctuation.

Exhibit C.1. Continued

It is representative of English language arts at the middle school level. In this part of the exam, students have an opportunity to show they can:

- Select details that clearly illustrate the writer's attitude or point

- Organize those details in ways that make them really understandable to a reader

- Observe basic conventions of writing (spelling, punctuation, etc.)

Preparing to Write
Youth is sometimes valued more in our culture than age and wisdom. Many products are sold using ads aimed specifically at young people. Many radio stations play music that interests young people. Sometimes we forget that older people can be very important in our lives. Older people may listen to our problems and offer helpful advice. They may have wisdom because they have lived a long time. They may even be good friends to someone your age.

Your Writing Task
Choose an older person who has helped you or been your friend. This person may be a neighbor, family member, or older friend. Write about this person, showing your readers what kind of person he or she is. Include specific incidents that show why this person is important to you. (An incident is an event that occurs in a few minutes, a few hours, or perhaps in a day.) Let your readers know how this older person has been important in your life.

About a decade ago, I would beg my mother to take me to the grey house with the green shutters everyday. Years later, I saw the same thing that I felt in my sister's eyes. It's not hard to see why we liked Mrs. Ryan so much.

I would cross the street with Anna Felicia, my favorite doll, clutched in my arms. The clothes she was wearing had been knitted by Mrs. Ryan and that's part of what made Anna special to me.

When I knocked on the door, I would be greeted with a smile and a "Hello Debbie. How are you and Anna feeling today?" everytime I visited her enchanting home.

She would put up with me for hours. I would look at all her pictures. Mrs. Ryan had at least a million of them. I would ask her questions about every person that I saw. Eventually, I began to recognize some of them. She

her family so ... who had born. From I wanted ... couldn't ... that her ... I loved ... he had a ... rang which ... from time ... moment ... smile to ... my music. ... began ... ... She ... made ... much. ... Started ... Ryan's ... her ... lid. ... ght ... to ... understood ... as ... ... A ... that ... knew ... had

Exhibit C.2. Integrated Reading and Writing Task Sample

The Integrated Reading and Writing Task is designed to see how well students understand what they read and how well they can write. After reading a passage, students answer several questions about the passage and also use the information they read to write a short essay. In this middle-grade-level task, students have a total of 45 minutes to do the following:

- Read a short information passage

- Answer three short-answer questions about the passage

- Write a short text-based essay in which they draw on both the passage and their own knowledge outside the text to explain an idea

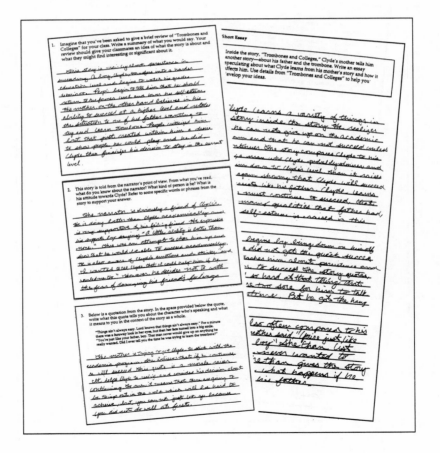

The *New Standards Mathematics Reference Examination* includes
extended open-ended and short-answer items measuring:

- Conceptual Understanding

- Mathematical Skills and Tools

- Problem Solving and Reasoning/Mathematical
  Communication

Many tasks are derived from real-life situations, so that in con-
structing responses students can see connections between the skills
they are learning and the world outside school.

Three levels of the examination are available in English and
Spanish—elementary, middle, and high school—developed to be
administered at the end of fourth, eighth, and tenth grades, respectively. It is expected that some students might achieve these levels
earlier and others later than these grades.

The items are referenced to *New Standards Performance Standards*
in the following areas:

- Arithmetic and number concepts

- Geometry and measurement concepts

- Function and algebra concepts

- Statistics and probability concepts

- Problem solving and mathematical reasoning

- Mathematical skills and tools

- Mathematical communication

Students take the examination over three class periods, and the
student-constructed responses are scored holistically and dimen-
sionally.

Exhibit C.3. Conceptual Understanding Sample "Counting Raisins"

In this task, students are asked to predict how many raisins might be in a small box of raisins. To make their prediction, students need to interpret a line plot that shows how many raisins were found in 11 boxes of raisins that have already been counted. This task is designed to assess conceptual understanding of statistics and probability concepts and is representative of a mathematics task at the elementary level.

In school, Marcus's class did a lesson with counting raisins in small boxes. Students counted the raisins in 11 different boxes. The teacher made a graph below of what they did.

The teacher said, "Study the graph and predict how many raisins you think you might find in the next small box."

2) What is your prediction?
    Explain how you decided on your prediction.

I think in the next box you will find 29 raisins because: If there are 2 boxes with 28, only one with 29, three with 30 in them, and 2 with 31.
I think the company hoped to get 28–31 raisins in a box. Therefore the next box should have 29 or 30.

Exhibit C.4. Mathematical Skills and Tools Sample "Life Expectancy"

This middle-grade-level sample is a set of three, linked five-minute tasks in which students are asked to read and interpret a graph showing the relationship between birth rate and life expectancy in a number of countries. It is designed to assess aspects of conceptual understanding as described in the Statistics and Probability performance standard. It also assesses mathematical skills and mathematical communication.

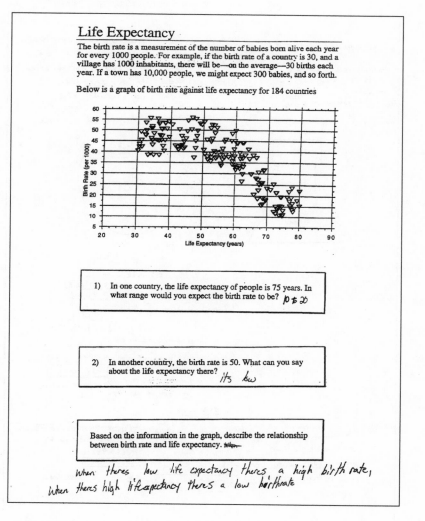

Life Expectancy

The birth rate is a measurement of the number of babies born alive each year for every 1000 people. For example, if the birth rate of a country is 30, and a village has 1000 inhabitants, there will be—on the average—30 births each year. If a town has 10,000 people, we might expect 300 babies, and so forth.

Below is a graph of birth rate against life expectancy for 184 countries

1) In one country, the life expectancy of people is 75 years. In what range would you expect the birth rate to be? *10 to 20*

2) In another country, the birth rate is 50. What can you say about the life expectancy there? *It's low*

Based on the information in the graph, describe the relationship between birth rate and life expectancy.

When theres low life expectancy theres a high birth rate, When theres high life expectancy theres a low birthrate

Exhibit C.5. Problem Solving and Reasoning Sample "Snark Soda"

This high school level task assesses the ability of students to model a familiar situation using basic concepts of volume from solid geometry. Students are asked to find a good approximation of the volume of liquid in a bottle by modeling the shape of the bottle with geometric solids. This task requires the student to visualize in three dimensions, make accurate measurements, and choose sensible shapes in their calculations.

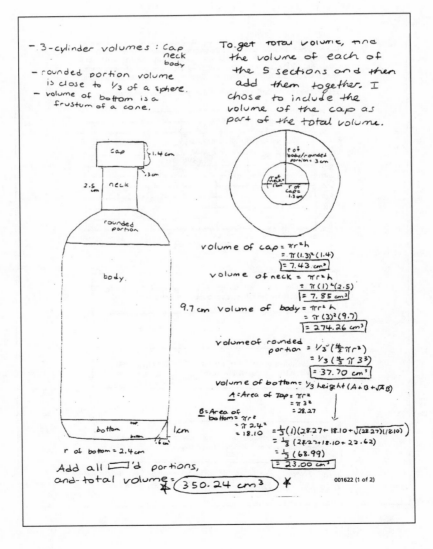

- 3-cylinder volumes : Cap
                 neck
                 body
- rounded portion volume is close to 1/3 of a sphere.
- volume of bottom is a frustum of a cone.

To get total volume, find the volume of each of the 5 sections and then add them together. I chose to include the volume of the cap as part of the total volume.

volume of cap = $\pi r^2 h$
          = $\pi(1.3)^2(1.4)$
          = 7.43 cm³

volume of neck = $\pi r^2 h$
          = $\pi(1)^2(2.5)$
          = 7.85 cm³

volume of body = $\pi r^2 h$
          = $\pi(3)^2(9.7)$
          = 274.26 cm³

volume of rounded portion = $1/3(\frac{4}{2}\pi r^2)$
          = $1/3(\frac{4}{2}\pi 3^3)$
          = 37.70 cm³

volume of bottom = 1/3 height $(A + B + \sqrt{AB})$
A = Area of Top = πr^2
          = $\pi 3^2$
          = 28.27

B = Area of bottom = πr^2
          = $\pi 2.4^2$
          = 18.10

= $\frac{1}{3}(1)(28.27 + 18.10 + \sqrt{(28.27)(18.10)})$
= $\frac{1}{3}(28.27 + 18.10 + 22.62)$
= $\frac{1}{3}(68.99)$
= 23.00 cm³

r of bottom = 2.4cm

Add all ▭'d portions, and total volume = 350.24 cm³ ✱

001622 (1 of 2)

Information Provided by the *Reference Examinations*

Student scores on the examinations are reported by performance levels referenced to the standards. That is, student achievement on each content-area cluster, e.g., mathematical skills and tools, is reported in relation to one or more of the performance standards. Reporting students' scores in this way provides rich and comprehensive information about students' achievement compared to high standards.

The examinations are professionally scored at the Performance Assessment Scoring Center of Harcourt Brace Educational Measurement by individuals trained and experienced in the holistic evaluation of student-constructed responses, according to New Standards guidelines.

A variety of score reports are available as packages and options to provide information about student, classroom, school, and district performance on the Mathematics and English Language Arts Examinations separately or combined.

The score reports are formatted in a unique way. The relevant standards are summarized across the top of the report in their main categories. Just below, a score is reported for each of the categories. This is an individual score if the report is for an individual student, or an average if for a group of students—say for a class, a grade in a school, or that grade for an entire district. Then, below that appears a statement offering advice as to what the student or students need to work on in order to improve the score. There are no statements about arcane issues such as stanines. There are no comparisons to the work of other students. The reports clearly and plainly show what the standards are, how the performance compares to the standards, and what must be done to improve the performance. The whole report form is designed to enable students, teachers, and parents to understand how the student is doing and what must be done in order to do better. The score report is a very good indicator of New Standards' commitment not only to accurate measures, but also to a system that will result in steady improvement in achievement if the student is willing to make the effort.

Resource D
Resources for Standards-Based Education

The following list of resources for standards-based education is in no sense complete. There are many other organizations whose claims in this arena are at least as strong. But we offer it to those who are seeking a place to start in the knowledge that they will be quickly led to many other sources of help and inspiration. If you have the time and inclination, please let us know about other organizations whose assistance you have found particularly useful.

Center for Leadership in School Reform
950 Breckenridge Lane, Suite 200
Louisville, KY 40207
502/895–1942
e-mail: info@clsr.org
Web site: www.clsr.org
The Center for Leadership in School Reform was designed to encourage and support the transformation of existing rules, roles, and relationships that govern the way time, people, space, knowledge, and technology are used in school.

Center for the Study of Social Policy
1260 Eye Street, NW, Suite 503
Washington, DC 20005–3822
202/371–1565

The Center for the Study of Social Policy assists government at all levels in improving human services for low-income and other disadvantaged populations. The center seeks to promote systemic reform in human services through changes in financing, administration, and delivery of services.

Coalition of Essential Schools
Box 1969
Brown University
Providence, RI 02912
401/863–3384
Web site: www.ces.brown.edu
The Coalition of Essential Schools is a national reform movement with a focus on classroom practice. Based on nine Common Principles, the CES strives to measure the long-term impact of school reform on the lives of students.

Comprehensive Math and Science Program
Columbia University School of Engineering
51 Astor Place
New York, NY 10003
212/228–0950
e-mail: cmsp@aol.com
The Comprehensive Math and Science Program uses a ground zero/mastery approach to give middle-school students the chance to achieve at high levels and build strong academic foundations for high school work.

Core Knowledge Foundation
2012-B Morton Drive
Charlottesville, VA 22903
804/977–7550
e-mail: coreknow@comet.net
Web site: www.coreknowledge.org

The Core Knowledge Foundation enables schools to achieve greater excellence and fairness by helping children establish strong, early foundations of knowledge; conducts research on curricula; offers model content guidelines; and develops resources based on those content guidelines.

Council for Basic Education
1319 F Street, NW, Suite 900
Washington, DC 20004–1152
202/347–4171
e-mail: info@c-b-e.org
The Council for Basic Education (CBE) promotes a curriculum strong in the basic subjects: English, history, geography, government, mathematics, sciences, foreign languages, and the arts, for all children. CBE advocates the development of high academic standards in K–12 education.

Different Ways of Knowing
The Galef Institute
11050 Santa Monica Boulevard, 3rd Floor
Los Angeles, CA 90025–3594
310/479–8883
Web site: www.galef.org
Different Ways of Knowing connects professional development for teachers and administrators to a content-rich interdisciplinary curriculum centered on powerful social studies themes. The themes are a springboard for deep and rigorous learning of mathematics and science concepts.

The Efficacy Institute
128 Spring Street
Lexington, MA 02173
617/862–4390
The Efficacy Institute is committed to serving children and the peo-

ple who serve them. They work to release the inherent intellectual capacity of all children, especially children of color, and to affirm their right to learn.

Foxfire Fund
P. O. Box 541
Mountain City, GA 30562
706/746–5318
Foxfire works teacher-to-teacher to disseminate an active, academically sound, learner-centered approach to education. Through courses offered by the twenty national Foxfire teacher networks, teachers are encouraged and equipped to use this approach in their classrooms.

Institute for Learning
Learning Research and Development Center
University of Pittsburgh
3939 O'Hara Street
Pittsburgh, PA 15260
412/624–7926
e-mail: *Bee@vms.cis.pitt.edu*
The Institute for Learning at the Learning Research and Development Center, University of Pittsburgh, helps schools and school systems create high-performance learning environments. The Institute serves as a think tank, design center, and educator of cadres of school professionals.

National Alliance for Restructuring Education
National Center on Education and the Economy
700 11th Street, NW, Suite 750
Washington, DC 20001
202/783–3668
A program of the National Center on Education and the Economy, the National Alliance provides comprehensive tools, technical

assistance, and professional development to support standards-based reform for schools, for school districts, and for states. The Alliance's range extends from policy to the details of practice, from the largest school districts to the smallest rural schools. The Alliance is working in over 300 schools in twenty districts in fourteen states. Its goal is to enable its partners to implement the ideas described in this book.

National Board for Professional Teaching Standards
26555 Evergreen Road, Suite 400
Southfield, MI 48076
248/351–4444
e-mail: info@nbpts.org
Web site: www.nbpts.org
The National Board for Professional Teaching Standards is an independent, nonprofit, nonpartisan organization governed by a sixty-three-member board composed of classroom teachers, school administrators, school board leaders, governors and state legislators, higher education officials, teacher union leaders, and business and community leaders. Their mission is to establish high and rigorous standards for what accomplished teachers should know and be able to do; to develop and operate a national, voluntary system to assess and certify teachers who meet these standards; and to advance related education reforms for the purpose of improving student learning in American schools.

National Center for the Accelerated Schools Project
Stanford University
CERAS 109
Stanford, CA 94305–3084
415/725–1676
e-mail: hf.cys@forsythe.stanford.edu
Web site: www-leland.stanford.edu/group/ASP/natlcenter.html
The Accelerated Schools Project is designed to improve schooling

for children in "at-risk" situations. Students are placed in accelerated school communities where staff, parents, administrators, students, district office representatives, and local community members accelerate learning by providing students with challenging activities.

National Center on Education and the Economy
700 11th Street, NW, Suite 750
Washington, DC 20001
202/783-3668
Web site: www.ncee.org
The National Center on Education and the Economy is a nonpartisan not-for-profit organization committed to the development in the United States of a standards-based education and training system. Through a series of major reports, the National Center has developed a policy agenda to serve this goal. Since its founding in 1988, it has been developing tools, technical assistance resources, and professional development programs designed to help people in many roles implement comprehensive programs of standards-based education and training. The National Center is home to New Standards, the National Alliance for Restructuring Education, and the Workforce Development Program. For a more extended description of NCEE, see the description at the beginning of the Resources section.

New American Schools
1000 Wilson Boulevard, Suite 2710
Arlington, VA 22209
703/908–9500
e-mail: info@hq.nasdc.org
Web site: www.naschools.org
New American Schools was founded to create great schools where students achieve at high levels, initially through new designs of schools and school systems, and now through implementation of those designs at the school and district levels. The current New American Schools designs include:

ATLAS Communities
Education Development Center
55 Chapel Street
Newton, MA 02160
617/969–7100
e-mail: Atlas @edc.org
Web site: www.edc.org/FSC/ATLAS
The ATLAS design centers on pathways—groups of schools
made up of high schools and feeder schools. Teams of teachers
in a pathway work together to design curriculum and assessments based on locally defined standards.

Audrey Cohen College
75 Varick Street
New York, NY 10013–1919
800/33-THINK
e-mail: JanithJ@aol.com
Web site: www.audrey-cohen.edu
The Audrey Cohen College system of education focuses student
learning on the study and achievement of meaningful purposes
for each semester's academic endeavors. An example of a
fourth-grade purpose is *We Work for Good Health*.

Co-NECT Schools
BBN Corporation
70 Fawcett Street
Cambridge, MA 02138
617/873–2683
e-mail: info@co-nect.bbn.com
Web site: co-nect.bbn.com
Co-NECT uses technology to enhance every aspect of teaching, learning, professional development, and school management. Schools are organized around small clusters of students,
and teaching and learning revolve around interdisciplinary

projects that promote critical skills and academic understanding, as well as integrating technology.

Expeditionary Learning Outward Bound
122 Mount Auburn Street
Cambridge, MA 02138
617/576–1260
e-mail: info@elob.ci.net
Web site: hugse1.harvard.edu/~elob
Expeditionary Learning draws on the power of purposeful, intellectual investigations, called learning expeditions, to improve student achievement and build character. Learning expeditions are long-term, academically rigorous, interdisciplinary studies requiring work both inside and outside the classroom.

Los Angeles Learning Centers
315 West Ninth Street, Suite 1110
Los Angeles, CA 90015
213/622–5237
e-mail: exchange@lalc.k12.ca.us
Web site: www.lalc.k12.ca.us
The Los Angeles Learning Centers design is a comprehensive K–12 model for urban schools. The curriculum and instruction are designed to ensure that all students are taught in a K–12 community, enabling new strategies to overcome barriers by addressing the health and well-being of students and their families.

Modern Red Schoolhouse Institute
208 23rd Avenue North
Nashville, TN 37203
615/320–8804
e-mail: skilgore@mrsh.org
Web site: www.mrsh.org
The Modern Red Schoolhouse Institute strives to help all students

achieve high standards through the construction of a standards-driven curriculum; use of traditional and performance-based assessments; establishment of effective organizational patterns and professional development programs; and implementation of effective community involvement strategies.

National Alliance for Restructuring Education. See earlier description in Resource D.

Roots and Wings
Elementary School Program
Center for Research on Effective Schooling
for Students Placed At Risk (CRESPAR)
Johns Hopkins University
3505 North Charles Street
Baltimore, MD 21218
800/548–4998
e-mail: bcoppersm@csos.jhu.edu
Web site: www.csos.jhu.edu /sfa/
Roots and Wings, an elementary school design, builds on the widely used Success for All reading program and incorporates science, history, and math to achieve a comprehensive academic program.

New Standards
700 11th Street, NW, Suite 750
Washington, DC 20001
202/783–3668
A partnership of the National Center on Education and the Economy and the Learning Research and Development Center at the University of Pittsburgh, as well as seventeen states and half a dozen school districts, New Standards has developed student performance examinations in English language arts, mathematics, science, and applied learning. Matching performance examinations are available

in mathematics and English language arts. Performance examinations in science are under development, as are performance standards for primary learning.

Paideia Group Inc.
P.O. Box 3423
Chapel Hill, NC 27515
919/929–0600
The Paideia Group is a nonprofit group that disseminates information about the Paideia concept and provides a forum for discussion and networking among members. It provides regional workshops, national conferences, and technical assistance to schools and districts using the Paideia framework for school reform as well as a certification program for trainers that involves working with a mentor and developing a portfolio for certification.

Panasonic Foundation Inc.
One Panasonic Way, 3G-7A
Secaucus, NJ 07094
201/392–4131
The Panasonic Foundation works with school districts and state departments of education with which it enters into five-to-ten-year partnerships to promote district- and state-level systemic, school-based, and whole-school reform. The Foundation provides direct technical assistance—not grants—to districts or states and the schools in them.

Program for School Improvement
The University of Georgia
College of Education
124 Aderhold Hall
Athens, Georgia 30602
706/542–2516
e-mail: cglick@uga.cc.uga.edu

The Program for School Improvement develops collaborations with schools, districts, and states focused on sustained school renewal through the democratization of education. Its most noted initiative is the League of Professional Schools, a network of more than one hundred schools in Georgia, Nevada, and Washington.

School Development Program
55 College Street
New Haven, CT 06510
203/ 737–4016
e-mail: charlene.vick@yale.edu
Web site: info.med.yale.edu/comer/welcome.html
Based on the belief that "it takes a whole village to raise a child," the School Development Program (also referred to as Comer Schools) is committed to the total development of all children by creating learning environments that support children's physical, cognitive, psychological, language, social, and ethical development.

Success for All Program
Center for Research on Effective Schooling
for Students Placed At Risk (CRESPAR)
Johns Hopkins University
3505 North Charles Street
Baltimore, MD 21218
800/548–4998
e-mail: bcoppersm@csos.jhu.edu
Web site: www.csos.jhu.edu/sfa/
A schoolwide program for students in grades pre-K to 5, Success for All organizes resources to ensure that virtually every student in a Chapter 1 school will reach grade 3 with adequate reading skills. Components include: one-to-one tutoring, research-based reading instruction, preschool and kindergarten programs, cooperative learning, eight-week assessments to determine reading progress, and family support.

The Pew Network for Standards-Based Reform
Center for Family, School and Community
Education Development Center, Inc.
55 Chapel Street
Newton, MA 02160
617/969–7100

The Pew Network for Standards-Based Reform, a consortium of medium-size school districts, is designed to test the proposition that new standards and assessments, if accompanied by a substantial investment in teachers' professional development aimed at producing a districtwide culture of continuous reflection and improvement, can lead to significant gains in student performance.

Resource E
Glossary

Benchmarking The disciplined search for best practices. In contrast to conventional library research, benchmarking is conducted not by studying research literature but by identifying the organizations that are the best at what they do, determining what it is that makes them successful, and figuring out how to adapt their practices so that your organization can do better.

Certificate of Initial Mastery (CIM) A credential that signifies that its holder has met standards for student performance that are as high as those the best-performing nations expect of their students at about age sixteen. The CIM is predicated on the idea that all but the most severely disabled students should meet high standards for performance in core subjects and applied learning and that the job of schools is to ensure that all students reach that goal. Students earn their certificates by earning high scores on examinations, completing coursework, and completing a capstone project. In contrast to a high school diploma, which signifies only that a student has remained in school for a certain number of years, the CIM is a certificate of accomplishment: the standards for attaining it are fixed, and the time for doing so varies.

Charter school A school operated under state or district charter by teachers, parents, or other organizations. Charter schools are effectively free from most state and local regulation. In return, the schools must meet the conditions of the charter, or it can be revoked. About half the states and the District of Columbia have laws authorizing the creation of charter schools, although the laws vary widely in the extent of autonomy provided to the schools and the extent to which they are held accountable for performance.

Class teacher   A teacher who remains with a group of students for a number of years, providing academic support and ensuring a close relationship among students, their parents, and at least one adult in the school. The practice is common in several northern European countries; in Denmark, for example, students may stay with a class teacher for up to eight years, and many students there consider the relationship with the class teacher the best feature of their early schooling.

College and career options system   A system affording a range of high-quality training and education options to young people after they meet foundation academic and applied learning standards. The options include early entry to college and college-preparatory and Advanced Placement courses. They also include *professional and technical education programs* that embrace classroom work and work-based learning and lead to employer-recognized skill credentials. The classroom work can take place in regional technical vocational schools, community colleges, technical colleges, or proprietary schools. Many students who complete these professional and technical programs will have earned both the industry-recognized skill certificate and a postsecondary degree or certificate.

Designed to allow students to determine the course that is best suited for them, the options are also intended to be flexible enough that a student can move freely from one to another. This means that a student pursuing technical training can later enter a four-year college, and vice versa.

Concept books   Publications that accompany *extended lesson books* that provide ready reference for the major concepts in each subject area over a three-year grade span. Published in paperback form to remain students' property, the books contain an outline of the major concepts, examples of work that illustrate them, and reference materials, such as tables and formulas.

Content standards   Performance descriptions; see *performance standards*.

Course of study guides   Outlines of a year's work in a classroom, including the major topics students are expected to understand, the books they are expected to read, and the projects they are expected to complete. The guides build on one another sequentially and are designed so that students who complete their work successfully each year will achieve the standards at the end of each major juncture. Teachers using *extended lesson books* should use course of study guides to see how the lessons fit into a year's program.

Cross-age peer tutoring   The practice of enlisting older students to help teach younger pupils. This type of tutoring has proved enormously beneficial to both groups of students: the younger students gain by having supplemental instruction to help them in areas where they are weak, and the older students gain by using their knowledge to teach others, a strategy cognitive research has shown to be enormously powerful in developing students' understanding.

Culminating event   The final step in a standards-based unit of study, during which students use the knowledge and skills they developed in the unit to demonstrate their understanding in a public way, such as by making a presentation to community members. During the event, the audience participates with the teachers in evaluating whether the students have met the standards for the particular event.

Distinguished educator   Kentucky's version of what is described elsewhere in this glossary as probation manager.

End-of-course examination   An assessment administered upon the completion of a program of study, similar to a final exam. Unlike traditional final exams, though, standards-based end-of-course examinations do not vary from class to class or from teacher to teacher. Instead, a common examination is administered across all the classes in a given course in a school or district and scored using common criteria based on the standards. This approach enables a school district to determine how well each cohort of test takers meets its standards. The content of the exam is embodied in a *program of study*.

Extended lesson books   Publications that outline key lessons in the form of extended lessons for students in major topic areas in each subject at each grade level. The extended lessons, which build on one another, include two or three problems; some probing questions; examples of responses that meet the standards and some that do not meet the standards, with guidance; diagnostic *rubrics*; and maps to several syllabi, including commonly used textbooks.

The extended lesson books are explicitly linked to *performance standards*. Using these books, teachers provide students with the knowledge and skills they need to meet the standards and with opportunities to produce work of the desired caliber.

High-performance management   Organizing schools and school districts to produce high-quality results. The traditional form of management, created early in the twentieth century and codified by Frederick W. Taylor, was designed to produce the maximum amount of goods at the lowest possible cost. The principles of high-performance management, by contrast, emphasize high-quality results and involve setting goals for performance, giving the people closest to delivering a service the authority and resources they need to achieve the goals, and holding them strictly accountable for producing results.

Incentives   The rewards a system offers to those who are instrumental in raising student performance (including the students) and the consequences it provides for those who are not. Currently, the incentives in school systems often reward poor performance and penalize gains in performance. For example, schools get more resources if they fail than if they succeed, and they never shut down, even if they fail consistently.

A proper system of incentives rewards schools for producing excellent results and issues severe consequences for failing to perform.

"In rewards"   A status that indicates that a school in an accountability system has exceeded its performance target and is eligible for the financial and other honors that accrue in the system. In Kentucky, where the state sets performance targets for each school and measures performance against such targets, schools that are in rewards are eligible for cash bonuses of about $2,000 per teacher, which they can spend in any way they choose.

Leadership and management team   A group of teachers (and others) in a school designated as responsible for setting the direction for the school and inspiring the staff and community to work in that direction. Collectively, the team works with the principal to build a broad consensus around goals and plans; individually, each member makes sure a particular task—standards and assessment, English language arts, instructional technology, community services and supports, and so forth—gets carried out.

A leadership and management team is distinct from a governance team, which sets overall policy for the school but is rarely held accountable for producing results.

Master schedule   The daily schedule that indicates the classes to which students and teachers are assigned and when they are held. By changing the master schedule—for example, by providing long time blocks for English and mathematics—schools can effect major changes in instruction. But there is no point in making the schedule change if there is no corresponding change in instruction.

National Skill Certificates   Credentials being created by national industry groups under the auspices of the National Skill Standards Board, a panel set up by Congress. The skill certificates will signify that the holders have the skills needed to perform with high levels of competence in the specified occupations and professions. The standards will be broad-based, to prepare students for a wide range of occupations in industries requiring similar skills. Preparation for the certificates takes place in *professional and technical education programs*.

Performance standards   Written standards consisting of performance descriptions, samples of student work, and commentaries on that work. The performance description is a succinct narrative statement of what students are expected to know and be able to do that describes what is most essential to learn in each discipline and is confined to things that can actually be assessed (which leaves out, for example, such ideals as "love of learning"). Performance descriptions are often referred to as content standards.

Examples of actual student work are matched to the performance descriptions so that the reader has a vivid image of what it actually takes to meet the standard. The commentaries draw attention to features of the student work that are judged to meet the standard, along with the reasons that the expert graders made that judgment. This presents a clear picture of what it takes to meet the standard.

Probation manager   An educator from outside a school that is on academic probation who works closely with the principal to develop an improvement plan. For example, the Chicago district placed 109 schools with very low test scores on probation and gave them a year to raise scores above a designated threshold. Each school was assigned a probation manager and was required to affiliate with an external technical assistance network. After the first year, test scores rose sharply in most of the probationary schools, and the district levied sanctions against only seven high schools.

Professional and technical education programs Programs designed to prepare students to earn *National Skill Certificates* and qualify for high-skill employment or higher education. The programs combine structured training on the job site with class work. Such programs can be created in regional technical and vocational high schools, community colleges, technical colleges, and proprietary schools.

Professional development The search for information and professional competence that a faculty engages in to improve their capacity to help the students in their school meet the standards. As we see it, the priorities set by a school for the use of professional development should be determined by an analysis of the skills and knowledge the staff will need to carry out the school's plan.

Public engagement The enlistment of support for the educational program from parents and the public. Schools and school systems often fail to engage the public before announcing an education initiative and end up whipped by the backlash. Public engagement begins with listening to the public's concerns and making sure that these concerns are responded to. In that way, the public will share the schools' goals, and the schools can pursue them with the support of the people they need to ensure that the goals are met.

Reconstitution Breaking up the faculty and staff of a failing school and rebuilding it from scratch. A number of districts, including Chicago, New York City, and San Francisco, have implemented reconstitution plans that have shown results. In some cases, the district reassigns teachers to other schools in the district; in others, teachers may reapply for their old jobs. In either case, the idea is to destroy a dysfunctional environment and replace it with one committed to improvement.

Rubric A scoring guide that indicates the criteria on which a piece of student work will be evaluated, based on standards for student performance. Rubrics indicate the characteristics of work at each level of performance, from work that barely shows evidence of meeting the standard to work that meets the standard to work that exceeds the standard.

Students have a better chance of meeting standards if they have a well-developed understanding of what high-quality work looks like and how to produce it. Once developed, rubrics should be displayed prominently so that students, parents, and teachers are familiar with them and understand what constitutes standards-level work.

Site-based management   The practice, implemented in a number of districts, of shifting authority over school policies from the central office to local schools. The idea behind site-based management had its origins in the principles of *high-performance management*. But it has not been implemented well. In many cases, the authority of site-based management teams is quite limited, so they end up spending their time on trivial matters. In others, the site-based management teams were constituted as a governance mechanism, but one that is not held accountable for results. Members of these site-based management teams often feel more obligated to the constituencies that elected them than to the students. Some principals defer to the committees so that no one ends up feeling or being accountable for student performance. As we see it, it is fine to have site-based management teams, as long as they are clearly in charge (in which case they should make the key decisions and receive the rewards and be subject to the sanctions of the new incentive system), or the principal should be clearly in charge (in which case, that person should be subject to the rewards and sanctions). The first principle is to locate responsibility and authority in the same person or body that will be held accountable for results.

Standards-based education   A way of operating schools and education systems so that standards for student performance are at the center, and the sole objective for everyone in the system is ensuring that students meet the standards.

Standards-referenced assessment   Assessment to determine whether students have met preestablished standards. Standards-referenced assessment systems provide information about how students perform in terms of a set of standards. Thus student performance is not compared to that of other students or to a "national average" but rather to an absolute level of performance determined by the standards. Students are prepared for standards-referenced examinations by teachers who teach to the standards—not to any particular test.

The beauty of standards-based learning is its unifying or integrating quality. It ensures that curriculum, instruction, professional development, and assessment are all based on the same academic expectations and thus can fulfill the goal of raising achievement levels for all students.

Summer effect   The phenomenon whereby the learning of most low-income students deteriorates over the long break between June and September, whereas the learning of most high-income students increases over the same period. The best way to alleviate the effect is to extend the school year for students whose performance is low, to ensure that students are using their minds during the summer and not forgetting what they have learned the year before.

Tracking   The practice of grouping students by purported ability and providing them with an educational program deemed appropriate for that level of ability. American schools tend to send students down divergent tracks as early as first grade, when readers are placed into "ability" groups that face differing expectations.

The problem with tracking is that it is nearly impossible to jump from one track to another, and thus by the end of elementary school, students from different tracks have had very different educational experiences. At that stage, it would be nearly impossible for students from the lower track to meet the high standards expected of those in the upper track.

Vouchers   Certificates given to parents to enable them to send their children, at public expense, to private or religious schools. Voucher proponents claim that such systems will improve public education by injecting free-market competition into the system. Voucher opponents see no evidence that vouchers improve academic performance where they have been tried and claim that their widespread use will weaken or destroy the public schools.

Resource F
Annotated Bibliography

This book was not conceived of as a scholarly volume, but we thought that some of our readers might welcome some suggestions for further reading and some comments on those suggestions. We make no claim to completeness here. There are many other books and articles that you might profit from. But all of these are useful.

Other Works on These Topics

For a much fuller treatment of the historical background, economic context, and policy implications of the themes dealt with in this book, see Ray Marshall and Marc Tucker, *Thinking for a Living: Education and the Wealth of Nations* (New York: Basic Books, 1992).

Also, the recommendations in the following two reports led to the work that lies behind this book: Carnegie Task Force on Teaching as a Profession, *A Nation Prepared: Teachers for the 21st Century* (Washington, D.C.: Carnegie Corporation of New York, 1986); and Commission on the Skills of the American Workforce, *America's Choice: high skills or low wages!* (Rochester, N.Y.: National Center on Education and the Economy, 1990).

A book that sounds themes similar to those expressed in our own work but with different—and great—strengths is Richard Murnane and Frank Levy, *Teaching the New Basic Skills: Principles for*

Educating Children to Thrive in a Changing Economy (New York: Free Press, 1996).

Works from the Past

Four books have made a particularly deep impression on the way we have interpreted the history of American education in this book: Raymond E. Callahan, *Education and the Cult of Efficiency: A Study of the Social Forces That Have Shaped the Administration of Public Schools* (Chicago: University of Chicago Press, 1962); Lawrence A. Cremin, *The Transformation of the American School: Progressivism in American Education, 1876–1957* (New York: Knopf, 1961); Richard Hofstadter, *Anti-Intellectualism in American Life* (New York: Knopf, 1963); and David B. Tyack, *The One Best System: A History of American Urban Education* (Cambridge, Mass.: Harvard University Press, 1974).

Education in Other Countries

Much of what we told you about education in other countries comes from the notes we have made from our many trips to those countries. But there are many fine books about education abroad, and two that we have found particularly insightful on the subject of Asian education are Harold W. Stevenson and James W. Stigler, *The Learning Gap* (New York: Touchstone Press/Simon & Schuster, 1992); and Merry White, *The Japanese Educational Challenge: A Commitment to Children* (New York: Free Press, 1987).

Though billed as a study of American achievement, the recent Third International Mathematics and Science Study must go down as one of the finest international comparative studies of education ever undertaken and is must reading: *Pursuing Excellence: A Study of U.S. Eighth-Grade Mathematics and Science Teaching, Learning, Curriculum and Achievement in International Context* (Washington,

D.C.: U.S. Department of Education, 1996). Another volume in the same series applies to the fourth grade.

Performance Standards and Assessment

A number of good resources on the subject of performance standards and assessment have appeared recently. Three of our favorites are American Federation of Teachers, *Making Standards Matter* (Washington, D.C.: American Federation of Teachers, 1996); Diane Ravitch, *National Standards in American Education: A Citizen's Guide* (Washington, D.C.: Brookings Institution, 1995); and Robert Rothman, *Measuring Up: Standards, Assessment, and School Reform* (San Francisco: Jossey-Bass, 1995).

Most of the subject-matter teachers associations, in addition to the American Association for the Advancement of Science, the National Science Board, and several other organizations, have offered national standards for their disciplines.

The National Board for Professional Teaching Standards has issued performance standards for teachers in many disciplines and school levels that have strong implications for student performance standards.

Two school reform networks, the Core Knowledge Foundation and the Modern Red Schoolhouse Institute, have also developed standards in the core disciplines.

We cannot resist including a reference to our own performance standards, which include, besides the standards themselves, a lengthy discussion of the standards that ought to be used to judge performance standards, as well as a commentary on the nature of performance standards: *Performance Standards* (Washington, D.C.: New Standards, 1996) in three volumes, available from the National Center on Education and the Economy.

Vincent Breglio, of RSM Associates, conducted a series of focus groups for New Standards while the standards were being developed that proved immensely valuable in the development process. His findings are reported in a monograph: Vincent Breglio, *Community Reactions to New Standards* (Lanham, Md.: RSM Associates, 1995).

Vince's findings in this report are fully corroborated by an independent report from the Public Agenda Foundation, *Americans' Views on Standards: An Assessment by Public Agenda,* prepared for the 1996 Education Summit (New York: Public Agenda Foundation, 1996).

New Standards reference examinations in mathematics and English language arts at the fourth-, eighth-, and tenth-grade levels are available from Harcourt Brace Educational Measurement, San Antonio, Texas.

Curriculum and Instruction

In the area of curriculum and instruction, these books and their authors have had a decisive impact on our thinking: Jerome S. Brunner, *The Process of Education* (Cambridge, Mass.: Harvard University Press, 1963); Jerome S. Brunner, *Toward a Theory of Instruction* (Cambridge, Mass.: Harvard University Press, 1966); John Dewey, *The School and Society* (Chicago: University of Chicago Press, 1899); Lauren Resnick and Leopold Klopfer, "An Overview," in *Toward the Thinking Curriculum: Current Cognitive Research (1989 Yearbook of the Association for Supervision and Curriculum Development),* eds. Lauren Resnick and Leopold Kloper (Alexandria, Va.: Association for Supervision and Curriculum Development, 1989); and Alfred North Whitehead, *The Aims of Education* (Old Tappan, N.J.: Macmillan, 1929).

The Thinking Curriculum

With respect to the issue of reading, we think the following will give you a good account of the kind of balanced approach we have recommended: Marilyn J. Adams, *Beginning to Read: Thinking and Learning About Print* (Cambridge, Mass.: MIT Press, 1990).

By far the best book we know of on the uses and abuses of modern information technology in education is Seymour Papert, *Mindstorms: Children, Computers, and Powerful Ideas* (New York: Basic Books, 1980).

For a good example of the kind of professional development materials we think teachers need, see *Standards-Driven Curriculum: Course I* (Washington, D.C.: National Center on Education and the Economy, 1996).

For a good example of a curriculum designed to take students from wherever they are and bring them up to a high achievement level, we suggest that you write to Gil Lopez, director of the Comprehensive Math and Science Program (CMSP), at Columbia University's School of Engineering, 51 Astor Place, New York, NY 10003; (212) 228–0950; e-mail: cmsp@aol.com

Morality in Education

The first book we would recommend on the moral dimension in education is F. Clark Power, Ann Higgins, and Lawrence Kohlberg, *Lawrence Kohlberg's Approach to Moral Education* (New York: Columbia University Press, 1989). Kohlberg's work in schools focused on the moral decisions teachers and students face as they resolve problems such as cheating, stealing, and substance use. Kohlberg called for schools not to just teach about democratic citizenship (it is not what you say but what you do) but to act as and be democratic societies.

Also worthy of your attention are Thomas Lickona, *Educating for Character: How Our Schools Can Teach Respect and Responsibility* (New York: Bantam Books, 1992); Thomas Lickona, *Raising Good Children* (New York: Bantam Books, 1994); Thomas J. Sergiovanni, *Moral Leadership: Getting to the Heart of School Improvement* (San Francisco: Jossey-Bass Publishers, 1992); and Robert Coles, *The Moral Intelligence of Children* (New York: Random House, 1997).

Primary and Secondary Schools

The two best works we have read on elementary and middle school education in recent years are *It's Elementary*, (Sacramento, Calif.: Department of Education Task Force on Elementary Education, 1992); and Task Force on Young Adolescents, *Turning Points* (New York: Carnegie Corporation of New York, 1989).

The powerful image of the "shopping mall high school" was drawn directly from Arthur G. Powell, Eleanor Farrar, and David K. Cohen, *The Shopping Mall High School: Winners and Losers in the Educational Marketplace* (Boston: Houghton Mifflin, 1985).

Although Deborah Meier and Ted Sizer disagree with our advocacy of standards that come from outside the school and its faculty, their work is full of insights that should form part of the intellectual foundation of every educator. See Deborah Meier, *The Power of Their Ideas: Lessons for America from a Small School in Harlem* (Boston: Beacon Press, 1995); Theodore Sizer, *Horace's Compromise: The Dilemma of the American High School* (Boston: Houghton Mifflin, 1984); Theodore Sizer, *Horace's School: Redesigning the American High School* (Boston: Houghton Mifflin, 1992); and Theodore Sizer, *Horace's Hope: What Works for the American High School* (Boston: Houghton Mifflin, 1996).

Modern Management, Public Education, and Incentive Systems

Back in the early 1980s, David Kearns led Xerox out of almost certain collapse to become one of the toughest competitors in the world. When we read Gary Jacobson and John Hillkirk, *Xerox: American Samurai* (Old Tappan, N.J.: Macmillan, 1986), we kept seeing parallels to public education, both in the nature of the problems faced and the solutions that Kearns and his colleagues devised.

Much earlier, on reading Peter Drucker, *The Age of Discontinuity: Guidelines to Our Changing Society* (New York: HarperCollins,

1968), we realized that teaching is not a profession at all in Drucker's terms and will not be one until teachers take on all the characteristics of knowledge workers and do knowledge work in the ways that Drucker describes. The conception of how schools and districts should be organized, managed, and run that is described in our book owes a great intellectual debt to Drucker and the argument he makes here.

We have found the work of Lee Bolman and Terry Deal very valuable as we endeavored to apply modern management theory to the public schools. Deal has spent a professional lifetime working in both worlds, and the ease with which he moves between them is reflected in Lee G. Bolman and Terrence E. Deal, *Reframing Organizations: Artistry, Choice, and Leadership* (San Francisco: Jossey-Bass, 1991); Lee G. Bolman and Terrence E. Deal, *Leading with Soul: An Uncommon Journey of Spirit* (San Francisco: Jossey-Bass, 1995); and Lee G. Bolman and Terrence E. Deal, *Becoming a Teacher Leader: From Isolation to Collaboration* (Thousand Oaks, Calif.: Corwin Press, 1994).

For a sense of the contribution that David Hornbeck has made to recent American thinking about the use of incentives in public education, we suggest you take a look at House Bill 990, available in four volumes from the Kentucky Legislative Research Commission. If that seems too daunting, you might want to look at the much briefer undated monograph "Professional Responsibility Index," published by the School District of Philadelphia.

The Kentucky document reflects Hornbeck's first effort to apply modern ideas about incentives at the state policy level; the Philadelphia one transfers those ideas to the district level.

For a good general survey of current ideas and literature in the management and organization of American education, see Allan R. Odden, *Educational Leadership for America's Schools* (New York: McGraw-Hill, 1995).

Notes

Chapter One

1. Commission on the Skills of the American Workforce, *America's Choice: high skills or low wages!* (Rochester, NY: National Center on Education and the Economy, 1990).

2. E. L. Baker and R. L. Linn, "The Psychology of Educational Reform: Goal Three" In R. Short and R. C. Talley (Eds.), *A Psychology of Educational Reform: Psychological Perspectives on Improving America's Schools* (Washington, DC: American Psychological Association, forthcoming).

   Christopher T. Cross and Scott Joftus, "Are Academic Standards a Threat or an Opportunity?" (Reston, VA: *National Association of Secondary School Principals' Bulletin,* September 1997).

   Linda Darling-Hammond, *The Right to Learn: A Blueprint for School Reform* (San Francisco, CA: Jossey-Bass, 1997).

   Denis P. Doyle and Susan Pimentel, *Raising the Standard: An Eight-Step Action Guide for Schools and Communities* (Sherman Oaks, CA: Corwin Press, 1997).

   Chester E. Finn Jr., *We Must Take Charge* (New York: Free Press, 1991).

   John Murphy and Jeffry Schiller, *Transforming America's Schools* (Peru, IL: Open Court, 1992).

John O'Neil, "On the New Standards Project: A Conversation with Lauren Resnick and Warren Simmons" (Arlington, VA: *Educational Leadership*, February 1993).

Diane Ravitch, *National Standards in American Education: A Citizen's Guide* (Washington, DC: Brookings Institution, 1995).

Grant P. Wiggins, *Educative Assessment: Assessment to Inform and Improve Student Performance* (San Francisco: Jossey-Bass, forthcoming).

Dennie Palmer Wolf, "Portfolio Assessment: Sampling Student Work" (Arlington, VA: *Educational Leadership* 46, no. 7, April 1989).

3. Mark Musick, *Setting Education Standards High Enough* (Atlanta, GA: Southern Regional Education Board, 1996).

4. E. D. Hirsch, *The Schools We Need: Why We Don't Have Them* (New York: Doubleday, 1996).

5. Alfred North Whitehead, *The Aims of Education* (New York: Macmillan, 1929).

6. Vince Breglio, *Community Reactions to New Standards* (Lanham, MD: RSM Associates, 1995). (Monograph).

7. Public Agenda Foundation, *Americans' Views on Standards: An Assessment by Public Agenda* (New York: Public Agenda Foundation, 1996).

Chapter Two

1. *Pursuing Excellence: A Study of U. S. Eighth-Grade Mathematics and Science Teaching, Learning, Curriculum and Achievement in International Context* (Washington, DC: U.S. Department of Education, 1996).

2. L. B. Resnick, *Instruction and Learning Profile* (Pittsburgh: University of Pittsburgh, Learning Research and Development Center, forthcoming).

3. Sally Hampton, memorandum to authors, 1997.

4. National Center on Education and the Economy, *Standards-Driven Curriculum: Course I* (Washington, DC: National Center on Education and the Economy, 1997).

5. See Resource D: Resources for Standards-Based Education, Core Knowledge Foundation.

6. Harold W. Stevenson and James W. Stigler, *The Learning Gap* (New York: Touchstone/Simon & Schuster, 1992).

7. Learning in Motion, *Measurement in Motion* (Santa Cruz, CA: Learning in Motion, 1995).

8. ABC World Reference, *3–D Atlas 1997* (Texas: Eakin Publications, 1996).

9. Seymour Papert, *The Connected Family: Bridging the Digital Generation Gap* (Atlanta, GA: Longstreet Press, 1996).

Chapter Three

1. See Resource D: Resources for Standards-Based Education, Comprehensive Math and Science Program.

2. David Tatel, conversation with authors.

3. See Resource D: Resources for Standards-Based Education.

Chapter Four

1. Stephen R. Covey, *The Seven Habits of Highly Effective People* (New York: Fireside, 1990).

   Stephen R. Covey, *Principle-Centered Leadership* (New York: Simon and Schuster, 1990, 1991).

2. Marilyn J. Adams, *Beginning to Read: Thinking and Learning About Print* (Cambridge, MA: MIT Press, 1990).

   Jeanne S. Chall, Vicki A. Jacobs, and Luke E. Baldwin, *The Reading Crisis: Why Poor Children Fall Behind* (Cambridge: Harvard University Press, 1990).

3. James Kulick, Robert Bangert, and George Williams. "Effects of Computer-Based Teaching on Secondary School Students." *Journal of Educational Psychology, 75(1),* 1983.

4. L. B. Resnick and L. E. Klopfer (Eds.). *Toward the Thinking Curriculum: Current Cognitive Research (1989 Yearbook of the ASCD)*

(Alexandria, VA: Association for Supervision and Curriculum Development, 1989. Also in Spanish: Curriculum y cognition).

L. B. Resnick, *Education and Learning to Think,* (Washington, DC: National Academy Press, 1987).

5. Iris R. Weiss, Michael C. Matti, and P. Sean Smith, *Report of the 1993 National Survey of Science and Mathematics Education* (Chapel Hill, NC: Horizon Research, 1994).

Chapter Five

1. James Bryant Conant, *The American High School Today: A First Report to Interested Citizens* (New York: McGraw-Hill, 1959).

James Bryant Conant, *Comprehensive High School: A Second Report to Interested Citizens* (New York: McGraw-Hill, 1967).

2. Arthur G. Powell, Eleanor Farrar, and David K. Cohen, *The Shopping Mall High School: Winners and Losers in the Educational Marketplace* (Boston: Houghton Mifflin, 1985).

Afterword to the Paperback Edition
The America's Choice School Design

When *Standards for Our Schools* was first published in 1998, the National Center on Education and the Economy (NCEE), the organization we lead, was in the process of creating a new program called the America's Choice School Design. Our aim was to apply everything we had learned in the United States and abroad about using standards-based systems to raise student achievement, in order to create the most powerful school designs we could come up with. By "school design," we mean a specification for how such a school would be organized and led, what the standards would look like, how student progress would be assessed, what the curriculum would look like, what instructional materials would be used, how classrooms would be organized, what sort of pedagogy would be used, what would be done to enable students who are behind to catch up, how student discipline would be handled, and so on.

What this amounts to is taking the principles that have been discussed in this book and answering the question, "What would a school look like and how would it be run if it was designed to implement these principles?"

We put together designs for elementary schools, K–8 schools, middle schools, and high schools. We aimed to design schools that we would love to have our own children attend but that would also be great schools for students who do not have the advantages our children have and that would enable such students to meet high standards no matter what their level of accomplishment was when they entered the school. That is a tall order.

We also set out to develop the capacity to deliver the technical assistance, training, and professional development that states, districts, and schools implementing the designs would need in order to be successful. You might ask why that was necessary. Surely any competent educator could act on the principles laid out in this book to come up with a design for implementing them, buy the necessary materials, figure out a way to train the faculty, and "just do it." We discovered that it is not so simple. The New Standards Project had to invest more than $40 million in the development of the kinds of standards and examinations that are needed to drive a high-quality standards-based education system.

When we had done that, the teachers who had been involved in that effort reported to us that despite the great quantity and variety of instructional materials available in the United States, they could not assemble a set that could be used to get their students to meet the standards. They turned out to be right. Because there is no agreement in this country, as there is in other countries, on which topics in each core subject in the curriculum are to be taught at particular grade levels, textbook publishers are forced to cram a very large number of topics between the covers of the text, each treated in a very cursory manner. What is mainly left out is the conceptual basis of the subject, the very thing on which real understanding depends. So we discovered that we had to create our own curriculum and instructional materials in English language arts and mathematics, another very large investment of time and money.

But even that was not enough. Our aim was to get all students up to high standards, no matter where they started, even if that was many grade levels behind. So we had to create curricula in English language arts and mathematics that included techniques and materials for greatly accelerating student progress for students who are substantially behind, which required not only more curriculum development but also the solution of many problems of school scheduling and classroom management.

These points are only illustrative. What we are getting at is that the actual implementation of a standards-based approach required a scale of investment of time and money in development that is beyond any school or district. And once the investment has been made in new materials, tools, and approaches to such things as scheduling and classroom organization, another large investment must be made in the development of effective ways to train school faculties to implement these tools well.

We started in the 1998–1999 school year with 47 schools. As this is being written, we are beginning the 2001–2002 school year with more than 460 schools in the network, a tenfold increase in three short years, making the America's Choice School Design network one of the fastest-growing comprehensive school designs in the nation. We have been roughly doubling in size each year we have been in operation.

Performance Standards

It will come as no surprise to readers of this book that the designs begin with the use of the New Standards performance standards. We use them to complement the standards of the states in which we work. Recalling from the early chapters in this book the distinction between content standards and performance standards, content standards are narrative statements of what students should know and be able to do. Typically, state standards are content standards. Performance standards are built around examples of student work that meet the standards. In our work in America's Choice schools, school faculties use the state standards to determine what topics they need to address and the performance standards to provide examples of what student work needs to look like to meet the standard. Everywhere we work, students who do well on the New Standards performance standards and reference examinations also do well on their state standards and accountability tests.

When we started the America's Choice School Design program, we asked the Consortium for Policy Research in Education (CPRE), one of the most respected independent evaluation organizations in education, to evaluate the America's Choice program. Their first report was issued in January 2001. The report focused on an analysis of the performance of America's Choice schools in three districts: Plainfield, New Jersey; Duval County (Jacksonville), Florida; and Rochester, New York. In each case, the CPRE team compared the performance of fourth-grade students in America's Choice schools with the performance of fourth graders in schools in the same district with comparable student bodies with respect to the proportion of students reaching the state standards. The results are shown in Figures AF.1, AF.2, and AF.3.

Figure AF.1. Percentage of Fourth Graders Meeting the Standard in English Language Arts on State Accountability Test in Plainfield, New Jersey

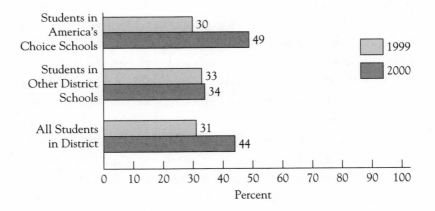

Figure AF.2. Percentage of Fourth Graders Meeting the Standard in Writing on Florida FCAT Test in Duval County (Jacksonville), Florida

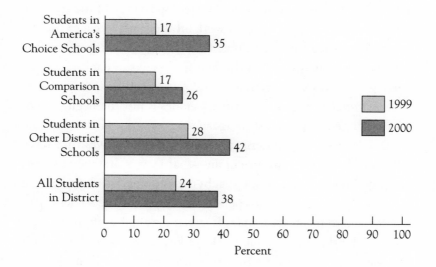

Figure AF.3. Percentage of Fourth Graders Meeting the Standard on New York State Language Arts Test in Rochester, New York

Curriculum Built Around the Standards

Over the last several years, NCEE's development team has been working hard to build one of the most highly aligned and most powerful instructional systems anywhere. The America's Choice curriculum materials are closely matched, of course, to the standards and assessments. They eliminate everything but the key topics that are needed, and those topics are studied in considerable depth, so that students focus only on what is most important and have time to thoroughly master one topic before going on to the next.

The New Standards literacy standards for the primary grades have attracted national acclaim. We have built a two-and-one-half-hour block for literacy around those standards. For half an hour every day, the students work on their skills—mainly phonics. Then there is an hour of readers workshop and an hour of writers workshop. We have worked out a standard set of classroom rituals and routines so that the class will settle into a regular rhythm that allows the teacher to work with the whole group for a defined part of the class time and with individuals and small groups in other parts of the schedule. These routines are designed so that all of the students are fully engaged in meaningful work all the time. Because the rituals and routines are common across classrooms, neither students nor teachers have to spend the first few weeks of each new year learning how to work together.

The literacy program for primary grades is just the beginning of our complete K–10 English language arts program. Following the primary literacy component, the program follows what we have called our hundred-day curriculum—that is, it is designed so that, when it is taught by average teachers to average students in one hundred days of regular class periods every year, those students can be expected to meet the standards, given reasonable effort on their part. Students read multiple works of key authors, studying their development and learning how they used particular literary techniques to achieve their effects. They also work to master a variety of genres, starting in each case with the basics and becoming progressively more sophisticated as they go through the grades. Grade by grade, they learn to compare their work to the standards, using rubrics to make the comparisons, and they get better and better at identifying what they need to do to be better and better readers and writers. All the way along, the work in their reading and writing workshops is complemented by steady development of their skills in areas from spelling to diction. Because the students are expected to meet the standards, they will become able readers and writers in a variety of genres ranging from narrative fiction and poetry to the kinds of reports that people write and read in the workplace.

In mathematics, our aim was to develop a curriculum that would enable all students to master introductory and intermediate algebra, geometry, statistics, and probability and to study calculus in high school should they choose to do so. The emphasis throughout is on students' mastery of skills and core concepts, as well as their ability to apply what they know to real-world problems of a kind that they have not seen before.

Safety Nets Built into the Curriculum

One of the toughest challenges we faced was to design curriculum and instructional materials that would enable students who are far behind to catch up. The idea is to create a series of safety nets for students, set up so that a student who needs only a little help may use only one layer of the safety net, whereas a student who needs a lot of help may take advantage of many layers of the safety net system.

The hundred-day curriculum provides the first safety net. There are 180 days in the average school year. About 30 of those days are used for noninstructional purposes. If only 100 days of the balance are used for the hundred-day curriculum, that leaves 50 days for the teacher to supplement the core curriculum. But if the students are unable to reach the standard in 100 days, then there are up to 50 additional days available for the teacher to go over the material in a different way, in more depth, or more slowly, doing whatever is necessary to make sure no one is left behind.

But that may not be enough. We will take one very important example: middle school and high school students who failed to become proficient readers in elementary school. These students account for a very high proportion of high school dropouts, students with discipline problems, and people who go on to spend much of their life behind bars. There are high schools in the United States at which 80 percent or more of the students do not read well, and there are very few high schools without any students who are not proficient readers.

For these students and for students who enter secondary school equally far behind in mathematics, we have created double-period courses designed to get them back on track. We built on the best research available to create a curriculum that gives middle school and high school teachers the skills and knowledge they need to make sure that every one of their students reads and reads well.

The corresponding course in our math curriculum is designed to make sure that students who end elementary school not really understanding the math they have studied get what they need to really understand the basic concepts underlying the algebra and geometry that will be at the center of our middle school mathematics curriculum. American students do quite well when they are asked to perform arithmetic calculations in a form just like the form of the problems they worked in elementary school. But they tend to fall apart when they get to middle school algebra and geometry, because they do not really understand the concepts underlying the arithmetic they studied. For the same reason, they often have trouble applying the arithmetic skills they have to unfamiliar kinds of problems. This lack of understanding of basic mathematical concepts can be just as devastating in its effects on students' capacity to go on in mathematics as the lack of decoding and basic comprehension skills can be in the reading arena. Therefore, these special double-period courses are extremely important components of our safety net program.

Even the double-period courses may not be enough for some students, so to these initial layers of the safety net we added tutoring programs before and after school and on Saturdays. These tutoring programs are designed to match the curriculum that the students get during the school day, including the double-period catch-up courses, so that they will have the maximum effect on student learning.

Innovative Use of Faculty

Instruction is at the core, but there is a lot more to a great school than its instructional program, just as there is a lot more to students than their cognitive development. We introduce the idea of the class teacher (described in Chapter Four) in the elementary school and retain that feature of the design right through the high school. The elementary school design also includes the idea of specialization among elementary teachers that we described in Chapter Four.

In the middle school design, because American middle schools are typically much larger than in other countries and American students are much more likely to become alienated and lost, we focus not just on the cognitive needs of the students but also on creating a school environment in which students get the kind of personal attention from the faculty that they need at that age. We strongly advocate building middle schools and high schools of no more than six hundred students, so that the faculty and student body can become a genuine community in which the students feel that the adults know who they are and really care about them and their development. Ideally, these smaller learning environments can be created in separate buildings. When that is not possible, we advocate creating multiple autonomous schools within a larger school building. If, for some reason, that cannot be done, we advocate creating a house system that provides a small learning community for the faculty and students assigned to each house of about four hundred students.

The same elements are present in the high school design. In the high school, the class teacher also becomes an adviser to the students in his or her class, taking on some of the responsibilities of the guidance staff for students who are very well known to that teacher.

Get Students Ready for College Without Remediation

The goal of the whole program, from kindergarten through high school, is to get all the students ready for college without remediation. That standard—ready for college without remediation—is not just a slogan; it is an academic standard that must be met in order to progress from the lower-division program to the upper-division program in high school. Prior to meeting this standard, from kindergarten through the end of the lower division, all students are expected to take the same core curriculum, because they are all striving to meet the same standard.

When the students reach that standard, around the end of their sophomore year in high school, they receive an Academic Foundation Certificate. They then have choices they can make. If they stay in high school—and the vast majority will—they go on in the upper division to what we call an "early college academy." One of these early college programs is a fairly traditional but demanding college-prep program that includes several Advanced Placement courses and is focused on the humanities. A variation on this theme incorporates many of the same courses as are found in the Humanities Early College Academy but focuses instead on science, technology, and mathematics. This is the Mathematics and Science Early College Academy. The third choice is the Applied Learning and Technology Early College Academy. The academic standards in this academy are as high as in the other two alternatives, but the pedagogy is very different. Much of the work is problem-based and project-based, and the students learn a lot about how to manage their own learning. To successfully complete an upper-division early college program, the student will have to meet the standard in the required courses and successfully complete a major project.

Some students will not meet the standards for the Academic Foundation Certificate by the end of their sophomore year and will need to take more time to do it. A few may drop out. Our high school design includes a design for a dropout recovery program— the Center for Independent Studies. The aim is to make sure, one way or another, that all students complete and that all meet the standards for the Academic Foundation Certificate.

It is also true that some students who meet the standards for the Academic Foundation Certificate will have picked out a skilled trade or occupation that they wish to train for. Since these students have already met a standard that qualifies them to go to college without remediation, according to the America's Choice design, they can go on to a community college or technical college to get a two-year degree in the technical arena they are interested in. As we pointed out earlier in this book, it is our opinion that high schools cannot successfully be all things to all students. It is no longer possible for any but the exceptional American high school to offer the quality of equipment and teaching staff necessary to support the up-to-date courses that graduates would need to qualify for good jobs in highly technical trades and occupations. Students who graduate from these two-year programs will get their high school diploma when they get their associate degree.

Leadership and Professional Development

We have given a lot of thought to the leadership structure of America's Choice schools. In the elementary schools, one faculty member becomes the primary coach and another becomes the upper elementary coach. The primary coach is mainly responsible for leading the implementation of the primary literacy program. The upper elementary coach is responsible for implementation of the design in the upper grades. These are full-time positions. Another faculty member, who may not be full-time in this position, is responsible for coordinating implementation of the program with parents and the larger community. The leadership team for the school consists of the principal, these three people, and anyone else the principal thinks appropriate.

In the middle schools, the leadership team includes the principal, a design coach, a parent and community coordinator, a literacy coach, a math coach, a science lead, and other department representatives. In this scheme, the design coach works with the principal to pull together all the elements of the design in the school. The high school leadership team looks much like the middle school team, though it will usually be larger because the organizational structure of the school is more complex.

The people serving in the roles we have just described are crucial to the implementation of the design. This is true of the principal in obvious ways. But it is also true of the others, because both the principal and the other people named have extensive training from the America's Choice staff over a period of years and most have formal roles in training and supporting the faculty of their own school.

The common complaint about professional development is that it is unrelated to the ongoing work of the school, given once, and never subsequently supported. America's Choice training is just the opposite. First, the implementation of the design takes place over a period that generally ranges from three to five years, proceeding through a series of stages during that period. A school does not move on to the next stage until it can show that it has mastered the preceding stage. The people who hold the roles just described receive continual support for their professional development throughout the implementation period. One approach used by the America's Choice program employs many of the principles of effective apprenticeship. Participants are introduced to a new technique or tool and given a chance to see how it is used by someone who is very experienced with it, as well as an opportunity to interact with that person and their colleagues to discuss the technique, its research basis, and the ways that it can be used in a variety of circumstances. They then return to their school to try it out with real students. In the next session, they gather once again with faculty members from other schools and discuss the work produced by their students when they tried out the new material or technique. This inevitably leads to an intense discussion of the student work and the teaching strategies that produced it. Then the whole process is repeated as new material or another technique is introduced. This apprenticeship style of learning characterizes virtually all of our work with school faculties.

Other approaches include regular faculty study groups that might focus on analysis of a relevant issue or introduce a new element of the program so that its implementation can be planned by the faculty for that particular subject. Or a teachers meeting might focus on the analysis of performance data for students in a particular subject at a particular grade level, with the aim of identifying weaknesses in their performance and agreeing on the strategies to be used to address those weaknesses. Sometimes the whole faculty might gather for a session of the Book of the Month Club, in which the principal chooses a book for the whole school to focus on each month, which gives the principal a chance to make a personal statement about what he or she values most and thereby to seize the moral leadership of the school.

Standards are always present. Examples of student work that meets the standards are the constant ingredient in the professional development and, indeed, in the life of the school. What does work that meets the standards look like? Let's hang students' work that meets the standards in our classrooms and in the hallways, so that everyone knows how proud we are of what we are accomplishing. How did you get your kids to do that? How can I get my kids to do that? How can I get more kids to do that? Look at how many more of my kids can do that this year than last year!

Training of the principal, coaches, and coordinators is an essential ingredient of the implementation plan, but it is not just a matter of training them and hoping that something useful will happen in the school. The literacy coaches, for example, are expected and trained to select a particularly promising teacher and to work with that teacher to establish a model of literacy teaching in that teacher's classroom. When that is done, the coach moves on to the next teacher in that grade level, until all the classrooms at that grade level are model classrooms. Then the process is repeated, grade by grade, until all the classrooms have been fully engaged in the process.

A Design That Works

There is much more to the unfolding of the design in a school than the process just described. There is the school planning process, in which the school faculty are trained to analyze carefully the data on student performance against the standards and to use that analysis to focus the resources of the school on those areas where the students need the most help to reach the standards. There is the work with the master schedule, to make sure that the highest-priority needs of the students drive the schedule rather than the needs of the schedule driving the allocation of faculty resources to the students. There is the 25 Book Campaign, a commitment to making sure that every student reads twenty-five books a year, which is not only a tool for expanding the working vocabulary of the students and a vital ingredient in the crucial process of deepening reading comprehension, but also a hugely successful way to get the community behind the school. Of course, there is much more.

The America's Choice School Design is being used in tiny schools serving the Mohawk Nation on New York State's border with Canada, as well as in large schools in Brooklyn. There are America's Choice schools in the coalfields of the Cumberland Plateau in deeply rural Kentucky as well as in the inner city in Newark, New Jersey. There is an America's Choice school in St. Paul, Minnesota, serving students who come mostly from families of Southeast Asian Hmong highlanders. More than a third of the schools in Duval County (Jacksonville), Florida, the sixteenth-largest school district in the United States, are America's Choice schools, as well as a large proportion of the low-performing schools in Georgia. Many of the first America's Choice schools are in Hawaii, and a swiftly growing number in Los Angeles are among the newest.

There are America's Choice schools serving students who live in the depths of rural and urban poverty and others serving students from well-kept, affluent middle-class suburban homes. The program is working to lift students without hope onto a path that will give them the skills and knowledge they need to live lives well worth living. And the program is enabling schools that were doing very well to do a lot better.

The message of *Standards for Our Schools* is, in fact, a message of hope. These are jaded times. It is fashionable these days among commentators on the education scene to announce that too much is being expected of education, that it is doing about as well as it can, and that every reform is necessarily a mirage that, like all mirages, disappears on close inspection.

We don't agree. The data from the America's Choice school network show that the students in American schools—especially those suffering from poverty and neglect—can do far better than they have in the past. Teachers from America's Choice schools tell us that now, for the first time, they can see how all the pieces can be made to work in harmony, that they will not retire when they had planned to because, for the first time in a very long time, they can see real progress; they can see their students doing things they had never thought they could do. That is the dream of every teacher, and it is coming true for thousands of teachers in the America's Choice network. Whether you choose to join the America's Choice network or simply read this book and act on the principles we present here, we know that it can happen for you, too.

For more information about the America's Choice School Design, consult our web site at www.americaschoice.org.

Index

A

Aalborg Technical College, 178

Ability grouping: and elementary school education, 149–150; failure of, 32–35; origins of, in U.S., 33–34; universal standards versus, 43–44. *See also* Tracking

Academic Foundation Certificates, 344–345

Accelerated Schools, 132, 305–306

Accountability: alignment of authority with, 242–243; and central office versus school authority, 217–243; in Chicago Public Schools, 209–215; developing a system of, 237–243; in Edmonton, Alberta, school system, 220–230; incentives and, 230–232, 238–241, 248; in Kentucky school system, 230–232; models of, compared, 232–233; models of, synthesized, 233–236; organizational structure for, 242–243; student performance indicators for, 238. *See also* Governance; Responsibility, personal

Achieve, 42–43

Achievement: determinants of, 76–77; elementary school education and, 140–141

Adams, M., 143, 327

Adolescence, 199

Adult education, Certificate of Initial Mastery and, 39

Advanced Placement (AP) courses: ability grouping and, 34; in early college academy, 344; in proposed high school model, 193

Age of Discontinuity, The (Drucker), 328–329

Aims of Education, The (Whitehead), 58, 326

Algebra Readiness Test, 28

Alignment: of accountability with authority, 242–243; of assessment with standards, 46–47, 74–75, 321; of curriculum and instruction with standards, 73–99; of incentives, 127–128; of master schedule, 115–118; around standards, 74–99

Allocation system: alignment of, with accountability, 242; central office versus school authority over, 221–228, 231; faculty incentives and, 230–232; models of, compared, 232–233. *See also* Governance

American Association for the Advancement of Science, 42, 47, 325

American Federation of Teachers (AFT), 41, 325

American Montessori Program, 135. *See also* Montessori program

America's Choice: High Skills or Low Wages (Commission on the Skills of the American Workforce), 39, 323

America's Choice School Design program, 335–349; curriculum developed for, 336, 340–343; evaluation of, 338–339; goal of, 344–345; leadership for, 345–346; overview of, 335–337; and performance standards, 337–339; professional development for, 346–348; role of faculty in, 343–344; schools using, 337, 348–349; web site for, 349

Analysis. *See* Student performance analysis

Anti-Intellectualism in American Life (Hofstadter), 324

Applied learning: curriculum design and, 77–78; in Danish educational system, 181–183; in elementary school mathematics, 148–149; high school redesign for, 191–194; New Standards, listed, 256; New Standards example of, 280–290; standards and, 44, 49, 57–58, 256; vocational education and, 173–174, 181–183

Applied Learning and Technology Early Academy, 344–345

Apprenticeship: for student learning, 79–80; for teacher professional development, 120–121, 346–347

Apprenticeship work programs: in Denmark, 177–178, 185–186; and student motivation, 35–36; and vocational education, 172, 205–207

Asian countries: class teacher system in, 151, 155; student effort and achievement in, 77; student motivation in, 36–37, 38; student time outside of school in, 129. *See also* Foreign countries; Japan

Assessment: aligned to standards, 46–47, 74–75, 321; of Comprehensive Math and Science Program, 71–72; standardized, 198; of values-related standards, 83. *See also* New Standards assessment system

Association for Supervision and Curriculum Development, 326

Asturias, H., 60

ATLAS Communities, 307

Attendance problems, in vignette, 8

Audrey Cohen College, 307

Austin, J., 133–138, 144, 145, 157, 159, 161

Awards assemblies, 115

B

Baker, E., 42

Becoming a Teacher Leader (Bolman and Deal), 329

Beginning to Read: Thinking and Learning About Print (Adams), 327

Bell curve, 33–34

Bell South, 42

Benchmarking: of best practices, 163–165; defined, 313; of student performance to standards, 85–86, 115–117

Benchmarking, international, 39–40, 45, 59, 164–165. *See also* Asian countries; European countries; Foreign countries

Bennett, W., 209

Boeing, 42

Bolman, L. G., 329

Books, student access to, 146–145

Borthwick, A., 48

Breglio, V., 58–60, 325–326

Brunner, J. S., 326

Bryke, T., 211

Bush, G., 41

Bush administration: and New Standards performance standards, 47–48; and standards movement, 41

Business community, and standards movement, 42

C

California high schools: budgeting in, 103–104; interscholastic sports in, 101–105

California school system, curriculum framework of, 28–29

Callahan, R. E., 324

Cardinal Principles of Secondary Education, 1918, 73

Caring, 113–115, 150

Carnegie Task Force on Teaching as a Profession, 323

Carnegie units, 199

Celebrations, of student success, 115

Center for Independent Studies, 345

Center for Leadership in School Reform, 301

Center for the Study of Social Policy, 158, 301–302

Central office: accountability and, 209–215, 217–230, 233–237; allocation system for, 242; and charter schools, 236–237; in Chicago Public Schools, 209–215; duties of, 233–234; in Edmonton, Alberta, school system, 220–230; power of, historical background on, 217–220; role of, versus role of schools, 233–237; workings of, described, 220–224; workings of, redesigned, 224–230. See also Accountability; Governance; School districts

Certificate of Initial Mastery (CIM), 39–40, 204, 313; American standards movement and, 40–43; high school redesign and, 192–193, 197–200; implementing, in states and districts, 195, 200–201; standards for, 43–47; student motivation and, 39, 40, 44; vocational education redesign and, 196, 197

Character development: in elementary school, 139–142; in high school, 200; resources about, 327

Charter schools, 236–237, 313–314

Chicago Public Schools, 131; compared to Edmonton and Kentucky models, 232–233; reform of, 209–215

Chico, G., 213–214

Circumstances of learning, 78–79

Class size, 92–94

Class teacher system, 151–152, 314, 343; English teachers as, 153; and high school community, 199–200, 344; and K–8 schools, 154; and parent involvement, 155–156

Classrooms, standards-based, 84–87; instructional practices in, 92–94; instructional technologies in, 94–99

Clendenin, J., 42

Clinton, B., 42–43, 60, 147, 195

Clinton administration: and national examinations proposal, 60; reading volunteer program, 147; and standards movement, 42–43

Coalition of Essential Schools, 32, 132, 302

Codding, J. B., 25–29, 31, 32, 65–72, 169–174

Cognitive development, in elementary school, 141; language-related, 143–147; mathematics and, 148–149

Cohen, D. K., 191, 328

Collaboration: with community, 130–131; with industry, 171, 174, 200–203; with social service agencies, 156–158

College and career options system, 314. See also Vocational education

College Board, 25

College-prep program: in early college academies, 344–345; in vignette, 9; vocational combined with academic education and, 169–174, 175–188, 194–195, 314

Comer Schools, 132

Commentaries on student work, 50

Commission on the Skills of the American Workforce, 35, 39, 47, 323

Committee of Ten, 73–74

Community college courses, 11–13, 345

Community networking, 130–131

Compensation system, 241. *See also* Incentives

"Compost," 275–279

Comprehensive high school model: origins of, 190–191; as problem to be abolished, 190–194. *See also* High school

Comprehensive Math and Science Program (CMSP), 67–72, 91, 165, 302; contact information for, 302; elements of, 67–68; implementation of, 68–72; outcomes of, 71–72; scheduling and, 115–117

Computational skill, 148–149

Computer technology, 94–99

Conant, J. B., 190

Concept books, 88, 314–315

Conceptual mastery, 44, 49; and curriculum design, 77–78; in elementary school mathematics and science, 148–149; high school redesign for, 191–194; and teaching practice, 92–94

Co-NECT Schools, 307–308

Consortium for Policy Research in Education (CPRE), 338

Content standards, 315, 337

Contracts, parent-student-school, 129–130

Core beliefs, 159

Core Knowledge Foundation, 132, 302–303, 325

Council for Basic Education (CBE), 41–42, 303

Course of study guides, 88–89, 315

"Counting Raisins," 296

Covey, S., 142

Cremin, L. A., 324

Cross, C., 42

Cross-age peer tutoring, 315. *See also* Student tutoring

"Cubes," 61–62, 266, 267–269

Culminating event, 315

Curriculum: aligned around universal high standards, 73–99; apprenticeship model and, 79–80; circumstances of learning and, 78–79; coverage versus core-mastery focus of, 73–76, 190–191; in Danish schools, 178; deep, 77–78; developed for America's Choice schools, 336, 340–343; development and implementation of, in vignette, 65–72; English language arts example of, 84–87; for high school students working towards Certificate of Mastery, 197–200; historical background of American, 73–74; hundred-day, 340, 341–342; instructional materials and, 87–91; instructional practice and, 92–94; instructional technology and, 94–99; principles for, 76–80; resources about, 326–327; revolution in thinking on, 74–76, 80; safety nets in, 341–343; sources of, 91; standards-based classroom and, 84–87; student performance analysis and, 85–86

Curriculum frameworks, 74, 90

Curriculum reform networks, 91, 325

Customer satisfaction orientation, 227

D

Daimler-Benz factory, 35–36

Daley, R., 210, 213

Darling-Hammond, L., 42

Daro, P., 48, 60, 87–88, 125

Deal, T. E., 329

Democracy, standards and, 57–58

Denmark: educational system of, 175–190; primary school education in, 140–142; vocational combined with academic education in, 175–190, 194–195

Dewey, J., 139, 326

Different Ways of Knowing, 303
Disadvantaged students. *See* Low-income students
Disciplinary societies: and performance descriptions, 49; and standards movement, 42, 45, 46, 47; and standards selection, 48, 255. *See also* Professional societies
Discipline, school, 111–113
Distinguished educator, 315
Double-period courses, 342–343
Doyle, D., 42
"Drift Aways," 261–266, 363–367
Dropout rate, in vignette, 8
Dropout recovery program, 345
Drucker, P., 328–329
Duval County (Jacksonville), Florida, school district, 338, 339, 348–349

E

Early college academies, 344–345
Eastman Kodak, 42
Edmonton (Alberta, Canada) school system: central office of, 220–230; compared to Chicago and Kentucky models, 232–231; redesign of, 224–230
Educating for Character (Lickona), 327
Education and the Cult of Efficiency (Callahan), 324
Educational Equality Project (College Board), 25
Educational Leadership for America's Schools (Odden), 329
Efficacy Institute, 303–304
Effort, as determinant of achievement, 76–77
Electives, 198
"ElectroHawk 1," 280–290
Elementary Algebra Diagnostic Test, 28
Elementary and Secondary Education Act of 1965, 218
Elementary school: America's Choice curriculum materials for, 340–341; character-related versus cognitive goals of, 139–142; class teacher system for, 151–152, 343; English language instruction in, 143–147; health and physical fitness in, 149; leadership team in, 345–346; mathematics instruction in, 148–149; New Standards math standard example in, 50, 51–52; parent involvement in, 136–137, 155–156; resources about, 328; specialist teachers in, 152–153, 343; study skills instruction in, 150–151; universal high standards in, 149–150; vignette of, 133–138
Elementary school network, 91
Elitism, 34
E-mail, for parent-teacher communication, 155–156
Employer outreach, 204–207
Employer perspective, 10–11
Employment outlook/prospects: and high school preparation, 14–15, 17–18; and student motivation, 35–38; and universal high standards, 34–35
End-of-course examination, 315–316
English language arts standards: curriculum based on, 84–87, 340–341; example of high school, 50, 52–56; New Standards, listed, 255; New Standards examples of, 257–266; for reading, 146, 257–261; reference examinations for, 292–294
English language instruction: balanced approach to, 143–145; in elementary school, 143–147, 340; high school curriculum for, 84–87, 340–341; for non-English speakers, 147; support mechanisms for, 145–147. *See also* Reading; Writing
European countries: ability grouping and, 34, 150; class teacher system in, 151, 153, 154, 155; K–8 schools in, 154; primary school education in, 141; student motivation in, 35–36, 38. *See also* Denmark; Foreign countries

Examinations. *See* Reference
   examinations
Expectations, high: in elementary
   school, 149–150; in other countries, 32–33; and universal standards, 43–44, 248–249
Expectations, low: Certificate of Initial Mastery and, 39, 40; and elementary school education,
   149–150; failure of system based
   on, 32–35, 252; historical background of, 33–34
Expeditionary Learning Outward
   Bound, 308
Extended lesson books, 88, 314, 316
Extended lesson planning, 85–86
Extended schedule: for low-income
   elementary school students, 138,
   145; for low-income high school
   students, 117–118; for low-
   performing students, 150

F

Family resource centers, 156–158; in
   Kentucky, 137–138, 157, 158
Farrar, E., 191, 328
Finn, C., Jr., 42
Fisher, G., 42
Floater teachers, 124–125
Folkeskole, Danish, 140–141,
   175–176, 179, 180, 192, 198
Foreign countries: ability grouping
   and, 34; high standards and
   expectations in, 32–33; internationally benchmarked standards
   and, 39–40, 45, 59; primary school
   education in, 139–142; student
   motivation in, 35–37, 38; studies
   of, 324–325. *See also* Asian countries; Benchmarking, international;
   European countries
Foxfire Fund, 304

G

Galef Institute, 132
General math curriculum, limitations
   of, 65–66

Gerstner, L., 42
Goal-seeking behavior, 158–159.
   See also Results orientation
Governance: accountability and,
   217–237; accountability system
   design and, 237–243; central office
   proposed role in, 233–234; central
   office redesign and, 224–230; central office versus school authority in,
   217–230, 233–237; central office
   traditional role in, 217–224; in
   Chicago Public Schools, 212–213,
   232–233; in Edmonton, Alberta,
   school system, 220–230, 232–233;
   industrial model of, 217–218; in
   Kentucky school system, 230–233;
   versus leadership and management,
   109; models of, compared, 232–233;
   models of, synthesized, 233–237;
   organizational structure for,
   242–243; proposed role of schools
   in, 235–236; of vocational institutions, 196. *See also* Accountability;
   Management, school
Graffiti, 112, 113
Graphic Arts Academy, 169–174,
   202, 203–204
Gymnasium, Danish, 176–177, 193;
   example of, 181–183

H

Hampton, S., 60, 84, 87–88, 125
Harvey, P., 209–215
Hay, S. M., 90
Health, elementary school education
   and, 149
Hefferan Elementary School, 209–210
Higgins, A., 327
High school(s): Academic Foundation
   Certificates in, 344–345; class teach-
   ers in, 344; community houses
   within, 199–200; comprehensive
   model of, 190–194; curriculum of,
   for students working towards
   Certificate of Mastery, 197–200;
   curriculum-standards alignment in,
   73–99; English standards in, exam-

ple of, 50, 52–56; leadership and management of, 101–132, 346; low achievement in, 1–15, 25–29; parent involvement in, 128–131; principal as instructional leader in, 125–127; proposed redesign of, 190–200; resources about, 328; role of, in countering bad influences, 199–200; role of, in vocational education reform, 203–208; size of, 343; standards-setting for, 31–63; vocational education and, 175–208. *See also* Pasadena High School

High school diploma: Certificate of Initial Mastery versus, 39–40, 197; role of, in proposed reform, 197

High school dropouts: poor reading skills of, 342; program for recovering, 345

High school graduates, prospects for, 14–15, 17–18

High-performance management, 316. *See also* Management

Hillkirk, J., 328

Hirsch, E. D., 49, 91

Hofstadter, R., 324

Home visits, 130

Honda, 169

Horace's Compromise: The Dilemma of the American High School (Sizer), 328

Hornbeck, D., 230, 329

House system, 114, 343

Humanities Early College Academy, 344

Hundred-day curriculum, 340, 341–342

I

IBM, 42

Implementation strategies, 165–166

"In rewards," 317

Incentives: accountability and, 229–230, 248; alignment of, 127–128; authority and, 229–230; defined, 316–317; developing a system of, 238–241; for district support staff, 241; for faculty and staff,

239–240; informal and intrinsic, 128, 229–230, 232; in Kentucky model, 230–232; models of, compared, 233; for schools, 240–241; for students, 238–239. *See also* Student motivation

Independent Writing Task, 292–293

Individualized and whole-class instruction, 92–94

Industry partnerships, 171, 174, 201–204; and employer outreach, 204–207

Institute for Learning, 304

Instructional design: aligned around universal high standards, 73–99; instructional materials and, 87–91; instructional practice and, 92–94; instructional technology and, 94–99; resources about, 326; standards-based classrooms and, 84–87. *See also* Curriculum

Instructional leadership, of principal, 125–127

Instructional materials, 87–91; audit and analysis of, 90; customizing, 90–91; development of, 89–91; elements of, 87–89; sources of, 91

Instructional practice, 92–94

Instructional technology, 94–99, 326

Integrated curriculum, 77

Integrated Reading and Writing Task, 294

International Baccalaureate Program, 193

It's Elementary, 328

J

Jacobson, G., 328

Japan: ability grouping and, 150; classroom size in, 92; primary school education in, 139–141, 142; student motivation in, 36–37; study skills instruction in, 150–151; teaching practice in, 92–94, 118, 150

Japanese Educational Challenge, The: A Commitment to Children (White), 324

"Jeff" vignette, 2–15
Jobs for the Future, 202
Johnson, A., 211
Journals, 122

K

Kearns, D., 328
Kennedy Elementary School, 144,
145, 159, 161, 166; vignette of,
133–138
Kentucky Council of School Perfor-
mance Standards, 230
Kentucky Distinguished Educator,
231–232
Kentucky Education Reform Act
(KERA), 137–138, 145, 230–232
Kentucky Family Resource Centers,
137–138, 157, 158
Kentucky school system: compared to
Chicago and Edmonton models,
232–233; model of, 230–232
Kimbrough, T., 210–211
K–8 schools, 153–154
Klopfer, L., 326
Knowledge, engagement in, 78–79.
See also Applied learning; Concep-
tual mastery
Kohlberg, L., 327

L

Lawrence Kohlberg's Approach to Moral
Education (Kohlberg et al.), 327
Leadership, school: versus governance, 109; for implementing
America's Choice School Design,
345–346; instructional, 125–127;
versus management, 107; schools'
need for, 107–108; teams for,
108–111, 345–346. See also
Management; Principals
Leadership and management team,
108–111; composition of, 110,
345–346; defined, 317; and incentives alignment, 128; and master
schedule, 119; member selection
for, 110–111; and professional

development program, 119, 123;
and school rule-setting, 111–112;
tasks of, 109–110; and teacher
recruitment, 123–124
Leading with Soul (Bolman and Deal),
329
Learning: love of, 139–141; principles
of, 76–80
Learning Gap, The (Stigler and
Stevenson), 92, 324
Learning in Motion, 96
Learning organization, 188
Learning Research and Development
Center, University of Pittsburgh,
47, 252
Learning through teaching, 78–79
LEGO-Logo, 98–99
Levy, F., 323–324
Lickona, T., 327
"Life Expectancy," 297
Linn, R., 42
Literature-based instruction, 144
Lopez, G., 67, 91, 327
Los Angeles Learning Centers, 308
Love of learning, development of,
139–142
Low-income students: agency col-
laboration and, 158; elementary
school vignette of, 133–138;
extended scheduling for, 117–118,
138, 145; family resource centers
and, 156–158; funding for, 117;
language learning support for,
145–147

M

MacArthur Foundation, 47
Making Standards Matter (American
Federation of Teachers), 325
Management, school: assistance networks for, 131–132, 215; duties of,
235–236; versus governance, 109;
high-performance, 316; versus leadership, 107; for master schedule
alignment, 115–118; for
parent/guardian involvement,

128–131; resources about, 328–329; for safety and orderliness, 111–113; for supportive environment, 113–115; for teacher excellence, 118–125; teams for, 108–111. *See also* Accountability; Governance; Leadership; Leadership and management team

Marshall, R., 323

Martinez, P., 211

Mass production system, 33, 92

Massachusetts Institute of Technology (MIT) media lab, 98

Master schedule, 348; changing of, for standards alignment, 115–118; defined, 317; professional development and, 119; in vignette, 101–105

Master teachers, 121

Mathematics and Science Early College Academy, 344

Mathematics curriculum: developed for America's Choice schools, 341; safety nets built into, 342–343; selection and development of, in vignette, 65–72

Mathematics instruction, elementary school, 148–149

Mathematics placement, in high school vignette, 25–29

Mathematics preparation, inadequacy of, 11, 25–29

Mathematics standards, 256; elementary school example of, 50, 51–52; New Standards, listed, 256; New Standards examples of, 266–274; reference examinations for, 295–298

Mathematics teacher recruitment, 69–70

Measurement in Motion, 96–97

Measuring Up: Standards, Assessment, and School Reform (Rothman), 325

Meier, D., 328

Middle school: K–8 school alternative to, 153–154; leadership team in,

346; mathematics preparation in, 25–29; problems of, 153–154; resources about, 327–328; size of, 343. *See also* Elementary school

Mindstorms: Children, Computers, and Powerful Ideas (Papert), 327

Minnesota, postsecondary opportunity in, 197

Mission: defined, 159; getting agreement on, 159, 161

Modern Red Schoolhouse Institute, 308–309, 325

Montessori, M., 134, 146

Montessori program, 134–135, 146; elementary school implementation of, 135–137; phonics and, 144

Montessori teacher certification, 135

Moral responsibility to children, 247–250

Morality in education, resources about, 327. *See also* Character development; Values

Motivation. *See* Student motivation

Multimedia: instructional, 96–99; for standards-driven instructional design, 90–91

Murnane, R., 323–324

Murphy, J., 42

Musick, M., 43

N

Nation Prepared, A: Teachers for the 21st Century (Carnegie), 323

National Alliance for Restructuring Education, 131–132, 202, 215, 252, 304–305, 309

National Alliance of Business, 202

National Assessment of Educational Progress (NAEP), 43

National Board for Professional Teaching Standards, 42, 305, 325

National Center for the Accelerated Schools Project, 132, 305–306

National Center on Education and the Economy, 35, 47, 131–132,

National Center on Education and the Economy (*continued*) 220, 251–253, 306; contact information for, 253, 306; curriculum development work of, 87–88; policy work of, 251; professional development programs of, 252–253; technical assistance work of, 252; tool development work of, 251–252. *See also* National Alliance for Restructuring Education; New Standards

National Centers of Excellence in the United States, 210

National Council of Teachers of English, 42, 47

National Council of Teachers of Mathematics, 42, 49, 255

National Education Association, 73

National Education Goals Panel, 41

National Education Summit: First, 41; Second, 42

National examinations, 60

National Governors' Association, 42

National Science Board, 42, 325

National Science Foundation, 60, 67, 91, 165

National skill certificates, 196–198, 318

National Skill Standards Board, 195, 196, 202, 318

National Standards in American Education: A Citizen's Guide (Ravitch), 325

Natural ability, as determinant of achievement, 76–77. *See also* Ability grouping

New American Schools, 91, 132, 306–309

New Standards, 251–252, 309–310, 325–326, 336; contact information for, 309

New Standards assessment system, 291–299; development of, 60; evolution of, 47–48. *See also* Assessment; Reference examinations

New Standards English Language Arts Reference Examination, 292–294

New Standards Mathematics Reference Examination, 295–298

New Standards performance standards, 42, 81, 255–290, 325–326; for applied learning, 256, 280–290; classrooms based on, 84–87; competitiveness of, 59; development of, 48–59, 204; for English language arts, 50, 52–56, 146, 255, 257–266; evolution of, 47–48; examples of, 51–56, 257–290; format for, 49–50; for literacy, 340–341; local application of, 60, 62–63, 81–83; for mathematics, 50, 51–52, 256, 266–274; names of, listed, 255–256; overview of, 255–257; parts of, 255, 257; public input in, 58–59; qualities of, 57; for reading, 257–261; for science, 256, 275–279; and values, 81, 82. *See also* Reference examinations; Standards; Universal high standards

O

Occupational skill standards, 196–197, 203–204

Odden, A. R., 329

Orderliness, 111–113

Organizations, for standards-based education, 301–312

Østerlund, R., 187–188

P

Paideia Group Inc., 310

Panasonic Foundation Inc., 310

Papert, S., 98, 327

Parent/guardian involvement: in elementary school, 136–137, 155–156; in governance, 209, 210; in high school, 128–131; and middle school problems, 153–154; in reading practice, 145–146

Parry, A., 220–224

Pasadena High School (PSH), 31–32, 162, 165; Graphic Arts Academy at, 169–174, 202, 203–204; master schedule changes in, 101–105, 115–116; mathematics curriculum selection and implementation in, 65–72; mathematics placement problems in, 25–29

Peer tutoring. See Student tutoring

Performance Assessment Scoring Center, 299

Performance descriptions, 49, 255, 257. See also New Standards performance standards

Performance standards, 46, 318, 337–339. See also New Standards performance standards; Standards; Universal high standards

Phonics-based instruction, 143–145

Physical fitness, in elementary school, 149

Plainfield, New Jersey, school district, 338

Plains states, vignette from, 1–15

Planning system, for student performance improvement, 158–167, 348

"Points and Segments," 266–267, 269–274

Politics: corruption and, 217–218; necessity of, 213–214

Powell, A. G., 191

Power, F. C., 327

Power of Their Ideas, The: Lessons for America from a Small School in Harlem (Meier), 328

Preparation: Danish model of, 175–190; inadequate, 2–15; proposed educational reform and, 190–208

Preschool program, 136–137, 156

Principals: authority of, 224, 226–227, 232; instructional leadership of, 125–127; role of, in implementing America's Choice School Design, 346; and school management, 108–111; successful, central office versus principals' perspectives on,

219; traditional role of, in governance, 219

Printing Industry Association (PIA) of Southern California, 169–170

Probation list, 214–215, 239–240

Probation managers, 214–215, 239–240, 318

Process of Education, The (Brunner), 326

Professional and technical education programs, 319; standards for, 195, 196, 203–204. See also Vocational education

Professional development, defined, 319. See also Teacher professional development

Professional societies: and New Standards performance standards, 47–48, 255; and performance descriptions, 49; and standards movement, 42, 45, 46, 47. See also Disciplinary societies

Program for School Improvement, 310–311

Proud to Read Aloud, 210

Public Agenda Foundation, 59, 326

Public educational system reform: accountability and, 209–215, 217–243; accountability system for, 237–243; central office and, 237–243; Danish educational model and, 175–190; high school redesign and, 190–194; proposal for restructured schools and, 190–208; rationale for, 18–23; standards-based, 46–47; support for, organizing, 200–201; vocational education and, 194–197

Public engagement, defined, 319

Public support: for Certificate of Initial Mastery, 200–201; for curriculum reform, 75; for New Standards, 58–59; and public engagement, 319; for standards, 44–45

Q

Quality indicators, in standards-based classroom, 87

R

Raising Good Children (Lickona), 327
Ravitch, D., 41, 42, 325
Reading: dropouts' poor skills in, 342; New Standards example of, 257–261; reading list for, 259–261; reference examination for, 294; support mechanisms for, 145–147. *See also* English language instruction
Reading Is Fundamental, 147
Reading Recovery program, 137
Real-world problems. *See* Applied learning
Reconstitution, 319
Reference examinations, 60, 61–62, 291–299, 326; for English language arts, 292–294; information provided by, 299; for mathematics, 295–298; overview of, 291–292; scoring of, 299
Reframing Organizations (Bolman and Deal), 329
Resnick, L., 47, 76, 326
Resources, for standards-based education, 301–312
Responsibility, personal: development of, in elementary school, 139–141; of parents versus school, 153–154, 155; for standards-based reform, 246–250; of students, for meeting standards, 86–87; of teachers, for professional development, 121–122. *See also* Accountability
Results orientation: in elementary school, 138; in planning to improve student performance, 158–167; and principal authority, 227; in school management, 107–132
Rewards: alignment of, 127–128; for schools, 240–241. *See also* Incentives
Rochester, New York, school district, 338, 339
Rochester City School District, 206–207

Romer, R., 41
Roots and Wings, 309
Rothman, R., 325
Rubrics, 319–320

S

Sable, M., 90
Safety, 111–113
Safety nets, in curriculum, 341–343
Sandwich program, Danish, 177–178, 181; example of, 184–187
Satisfaction surveys, 227
Saturday programs, 117, 145, 150. *See also* Extended schedule
Scarsdale High School, 207–208
Scheduling. *See* Extended schedule; Master schedule
School and Society, The (Dewey), 326
School assistance networks, 131–132, 215
"School Bond Levy," 50, 52–56
School councils, 220, 226; in Kentucky school system, 230–231, 232
School design, defined, 335. *See also* America's Choice School Design program
School Development Program, 311
School districts: accountability and governance in, 209–215, 217–243; role of, in educational reform, 190–197, 200–201. *See also* Accountability; Central office; Governance
School environment: class teacher system and, 151–152; safe and orderly, 111–113; supportive and caring, 113–115
School management. *See* Management, school
School rules, 111–113
School security, 111–113
School size, optimum, 114, 343
School structure, 109, 114
School year, extended schedule for, 117–118, 321

Shrontz, F., 42

Schwartz, B., 41–42

Science instruction, elementary school, 149

Science standards: New Standards, listed, 256; New Standards example of, 275–279

Selden Design Teams, 132

Self-confidence development, in elementary school, 139–142

Self-image, student, 82

Shanker, A., 41

"Sharing 25," 50, 51–52

Shopping Mall High School, The (Powell et al.), 191, 328

Simon, P., 210

Site-based management, 108–109, 219–220, 320

Size: class, 92–94; school, 114, 343

Sizer, T., 328

"Snark Soda," 298

Social service agency collaboration, 156–158

Social skills development, in elementary school, 139–142

Software, instructional, 95–99

Southern Regional Education Board, 43

Specialist teachers, 152–153, 343

Sports, in California high schools, 101–105

Sports coaches, 102–103

Staffing: and master schedule changes, 116; for new curriculum implementation, 69–71

Stage, E., 60

Standards: comprehensive approach to, 20–23; inadequate, in vignette, 6–15; introduction of, 20–21; performance, 46, 318, 337–339; rationales for, 32–38; for professional and technical programs, 195, 196, 203–204; resources about, 325–326; standards for, 43–47, 48. See also Certificate of Initial Mastery; New Standards performance standards; Universal high standards

Standards movement: evolution of, 40–43; status and critique of, 43–47

Standards-based classroom, 83–87

Standards-based education, 21–23; commitment to, 245–250; defined, 320; organizational resources for, 301–312. See also Universal high standards

Standards-Driven Curriculum, 327

Standards-referenced assessment, defined, 321. See also Assessment

Stanford Achievement Tests, 31

State standards, 43; assessment and, 47; limitations of, 45–46, 47; and standards movement, 41–42; and standards selection, 48; and students in America's Choice schools, 337–339; for values, 45–46

States: and academic certificate implementation, 200–201; and vocational education reform, 190–197, 200–203

Stevenson, H. W., 92, 324

Stigler, J. W., 92, 93, 324

Strategies for student performance improvement: implementation of, 165–166; selection of, 162–165

Strembitsky, M., 220–230

Student motivation: Certificate of Initial Mastery and, 39, 40, 44; developing incentives for, 238–239; in foreign countries versus U.S., 35–37, 38; problem of low, 35–38

Student performance analysis: assignments based on, 85–86; benchmarked to standards, 85, 115–117; and master schedule, 115–117; and professional development, 120, 121; selecting indicators for, 161–162

Student performance improvement planning, 158–167

Student performance indicators, 161–162, 238

Student performance targets, 162

Student time, outside of school, 129
Student tutoring: benefits of, 78–79;
    in Comprehensive Math and Sci-
    ence Program, 71; cross-age, 315;
    for reading, 146
Student employment, 129
Student groups, high school, 199–200
Students, moral responsibility to,
    247–250
Student-teacher connections,
    113–115
Study skills instruction, 150–151
Substitute teachers, 124–125
Success: celebration of student, 115;
    and teacher professional develop-
    ment, 123
Success for All Program, 132, 311
Summer effect, 321
Summer school, 71, 117, 145, 150
Supportive environment, 113–115;
    class teacher system and, 151–152
Syracuse youth apprenticeship pro-
    gram, 206

T

Tatel, D., 121–122
Taylor, F. W., 316
Teacher licensing, aligned to stan-
    dards, 75
Teacher preparation, aligned to stan-
    dards, 75
Teacher professional development,
    118–125; in America's Choice
    School Design program, 346–348;
    apprenticeship approach to,
    120–121, 346–347; defined, 319;
    individual responsibility for,
    121–122; National Center on Edu-
    cation and the Economy programs
    of, 252–253; prevailing approach
    to, 118–119; resources for, 327; in
    results-oriented schools, 119–125
Teacher recruitment, 123–125; for
    Comprehensive Math and Science
    Program, 69–70; planning for,
    228–229

Teacher support, for standards, 44–45
Teacher teams, for assignment plan-
    ning, 85–86
Teacher training: for Comprehensive
    Math and Science Program, 70; for
    Montessori program, 135
Teachers: class, 151–152, 153, 154,
    199–200, 314; elementary school,
    151–153; floater, 124–125; and
    high school community, 199–200;
    low-performing, 122–124; special-
    ist, 152–153; substitute, 124
Teacher's guides, 88–89
Teachers' organizations: and national
    content standards, 255; and stan-
    dards movement, 41, 42. See also
    Disciplinary societies
Teacher-student connections,
    113–115
Teaching: aligned to standards,
    92–94; in Japanese versus Ameri-
    can classrooms, 92
Teaching the New Basic Skills: Principles
    for Educating Children to Thrive in a
    Changing Economy (Levy and Mur-
    nane), 323–324
Teams. See Leadership and manage-
    ment team; Teacher teams
Technical assistance, 131–132, 202,
    215, 251, 252
Technical programs. See Vocational
    education
Technology, instructional, 94–99, 327
Television, 129, 130
Textbooks: alternatives to, 87–91; and
    coverage-focused curriculum, 76;
    mathematics, 66
The Pew Charitable Trusts, 41–42, 47
The Pew Network for Standards-
    Based Reform, 312
Thinking for a Living: Education and the
    Wealth of Nations (Marshall and
    Tucker), 323
Third International Mathematics and
    Science Study (TIMSS), 76,
    324–325; elementary and middle

school findings of, 140, 141; web site of, 93

3–D World Atlas, 97–98

Toward a Theory of Instruction (Brunner), 326

Toward the Thinking Curriculum: Current Cognitive Research (Resnick and Klopfer), 326

Toyota Motor Corporation, Japan, 36–37

Tracking: Danish selection system versus, 187; defined, 321; in elementary school, 149–150; failure of, 32–35; origins of, in U.S., 33–34; universal standards versus, 22, 43–44; in vignette, 8–9. See also Ability grouping

Transformation of the American School, The: Progressivism in American Education (Cremin), 324

Truancy rate, in vignette, 8

Tucker, M. S., 47, 139–140, 323

Turning Points, 328

Tutoring programs: mathematics, 343; volunteer, 147. See also Student tutoring

25-Book Campaign, 348

Tyack, D. B., One Best System: A History of American Urban Education (Tyack), 324

U

U.S. Department of Education web site, 93

Universal high standards, 22, 31–63; versus ability grouping, 32–35; alignment around, 74–99; assessment aligned to, 46–47, 74–75, 320–321; classrooms aligned to, 84–87; curriculum design and, 73–80; in elementary school, 149–150; instructional materials aligned to, 87–91; instructional practice aligned to, 92–94; instructional technology aligned to, 94–99; internationally benchmarked, 39–40, 45; rationales for, 32–38; school management and, 107–132; setting, guidelines for, 81–83, 238; standards for, 43–47, 48; and student motivation, 35–38; student responsibility for meeting, 86–87; support for, 44–45; universality of, 45; usability of, 44; values and, 81–83. See also Certificate of Initial Mastery; New Standards performance standards; Standards; Standards-based education

Universities, Danish, 176, 183

University of California, 47

University of California, Los Angeles (UCLA), 27, 28

Usability, 44; of New Standards, 48–49, 5–58

V

Vallas, P., 213–214

Values: development of, in elementary school, 141–142; development of, in high school, 200; measures of, 83; and setting standards, 81–83; state standards for, 45–46

Videotapes, of Japanese classroom teaching, 93

Violence, 112–113

Vision: defined, 159; getting agreement on, 159, 161

Vocational education, 58, 175–208; academic combined with, 169–174, 175–188, 194–195, 314, 345; in Denmark, 175–190; in high school vignettes, 9–13, 169–174; high schools' role in reform of, 203–208; proposed redesign of, 194–208; school districts' role in reform of, 190–197, 200–201; standards for, 195, 196; states' role in reform of, 190–197, 200–203

Vouchers, 237, 322

W

"Walt Whitman High School"
    ("WW") vignette, 2–15
Wegmans Food Markets, 206–207
White, M., 324
Whitehead, A. N., 58, 79, 326
Whole language instruction, 143–145
Whole-class instruction, 92–94
Wiggins, G., 42
Word processors, 95–96
Work ethic, 10–11
Work samples, 50
Workforce Development program,
    202, 252
Writing: New Standards performance
    standard example of, 261–266; New
    Standards reference examinations
    for, 292–294; word processors and,
    95–96. *See also* English language
    learning

X

Xerox: American Samurai (Jacobson
    and Hillkirk), 328

Y

Yeats, W. B., 250